When the Movies
were Young

Biograph's studio, Eleven East Fourteenth Street, an old brownstone mansion of New York City, the home of movie romance. *(See p. 1)*
Frontispiece.

When the Movies were Young

by

Mrs. D. W. Griffith

(LINDA ARVIDSON)

WITH A NEW INTRODUCTION BY

Edward Wagenknecht

DOVER PUBLICATIONS, INC.
NEW YORK

Published in Canada by General Publishing Company, Ltd., 30 Lesmill Road, Don Mills, Toronto,
Ontario.
Published in the United Kingdom by Constable
and Company, Ltd., 10 Orange Street, London WC 2.

This Dover edition, first published in 1969, is an
unabridged and slightly corrected republication of
the work originally published by E. P. Dutton &
Company, New York, in 1925. A new Introduction
by Edward Wagenknecht has been written specially
for this edition. The Index is also a new feature of
the present volume. The eighteen additional Biograph stills following page xiv appear by courtesy
of The Museum of Modern Art Film Stills Archive.

Standard Book Number : 486-22300-0
Library of Congress Catalog Card Number: 69-16841

Manufactured in the United States of America
Dover Publications, Inc.
180 Varick Street
New York, N. Y. 10014

INTRODUCTION
to the Dover edition

FIRST published in 1925, when there were very few books available about motion pictures, *When the Movies Were Young* was one of the earliest volumes containing eye-witness testimony to the conditions under which early motion pictures were made. Now that the whole character of the cinema has been so radically altered that many persons find it impossible to distinguish between "adult entertainment" and pornography, and what was our closest approach to a folk drama has been destroyed—now, too, that the spontaneity and casual creativity which produced so much of the charm of early film-making has been smothered under tons of mechanical equipment and technological complications—many, I think, will echo the note on which the author closes, rejoicing that "I served my novitiate in a day when we could afford to be good fellows, and our hearts were young enough and happy enough to enjoy the gypsying way of things."

Her chronicle has an added claim to our attention because she writes of Biograph, the most honored trade name in film history. Though he is universally regarded as the most important and creative of all directors, D. W. Griffith's career has so far been most inadequately chronicled. Iris Barry's *D. W. Griffith, American Film Master* (1940), excellent as it is, is only a monograph, and Homer Croy's *Star Maker* (1959) contributes nothing. We may expect

that much will be added in the book by Griffith's leading
actress, Lillian Gish, scheduled for publication early in 1969.
And though Seymour Stern has for years been accumulating
plethoric materials for a definitive book on Griffith, so far
there have been no signs that these are being reduced to
publishable form. These circumstances would seem to make
it all the more important that we should not overlook material coming from any informed source.

To be sure, we must allow in this volume, as in all personal chronicles, for the writer's own point of view, but in
this case it is not very intrusive. Mrs. Griffith tells us very
little concerning her personal relations with fellow players
in her husband's company, and she leaves us largely to our
own inferences as to her attitude toward them. For that
matter, she is decidedly reticent about her relations with him.
Mostly she is on the set, describing how this, that, and the
other film was made, or this, that, and the other innovation
introduced, and this is exactly what we would require of her.

Is she accurate? Since I was not present in the Biograph
studio, I cannot of course vouch for her accuracy, but beyond
a few misspellings (which have been silently corrected in
this reprint), I have noticed few errors of fact. Complete
accuracy is not often achieved in motion picture reminis-
cences, nor, if the truth must be told, in books about the
movies which have been "researched" (I could even point
out a few in my own book *The Movies in the Age of Innocence.*) Mrs. Griffith misnames *The Battle at Elderbush
Gulch* (which she calls "The Battle of Elderberry Gulch")
and confuses its story with that of another film (I think *The
Massacre*). She credits Griffith with a film called "The Tell-
tale Heart," which he never made (*The Avenging Conscience*
was partly based on Poe's story of that title). She is in error

in stating that Thomas Meighan acted in films with Geraldine Farrar. She also seems to be under the impression that Rudyard Kipling wrote *A Fool There Was;* actually he wrote only the poem "The Vampire," which gave Porter Emerson Browne the basic idea for his play. Of course one must also allow for the time-lapse since the book was first published. The author's "now's" do not apply to the late sixties; it is considerably more than "nearly ten years" since Biograph folded; and though the building that housed the New York studio still stood when she wrote, it long ago disappeared, as historic buildings have a way of disappearing in New York. But none of this is her fault. She had no idea in 1925 that we should be reprinting her book in 1969, and it is, in a way, a tribute to her that this should be the fact.

There *is* a problem, however. Linda Arvidson and D. W. Griffith, who married in 1906, parted during the Biograph period, just when I do not know. They were not divorced until many years later, and the lady seems never to have been able to reconcile herself to her changed status, even after her former husband's second marriage. It is not without significance, then, that, as late as 1925, she should have signed her book as "Mrs. D. W. Griffith" rather than as Linda Arvidson Griffith. Most of the Griffith Biograph films in which she appeared were very early—1908 or 1909—and I have not noted anything later than *Enoch Arden* (1911). Miss Lillian Gish, who arrived at Biograph late in 1912, tells me that Mrs. Griffith was gone a year or more before this date. It is true that in 1914 Dorothy Gish played with her in one of the Klaw and Erlanger Biographs, *The Wife,* but by this time Griffith himself had left Biograph, and with this film he had nothing to do. The book, however, creates the impression that she was on the scene clear up to *The Birth of a*

Nation, and one cannot therefore but wonder where she got her information for the later years, and if she is less accurate here. I wish very much that I could answer these questions but I cannot.

When all is said and done, I think the most interesting thing about turning to such a book as this—or any book that catches the true flavor of the early movie days—is the extraordinary freshness of the life it describes. All this was only sixty years ago or less, and yet we must make an effort to go back to it, as if we were going back to the Elizabethan drama or the early eighteenth-century novel. These people were creating something fresh and new and exciting. What they were doing was not really much more experimental than what was to be done later in the early days of sound; but whereas the early sound films were a dismal bore because their makers were throwing everything that had been learned about picture-making out the window and starting anew on a false trail, the early silents are still exciting. They embodied something which for a brief span of years (after which it did not die but was murdered) had vitality and strength and beauty, and which therefore took hold of the heart of the American people and expressed their longings and dreams and aspirations as no art form had ever done before nor perhaps ever will again.

Edward Wagenknecht

CONTENTS

CHAPTER   PAGE

I. ELEVEN EAST FOURTEENTH STREET 1

II. ENDINGS AND BEGINNINGS 8

III. CLIMACTERIC—AN EARTHQUAKE AND A MARRIAGE . . 14

IV. YOUNG AMBITIONS AND A FEW JOLTS 22

V. THE MOVIES TEMPT 29

VI. MOVIE ACTING DAYS—AND AN "IF" 37

VII. D. W. GRIFFITH DIRECTS HIS FIRST MOVIE 45

VIII. DIGGING IN 53

IX. FIRST PUBLICITY AND EARLY SCENARIOS 62

X. WARDROBE—AND A FEW PERSONALITIES 71

XI. MACK SENNETT GETS STARTED 77

XII. ON LOCATION—EXPERIENCES PLEASANT AND OTHERWISE 82

XIII. AT THE STUDIO 90

XIV. MARY PICKFORD HAPPENS ALONG 99

XV. ACQUIRING ACTORS AND STYLE 108

XVI. CUDDEBACKVILLE 115

XVII. "PIPPA PASSES" FILMED 127

XVIII. GETTING ON 134

XIX. TO THE WEST COAST 143

XX. IN CALIFORNIA AND ON THE JOB 155

XXI. BACK HOME AGAIN 173

XXII. IT COMES TO PASS 184

XXIII. THE FIRST TWO-REELER 190

XXIV. EMBRYO STARS 202

XXV. MARKING TIME 208

XXVI. THE OLD DAYS END 221

XXVII. SOMEWHAT DIGRESSIVE 234

XXVIII. "THE BIRTH OF A NATION" 245

INDEX 257

LIST OF ILLUSTRATIONS

FACING PAGE

Biograph's studio, Eleven East Fourteenth Street . . *Frontispiece*

"Lawrence" Griffith 6

Linda Arvidson (Mrs. David W. Griffith) 7

Linda Arvidson (Mrs. Griffith), David W. Griffith and Harry
Salter, in "When Knights were Bold" 22

Marion Davies, Forrest Stanley, Ruth Shepley and Ernest Glendenning in "When Knighthood was in Flower" 22

Advertising Bulletin for "Balked at the Altar" 23

Biograph Mutoscope of the murder of Stanford White . . . 38

The first Biograph Girl, Florence Lawrence, in "The Barbarian" . 39

From "The Politician's Love Story" 39

The brilliant social world of early movie days 54

"Murphy's," where members of Biograph's original stock company
consumed hearty breakfasts 55

From "Edgar Allan Poe" 70

Herbert Pryor, Linda Griffith, Violet Mersereau and Owen Moore
in "The Cricket on the Hearth" 70

"Little Mary" portraying the type of heroine that won her a legion
of admirers 71

Register of Caudebec Inn at Cuddebackville 71

Caudebec Inn at Cuddebackville 86

From "The Mended Lute," made at Cuddebackville 86

Frank Powell, Mr. Griffith's first $10-a-day actor, with Marion
Leonard in "Fools of Fate" 86

Richard Barthelmess with Nazimova in "War Brides" . . . 87

From "Wark" to "work," with only the difference of a vowel . 102

Biograph's one automobile 102

Annie Lee. From "Enoch Arden," the first two-reel picture . 103

Jeanie Macpherson, Frank Grandin, Linda Griffith and Wilfred
Lucas in "Enoch Arden" 103

The vessel that was towed from San Pedro. From "Enoch
Arden" 103

The Norwegian's shack. From "Enoch Arden" 103

xiii

xiv LIST OF ILLUSTRATIONS

xiv   LIST OF ILLUSTRATIONS

FACING PAGE

A scene from "Mrs. Jones Entertains," released January 1909.
(See p. 74)

Harry Salter, Clara T. Bracey and Mary Pickford in "The Cricket on
the Hearth," released May 1909. *(See p. 92)*

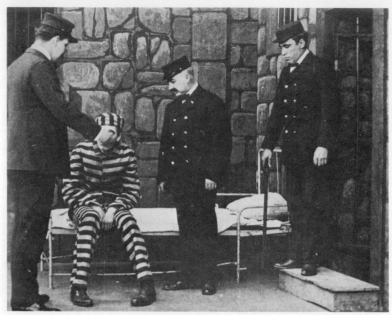

James Kirkwood and Mack Sennett in "A Convict's Sacrifice," released July 1909.

James Kirkwood, Marion Leonard, Arthur Johnson and Mack Sennett in "The Gibson Goddess," released November 1909.

Kate Bruce and J. Barney Sherry in "A Corner in Wheat," released
December 1909.

James Kirkwood and Marion Leonard, 1910.

Marion Leonard and Henry Walthall in "The House with Closed
Shutters," released August 1910. *(See p. 175)*

Linda Arvidson (Mrs. D. W. Griffith) and Arthur Johnson in "Fisher
Folks," released February 1911.

Blanche Sweet in "The Lonedale Operator," released March 1911.
(See p. 201)

Lionel Barrymore and Blanche Sweet in "Fighting Blood," released
June 1911.

J. Barney Sherry (lower left) in "The Last Drop of Water," released July 1911. *(See p. 197)*

Wilfred Lucas and Blanche Sweet in "The Blind Princess and the Poet," released August 1911.

Mabel Normand in "Her Awakening," released
September 1911.

Mabel Normand in "The Eternal Mother," released January 1912.

Dorothy Bernard and H. C. Mailes in "The Goddess of Sagebrush Gulch," released March 1912.

Dorothy Bernard in another scene from "The Goddess of Sagebrush Gulch."

Wilfred Lucas and Dorothy Bernard in "The Girl and Her Trust,"
released March 1912.

Lillian and Dorothy Gish in "An Unseen Enemy," released September
1912. *(See p. 228)*

WHEN THE MOVIES WERE YOUNG

CHAPTER I

ELEVEN EAST FOURTEENTH STREET

JUST off Union Square, New York City, there is a stately old brownstone house on which future generations some day may place a tablet to commemorate the place where David W. Griffith and Mary Pickford were first associated with moving pictures.

Here has dwelt romance of many colors. A bird of brilliant plumage, so the story goes, first lived in this broad-spreading five-story old brownstone that still stands on Fourteenth Street between Fifth Avenue and Broadway, vibrant with life and the ambitions and endeavors of its present occupants.

Although brownstone Manhattan had seen the end of peaceful Dutch ways and the beginning of the present scrambling in the great school of human activity, the first resident of 11 East Fourteenth Street paid no heed—went his independent way. No short-waisted, long and narrow-skirted black frock-coat for him, but a bright blue affair, gold braided and gold buttoned. He was said to be the last man in old Manhattan to put powder in his hair.

As he grew older, they say his style of dressing became more fantastic, further and further back he went in fashion's page, until in his last days knickerbockers with fancy buckles adorned his shrinking limbs, and the powdered hair became a periwig. He became known as "The Last Leaf."

A bachelor, he could indulge in what hobbies he liked. He got much out of life. He had a cool cellar built for the claret, and a sun room for the Madeira. In his impressive reception room he gathered his cronies, opened up his claret and Madeira, the while he matched his game-cocks, and the bets were high. Even when the master became very old and ill, and was alone in his mansion with his faithful old servant, Scipio, there were still the rooster fights. But now they were held upstairs in the master's bedroom. Scipio was allowed to bet a quarter against the old man's twenty-dollar note, and no matter how high the stakes piled, or who won, the pot in these last days always went to Scipio.

And so "The Last Leaf" lived and died.

Then in due time the old brownstone became the home of another picturesque character, Colonel Rush C. Hawkins of the Hawkins Zouaves of the Civil War.

Dignified days, when the family learned the world's news from *Frank Leslie's Illustrated Paper* and the *New York Tribune*, and had Peter Goelet and Moses Taylor for millionaire neighbors. For their entertainment they went to Laura Keene's New Theatre, saw Joe Jefferson, and Lotta; went to the Academy of Music, heard Patti and Clara Louise Kellogg; heard Emma Abbott in concert; and rode on horseback up Fifth Avenue to the Park.

Of an evening, in the spacious ballroom whose doors have since opened to Mary Pickford, D. W. Griffith, and Mack Sennett, the youths, maidens and young matrons in the soft, flickering light of the astral lamp and snowy candle, danced the modest cotillon and stately quadrille, the while the elders played whist. Bounteous supper—champagne, perhaps gin and tansy.

But keenly attuned ears, when they paused to listen, could already hear off in the distance the first faint roll of the drums in the march of progress. "Little Old New York" was growing up and getting to be a big city. And so the Knickerbockers and other aristocracy must leave their brownstone dwellings for quieter districts further uptown. Business was slowly encroaching on their life's peaceful way.

Another day and another generation. Gone the green lawns, enclosed by iron fences where modest cows and showy peacocks mingled, friendly. Gone the harpsichord, the candle, the lamp, to give way to the piano and the gas-lamp. Close up against each other the buildings now nestle round Union Square and on into Fourteenth Street. The horse-drawn street car rattles back and forth where No. 11 stands with some remaining dignity of the old days. On the large glass window—for No. 11's original charming exterior has already yielded to the changes necessitated by trade—is to be read "Steck Piano Company."

In the lovely old ballroom where valiant gentlemen and languishing ladies once danced to soft and lilting strains of music, under the candles' glow, and where "The Last Leaf" entertained his stalwart cronies with cock fighting, the Steck Piano Company now gives concerts and recitals.

The old house has "tenants." And as tenants come and go, the Steck Piano Company tarries but a while, and then moves on.

A lease for the piano company's quarters in No. 11 is drawn up for another firm for $5,000 per year. In place

of the Steck Piano Company on the large window is to
be read—"American Mutoscope and Biograph Company."

However, the name of the new tenant signified nothing whatever to the real estate firm adjacent to No. 11
that had made the new lease. It was understood that
Mutoscope pictures to be shown in Penny Arcades were
being made, and there was no particular interest in the
matter. The "Biograph" part of the name had little significance, if any, until in the passage of time a young actor
from Louisville, called Griffith, came to labor where labor
had been little known and to wonder about the queer new
job he had somewhat reluctantly fallen heir to.

The gentlemen of the real estate firm did some wondering too. Up to this time, the peace of their quarters had
been disturbed only by the occasional lady-like afternoon
concert of the Steck Piano Company. The few preceding
directors of the American Mutoscope and Biograph Company had done their work quietly and unemotionally.

Now, whatever was going on in what was once "The
Last Leaf's" gay and elegant drawing-room, and why did
such shocking language drift through to disturb the conservative transactions in real estate!

"Say, what's the matter with you—you're dying you
know—you've been shot and you're dying! Well, that's
better, something like it! You, here, you've done the shooting,
you're the murderer, naturally you're a bit perturbed, you've
lots to think about—yourself for one thing! You're not
surrendering at the nearest police station, no, you're beating
it, *beating* it, you understand. Now we'll try it again—
That's better, something like it! Now we'll take it. All
right, everybody! Shoot!"

The neighborhood certainly was changing. The language!

The people! Where once distinguished callers in ones and twos had come once and twice a week—now in mobs they were crossing the once sacred threshold every day.

It was in the spring of 1908 that David W. Griffith came to preside at 11 East Fourteenth. Here it was he took up the daily grind, struggled, dreamed, saw old ambitions die, suffered humiliation, achieved, and in four short years was well started on the road to become world famous as the greatest director of the motion picture.

For movies, yes, movies were being made where once "The Last Leaf" had entertained in the grand old manner. That was what the inscription, "American Mutoscope and Biograph Company," had meant.

But movies did not desecrate the dignity of 11 East Fourteenth Street. The dignity of achievement had begun. The old beauty of the place was fast disappearing. The magnificent old chandelier had given place to banks of mercury vapor tubes. There were no soft carpets for the tired actors' feet. The ex-drawing-room and ex-concert hall were now full and overflowing with actors, and life's little comedies and tragedies were being play-acted where once they had been lived.

Fourteenth Street, New York, has been called "the nursery of genius." Many artists struggled there in cheap little studios, began to feel their wings, could not stand success, moved to studio apartments uptown, and met defeat. But 11 East Fourteenth Street still harbors the artist; the building is full of them. Evelyn Longman, who was there when "old Biograph" was, is still there. On other doors are other names—Ruotolo, Oberhardt, John S. Gelert, sculptor; Lester, studio; The Waller Studios; Ye Studio of Frederic Ehrlich.

In the old projection room are now stacked books and plays of the Edgar S. Werner Company, and in the dear old studio, which is just the same to-day as the day we left it, except that the mercury tubes have been taken out, and a north window cut, presides a sculptor by the name of A. Stirling Calder, who has painted the old door blue and hung a huge brass knocker on it.

Now, when I made up my mind to write this record of those early days of the movies, I knew that I must go down once again to see the old workshop, where for four years David W. Griffith wielded the scepter, until swelled with success and new-gained wealth the Biograph Company pulled up stakes and flitted to its new large modern and expensive studio up in the Bronx at East 175th Street.

So down I went to beg Mr. Calder to let me look over the old place and take a picture of it.

My heart was going pit-a-pat out there in the old hallway while I awaited an answer to my knock. "Please," I pleaded, "I want so much to take a photograph of the studio just as it is. I'm writing a little book about our pioneering days here; it won't take a minute. May I, please?"

Emotion was quite overwhelming me as the memories of the years crowded on me, memories of young and happy days untouched with the sadness that years must inevitably bring even though they bring what is considered "success." Twelve years had gone their way since I had passed through those studio doors and here I was again, all a-flutter with anticipation and choky with the half-dreamy memories of events long past.

But don't be tempted to announce your arrival if you

"Lawrence" Griffith. (*See p. 12*)

Linda Arvidson (Mrs. David W. Griffith), as leading ingénue with Florence Roberts in stock in San Francisco. (*See p. 15*)

have ever been connected with a moving picture, for Mr. Calder has scarcely heard of them and when I insisted he must have, he said, with much condescension, "Oh, yes, I remember, Mr. Griffith did a Chinese picture; it was rather good but too sentimental." And he refused to let me take a picture of the studio for he "could not afford to lend his work and his studio to problematical publicity of which he had not the slightest proof."

I felt sorry Mr. Calder had come to reside in our movie nursery at 11 East Fourteenth Street, for we were such good fellows, happy and interested in our work, cordial and pleasant to one another.

The change made me sad!

CHAPTER II

BUT now to go back to the beginning.

It was a night in the summer of 1904 in my dear and fascinating old San Francisco, before the life we all knew and loved had been broken in two, never to be mended, by the disaster of the great fire and earthquake. At the old Alcazar Theatre the now historic stock company was producing Mr. Hall Caine's drama "The Christian."

In the first act the fishermaidens made merry in the village square.

Unknown to family or friends, and with little pride in my humble beginning, I mingled as one of the fishergirls. Three dollars and fifty cents a week was the salary Fred Belasco (David's brother) paid me for my bit of Hall Caine interpretation, so I, for one, had no need to be horrified some four years later when I was paid three dollars a day for playing the same fishermaiden in support of Mary Pickford, who, under Mr. Griffith's direction, was making Glory Quayle into a screen heroine.

Here at the old Alcazar were wonderful people I could worship. There was Oza Waldrop, and John Craig, and Mary Young, Eleanor Gordon, Frances Starr, and Frank Bacon. Kindly, sweet Frank Bacon whose big success, years later, as *Lightnin' Bill Jones,* in his own play "Lightnin'," made not the slightest change in his simple, unpretentious soul. Mr. Bacon had written a play called "In the Hills of California." It was to be produced for

8

a week's run at Ye Liberty Theatre, Oakland, California, and I was to play the ingénue.

One little experience added to another little experience fortified me with sufficient courage to call on managers of visiting Eastern road companies who traveled short of "maids," "special guests at the ball," and "spectators at the races." New York was already beckoning, and without funds for a railroad ticket the only way to get there was to join a company traveling that way.

A summing up of previous experiences showed a recital at Sherman and Clay Hall and two weeks on tour in Richard Walton Tully's University of California's Junior farce "James Wobberts, Freshman."

In the company were Mr. Tully and his then wife, Eleanor Gates, the author; Emil Kreuske, for some years now "Bill Nigh," the motion picture director; Milton Schwartz, who took to law and now practices in Hollywood; Dick Tully and his wife Olive Vail. Elmer Harris of the original college company did not go. Elmer is now partner to Frank E. Woods along with Thompson Buchanan in Mr. Wood's new producing company.

The recital at Sherman and Clay Hall on Sutter Street was a most ambitious effort. My job-hunting pal, Harriet Quimby, a girl I had met prowling about the theaters, concluded we were getting nowhere and time was fleeting. So we hit on a plan to give a recital in San Francisco's Carnegie Hall, and invite the dramatic critics hoping they would come and give us good notices.

The Homer Henley Quartette which we engaged would charge twenty dollars. The rent of the hall was twenty. We should have had in hand forty dollars, and between us we didn't own forty cents.

Harriet Quimby knew Arnold Genthe, and, appreciating her rare beauty, Mr. Genthe said he would make her photos for window display for nothing. Oscar Mauer did the same for me, gratis. Rugs and furniture we borrowed, and the costumes by advertising in the program, we rented cheaply.

We understood only this much of politics: Jimmy Phelan, our Mayor (afterwards Senator James H. Phelan) was a very wealthy man, charitably disposed, and one day we summoned up sufficient courage to tell him our trouble. Most attentively and respectfully he heard us. and without a moment's hesitation gave us the twenty.

So we gave the recital. We sold enough tickets to pay the Homer Henleys, but not enough to pay the debt to Mr. Phelan. He's never been paid these many years though I've thought of doing it often, and will do it some day.

However, the critics came and they gave us good notices, but the recital didn't seem to put much of a dent in our careers. Harriet Quimby soon achieved New York via *The Sunset Magazine*. In New York she "caught on," and became dramatic critic on *Leslie's Weekly*.

The honor of being the first woman in America to receive an aviator's license became hers, as also that of being the first woman to pilot a monoplane across the English Channel. That was in the spring of 1912, a few months before her death while flying over Boston Harbor.

Mission Street, near Third, was in that unique section called South-of-the-Slot. The character of the community was such, that to reside there, or even to admit of knowing residents there meant complete loss of social prestige. Mission Street, which was once the old road that led over blue and yellow lupin-covered hills out to the Mission Dolores of the Spanish Fathers, and was later the place where the elegantly costumed descendants of the forty-niners who had struck pay dirt (and kept it) strolled, held, at the time of which I speak, no reminder of its departed glory except the great romantic old Grand Opera House, which, amid second-hand stores, pawn-shops, cheap restaurants, and saloons, languished in lonely grandeur.

Once in my young life Richard Mansfield played there; Henry Irving and Ellen Terry gave a week of Shakespearean repertoire; Weber and Fields came from New York for the first time and gave their show, but failed. San Franciscans thought that Kolb and Dill, Barney Bernard, and Georgie O'Ramey, who held forth nightly at Fischer's Music Hall, were just as good.

At the time of the earthquake a grand opera company headed by Caruso was singing there. Between traveling luminaries, lesser lights glimmered on the historic old stage. And for a long time, when the theater was called Morosco's Grand Opera House, ten, twenty, and thirty blood-and-thunder melodrama held the boards.

At this stage in its career, and hardly one year before the great disaster, a young actor who called himself Lawrence Griffith was heading toward the Coast in a show called "Miss Petticoats." Katherine Osterman was the star. The company stranded in San Francisco.

Melbourne MacDowell, in the last remnants of the faded glory cast upon him by Fanny Davenport, was about to tread the sacred stage of the old Grand Opera House, putting on a repertoire of the Sudermann and Sardou dramas.

Frank Bacon, always my kind adviser, suggested I

should try my luck with this aggregation. So I trotted merrily down, wandered through dark alleyways, terribly thrilled, for Henry Irving had come this same way and I was walking where once he had walked.

I was to appear as a boy servant in "Fedora." I remember only one scene. It was in a sort of court room with a civil officer sitting high and mighty and calm and unperturbed on a high stool behind a high desk. I entered the room and timidly approached the desk. A deep stern voice that seemed to rise from some dark depths shouted at me, "At what hour did your master leave *Blu Bla?*"

I shivered and shook and finally stammered out the answer, and was mighty glad when the scene was over.

Heavens! Who was this person, anyhow?

His name, I soon learned, was Griffith—Lawrence Griffith—I never could abide that "Lawrence"! Though, as it turned out afterward, our married life might have been dull without that Christian name as a perpetual resource for argument.

Afterward, to my great joy, Mr. Griffith confided to me that he had taken the name "Lawrence" only for the stage. His real name was "David," "David Wark," but he was going to keep that name dark until he was a big success in the world, and famous. And as yet he didn't know, although he seemed very lackadaisical about it, I thought, whether he'd be great as an actor, stage director, grand opera star, poet, playwright, or novelist.

I wasn't the only one who thought he might have become a great singer. Once a New York critic reviewing a première of one of David Griffith's motion pictures, said: "The most interesting feature of Mr. Griffith's openings is to hear his wonderful voice."

"Lawrence" condescended to a little conversation now and then. He was quite encouraging at times. Said I had wonderful eyes for the stage and if I ever went to New York and got in right, I'd get jobs "on my eyes." (Sounded very funny—getting a job "on one's eyes.") Advised me never to get married if I expected to stay on the stage. Told me about the big New York actors: Leslie Carter, who had just been doing DuBarry; and David Belasco, and what a wonderful producer he was; and dainty Maude Adams; and brilliant Mrs. Fiske; and Charles Frohman; and Richard Mansfield in "Monsieur Beaucaire"; and Broadway; and Mrs. Fernandez's wonderful agency; and how John Drew got his first wonderful job through her agency at one hundred and twenty-five dollars a week!

I was eager to learn more of the big theatrical world three thousand miles away. I invited Mr. Griffith out home to lunch one day. A new world soon opened up for me— the South. The first Southerner I'd ever met was Mr. Griffith. I had known of the South only from my school history; but the one I had studied didn't tell of Colonel Jacob Wark Griffith, David's father, who fought under Stonewall Jackson in the Civil War, and was called "Thunder Jake" because of his roaring voice. He owned lots of negroes, gambled, and loved Shakespeare. There was big "Sister Mattie" who taught her little brother his lessons and who, out on the little front stoop, just before bedtime, did her best to answer all the questions the inquisitive boy would ask about the stars and other wonders.

This was all very different from being daughter to a Norseman who had settled out on San Francisco's seven hills in the winds and fogs.

The South began to loom up as a land of romance.

CHAPTER III

CLIMACTERIC—AN EARTHQUAKE AND A MARRIAGE

WHEN the Melbourne MacDowell repertory season closed, the stranded actors of the "Miss Petticoats" Company were again on the loose. While San Francisco supported two good stock companies, the Alcazar presenting high-class drama and the Central given over to melodrama, their rosters had been completed for the season and they offered rather lean pickings. But Lawrence Griffith worked them both to the best of his persuasive powers.

Early fall came with workless weeks, and finally, to conserve his shrinking treasury, our young actor who had been domiciled in the old Windsor Hotel, a most moderately priced place on Market and Fourth Streets, had to bunk in with Carlton, the stage carpenter of the MacDowell show, in a single-bedded single room. Mr. Carlton was on a social and mental plane with the actor, but his financial status was decidedly superior.

The doubling-up arrangement soon grew rather irksome. What with idle days, a flattened purse, and isolation from theatrical activities, gloom and discouragement enveloped young Griffith, although he never seemed to worry.

He had a trunk full of manuscripts—one-act plays, long plays, and short stories and poems! To my unsophisticated soul it was all very wonderful. What a cruel, unappreciative world, to permit works of genius to languish lonely amid stage wardrobe and wigs and greasy make-up!

On pleasant days when the winds were quiet and the fogs hung no nearer than Tamalpais across the Gate, we would hie ourselves to the Ocean Beach, where, fortified with note-book and pencil the actor-poet would dictate new poems and stories.

One day young Lawrence brought along a one-act play called "In Washington's Time." The act had been head-lined over the Keith Circuit. It had never played in San Francisco. He wondered if he could do anything with it.

It was approaching the hop-picking season. The stranded young actor's funds were reaching bottom. Some-thing must be done.

In California, in those days, quite nice people picked hops. Mother and father, young folks, and the children, went. Being the dry season, they'd live in the open; pick hops by day, and at night dance and sing.

Lawrence Griffith decided it would be a healthful, a colorful, and a more remunerative experience than picking up theatrical odd jobs, to join the hop pickers up Ukiah way. So for a few weeks he picked hops and mingled with thrifty, plain people and operatic Italians who drank "dago red" and sang the sextette from "Lucia" while they picked their portion. Here he saved money and got atmosphere for a play. Sent me a box of sweet-smelling hops from the fields, too!

A brief engagement as leading ingénue with Florence Roberts had cheered me in the interval, even though Fred Belasco made me feel utterly unworthy of my thirty-five dollar salary. "My God," said he when I presented my first week's voucher, "they don't give a damn what they do with my money."

However, Mr. Griffith soon returned to San Francisco. He hoped to do something with his playlet. Martin Beck, the vaudeville magnate, who was then manager of the Orpheum Theatre and booked acts over the Orpheum Circuit, said to let him see a rehearsal.

Such excitement! I was to play a little Colonial girl and appear at our own Orpheum Theatre in an act that had played New York, Boston, Philadelphia, Chicago, and other awesome cities. Mr. Beck booked for the week and gave us a good salary, but could not offer enough consecutive bookings to make a road tour pay, so that was that.

In the meantime Oliver Morosco had opened his beautiful Majestic Theatre in upper Market Street, with "In the Palace of the King." The New York company lacking a blind Inez, I got the part, and the dramatic critic, Ashton Stevens, gave me a great notice. In the next week's bill, "Captain Barrington," I played a scene which brought me a paragraph from Mr. Stevens captioned "An Actress with more than Looks." On the strength of this notice Mr. Morosco sent me to play ingénues at his Burbank Theatre in Los Angeles, at twenty-five dollars per week.

Barney Bernard was stepping out just now. He wanted to see what he could do away from the musical skits of Kolb and Dill. So he found a play called "The Financier." "Lawrence" Griffith had a little job in it. The hardest part of the job was to smoke a cigar in a scene—it nearly made him ill. But he had a good season, six weeks with salary paid.

That over, came a call to Los Angeles to portray the Indian, Alessandro, in a dramatization of Helen Hunt Jackson's famous novel "Ramona."

It was pleasant for us to see each other. We went out to San Gabriel Mission together. Mr. Griffith afterwards used the Mission as the setting for a short story— a romantic satire which he called "From Morning Until Night." His brief engagement over, "Lawrence" went back to San Francisco, and my Morosco season ending shortly afterward, I followed suit.

In San Francisco, Nance O'Neill was being billed. She was returning from her Australian triumphs in Ibsen, Sardou, and Sudermann. The company, with McKee Rankin as manager and leading man, included John Glendenning, father of Ernest; Clara T. Bracey, sister of Lydia Thompson of British Blonde Burlesque and Black Crook fame; Paul Scardon from the Australian Varieties and now husband of a famous cinema star, Betty Blythe; and Jane Marbury.

Mr. Griffith, hoping for a chance to return East with the company, applied for a job and was offered "bits" which he accepted. Then one day, Mr. Rankin being ill, Lawrence Griffith stepped into the part of the Father in "Magda." Miss O'Neill thought so well of his performance and the notices he received that she offered him leading parts for the balance of the season.

When in the early spring of 1906, the company departed from San Francisco, it left me with my interest in life decidedly diminished—but Lawrence Griffith had promised to return, and when he came back things would be different.

So, while the O'Neill company was working close to Minneapolis, I was "resting." I "rested" until eighteen minutes to five on the morning of April 18th, when something happened.

"Earthquake?"

"I don't know, but I think we had better get up," suggested my sister.

I sent Lawrence a long telegram about what had happened to us, but he received it by post. And then about a week later I received a letter from Milwaukee telling me that Miss O'Neill and the company were giving a benefit for desolate San Francisco, and that I had better come on and meet him in Boston where the company was booked for a six weeks' engagement.

So to Fillmore Street I went to beg for a railroad ticket to Boston, gratis. There was a long line of people waiting. I took my place at the end of the line. In time I reached the man at the desk.

"Where to?"

"Boston."

"What is your occupation?"

"Actress."

I thought it unwise to confide my matrimonial objective. No further questions, however. I was given a yard of ticket and on May 9th I boarded a refugee train at the Oakland mole, all dressed up in Red Cross clothes that fitted me nowhere.

But I had a lovely lunch, put up by neighbors, some fried chicken, and two small bottles of California claret. In another box, their stems stuck in raw potatoes, some orange blossoms off a tree that stood close to our tent.

Ah, dear old town, good-bye!

Every night I cried myself to sleep.

Thus I went to meet my bridegroom.

Boston!

Everything a bustle! People, and people, and people! Laughing, happy, chattering people who didn't seem to know and apparently didn't care what had happened to us out there by the bleak Pacific. I was so annoyed at them. Their life was still normal. Though I knew they had helped bounteously, I was annoyed.

But here HE comes! And we jumped into a cab—with a license, but no ring. In the unusual excitement that had been forgotten, so we had to turn back in the narrow street and find a jeweler. Then we drove to Old North Church, where Paul Revere had hung out his lantern on his famous ride (which Mr. Griffith has since filmed in "America"), and our names were soon written in the register.

The end of June, and New York! Just blowing up for a thunderstorm. I had never heard real thunder, nor seen lightning, nor been wet by a summer rain. What horrible weather! The wind blew a gale, driving papers and dust in thick swirling clouds. Of all the miserable introductions to the city of my dreams and ambitions, New York City could hardly have offered me a more miserable one!

We lived in style for a few days at the Hotel Navarre on Seventh Avenue and Thirty-ninth Street, and then looked for a "sublet" for the summer. I'd never heard of a "sublet" before.

We ferreted around and found a ducky little place, so cheap—twenty-five dollars a month—on West Fifty-sixth Street, overlooking the athletic grounds of the Y. M. C. A., where I was tremendously amused watching the fat men all wrapped up in sweaters doing their ten times around without stopping—for reducing purposes.

But we had little time to waste in such observations.

A job must be had for the fall. In a few weeks we signed with the Rev. Thomas Dixon (fresh from his successful "Clansman") ; my husband as leading man and I as general understudy, in "The One Woman." Rehearsals were to be called in about two months.

To honeymoon, or not to honeymoon—to work or not to work. Work it was, and David started on a play.

And he worked. He walked the floor while dictating and I took it down on the second-hand typewriter I had purchased somewhere on Amsterdam Avenue for twenty dollars. The only other investment of the summer had been at Filene's in Boston where I left my Red Cross sartorial contributions and emerged in clothes that had a more personal relation to me.

They were happy days. The burdens were shared equally. My husband was a splendid cook; modestly said, so was I. He loved to cook, singing negro songs the while, and whatever he did, whether cooking or writing or washing the dishes, he did it with the same earnestness and cheerfulness. Felt his responsibilities too, and had a sort of mournful envy of those who had established themselves.

Harriet Quimby was now writing a weekly article for *Leslie's,* and summering gratis at the old Oriental Hotel at Manhattan Beach as payment for publicizing the social activities of the place. Beach-bound one day, she called at our modest menage, beautifully dressed, with wealthy guests in their expensive car. As the car drove off, Mr. Griffith gazing sadly below from our window five flights up, as sadly said "She's a success."

The play came along fine, owing much to our experiences in California. One act was located in the hop fields, and there were Mexican songs that Mr. Griffith had first heard rendered by native Mexicans who sang in "Ramona." Another act was in a famous old café in San Francisco, The Poodle Dog. It was christened "A Fool and a Girl." The fool was an innocent youth from Kentucky, but the girl, being from San Francisco, was more piquant.

We'd been signed for the fall, and we felt we'd done pretty well by the first summer. I'd learned to relish the funny little black raspberries and not to be afraid of thunderstorms—they were not so uncertain as earthquakes.

And now rehearsals are called for Mr. Dixon's "The One Woman." They lasted some weeks before we took to the road and opened in Norfolk, Virginia, where we drew our first salaries, seventy-five for him and thirty-five for her. Nice, it was, and we hoped it would be a long season.

CHAPTER IV

YOUNG AMBITIONS AND A FEW JOLTS

BUT it wasn't.

After two months on the road we received our two weeks' notice. For half Mr. Griffith's salary, Mr. Dixon had engaged another leading man, who, he felt, would adequately serve the cause. So, sad at heart and not so wealthy, we returned to the merry little whirl of life in the theatrical metropolis of the U. S. A. We had one asset—the play. Good thing we had not frivoled away those precious summer weeks in seeking cooling breezes by Coney's coral strand!

Late that fall my husband played a small part in a production of "Salome" at the Astor Theatre under Edward Ellsner's direction. Mr. Ellsner was looking for a play for Pauline Frederick. Mr. Griffith suggested his play and Mr. Ellsner was sufficiently interested to arrange for a reading for Miss Frederick and her mother. They liked it; so did Mr. Ellsner; and so the play was sent on to Mr. James K. Hackett, Miss Frederick's manager at that time.

It was Christmas eve—our first. Three thousand miles from home, lonesome, broke.

In the busy marts of dramatic commerce poor little "D" was dashing hither and yon with his first-born. Even on this day before Christmas he was on the job. The festive

Linda Arvidson (Mrs. Griffith), David W. Griffith and Harry Salter, in "When Knights were Bold," Biograph's version of "When Knighthood was in Flower." *(See p. 34)*

Marion Davies, Forrest Stanley, Ruth Shepley and Ernest Glendenning, in Cosmopolitan's production of "When Knighthood was in Flower." *(See p. 34)*

FORM NO 1336   BULLETIN No. 164. RELEASED August 25, 1908

BALKED AT THE ALTAR

Biograph Comedy of a Near-wedding

LENGTH 703 FEET   PRICE, 14 CENTS PER FOOT.

Artemisia Sophia Stebbins was a lovelorn maiden who had delved deep into the mysteries of "Three Weeks," as well as being conversant with the teachings of Laura Jean Libbe Her one hobby was to possess a hubby Many there were whom she tried to hook but in vain, for truth to say Arte was of pulchritude a bit shy She had the complexion of pale rhubarb and a figure like a wheat sack Still her motto was *Vil desperandum*," and she was ever hopeful One thing in her favor her father Obediah Stebbins, avowed his aid Of the visitors who called at the Stebbins domicile Hezekiah Hornbeak seemed the most probable to corral so Artemisia set to work Hez at first was a trifle recalcitrant, but was soon subdued by Obediah s gun which we must admit possessed agregious powers of persuasion The day for the wedding was set and to the village church there flocked the natives to witness this momentous affair All was progressing serenely until the all-important question was put to Hezekiah and instead of answering ' Yea ' he kicked over the trace and tried to beat it His escape by way of he door was intercepted, so it happens that the little church is in sore need of a stained glass window for Hez took a portion of it with him in his haste. Out and over the lawn he gallops with the congregation close at his heels, Artemisia Sophia well in the lead Down from the terrace onto the road they leap and across the meadow until they come to a fence, on the other side of which are two boys shooting crap Over this hurdle they vault coming plump down on the poor boys, almost crushing the life out of them Regaining his equilibrium Hez forges on coming to the very acropolis of the town. The descent therefrom is decidedly precipitous and makes Hez hesitate for a moment, but only a moment, for the howling horde is still in pursuit; so down he goes in leaps and falls to the bottom followed by a veritable avalanche of human beings Owing to this mix up Hez has a chance to distance them a little and being almost exhausted he attempts to climb a tree, but too late for the gang is soon on him, and carry him back to the church where the ceremony is started again, and when he is asked that all important question he fairly yells "Yes, b'gosh!" Artemisia is now asked the question and to the amazement of all present she says "Not on your county fair tintype " and flounces haughtily out of the church, leaving poor Hezekiah in a state of utter collapse, surrounded by sympathizing friends

No 3465   **CODE WORD—Revesaste**

Advertising Bulletin for "Balked at the Altar," with Harry Salter, Mabel Stoughton, Mack Sennett, George Gebhardt and Linda Griffith. The release of all Biograph movies was similarly announced.   *(See p. 40)*

holiday meal I had prepared was quite ready. There were some things to be grateful for: each other, the comfortable two rooms, and the typewriter. The hamburger steak was all set, the gravy made, and the potatoes with their jackets on, à la California camp style, were a-steaming. The little five-cent baker's pie was warming in the oven and the pint bottle of beer was cooling in the snow on the window ledge. And some one all mine was coming.

We sat down to dinner. Couldn't put the plates on the table right side up these days, it seemed. Had no recollection of having turned my plate over. Turned it right side up again.

I wished people wouldn't be silly. I supposed this was a verse about Christmas. But why the mystery? Wonderingly, I opened the folded slip of paper. Funny looking poetry. Funny look on D's face. What was this anyhow? Looked like an old-fashioned rent receipt. But it didn't say "Received from ———." It said "Pay to ———," "Pay to the order of David W. Griffith seven hundred dollars," and it was signed "James K. Hackett."

"Oh no, you haven't *sold the play!*"

Yes, it was sold; the check represented a little advance royalty. And were the play a success we would receive a stipulated percentage of the weekly gross. (I've forgotten the scale.)

Oh, kind and generous Mr. Hackett!

Isn't it funny how calm one can be in the big moments of life? But I couldn't grasp it. Christmas eve and all! An honest-to-God check on an honest-to-God bank for seven hundred whole dollars. Was there that much money in the whole world?

Now came wonderful days—no financial worry and no

job-hunting. True, we realized the seven hundred would not last indefinitely. But to accept a job and not be in New York when rehearsals for the play were called, was an idea not to be entertained. So, to feel right about the interim of inactivity, David wrote yards of poetry and several short stories. And John A. Sleicher of *Leslie's Weekly* paid the princely sum of six dollars for a poem called "The Wild Duck."

A bunch of stuff was sent off to *McClure's*, which Mr. McClure said appealed to him very much—though not enough for publication. He'd like to see more of Mr. Griffith's work.

And the *Cosmopolitan*, then under Perriton Maxwell's editorship, bought "From Morning Until Night" for seventy-five dollars. Things were looking up.

In Norfolk, Va., a Centennial was to be held in celebration of the landing on Southern soil of the first of the F. F. V.'s, and a play commemorating the event had been written around Captain John Smith and Pocahontas. Mr. Griffith accepted a part in it. The six weeks' engagement would help out until the rehearsals of his own play were called. But Pocahontas's financial aid must have been somewhat stingy according to the letter my husband wrote me in New York. We had felt we couldn't afford my railroad fare to Norfolk and my maintenance there. It was our first separation.

And this the letter:

DEAR LINDA,

I am sending you a little $3 for carfare. I would send more but I couldn't get anything advanced, so I only send you this much.

I'll get my salary, or part of it, rather, Monday, so I'll send you more then and also tell you what I think we should do. I would like to go to Miss ———— if we could get it for $6 a week, or $25 a month but I don't like to pay $7.50, that's too strong if we can do cheaper. Of course, if we can't we can't and that's all there is to it. Let me know as soon as you get this money as I am only sending it wrapped up as I don't want you to have to cash so small a check as $3, so that's why I am sending it this way.

I bet you I get some good things out of this world for her yet, just watch me and see. . . .

Her husband,

David

Pocahontas flivvered out in three weeks. But as Shakespeare says, "Sweet are the uses of adversity." While Mr. Griffith was away, I found time to make myself a new dress. In a reckless moment I had paid a dollar deposit on some green silk dress material at Macy's, which at a later and wealthier moment I had redeemed. So now I rented a sewing machine and sewed like mad to get the dress done, for I could afford only one dollar-and-a-half weekly rental on the old Wheeler and Wilson.

By the time "A Fool and A Girl" was to open in Washington, D. C., there was just enough cold cash left for railroad fare there. Klaw and Erlanger produced the play under Mr. Duane's direction, and Mr. Hackett came on to rehearsals in Washington. Fannie Ward and Jack Deane played the leading parts. Here they met and their romance began, and according to latest accounts it is still thriving. Alison Skipworth of "The Torch Bearers" and other successes, was a member of the cast.

The notices were not the best nor the worst. They

are interesting to-day, for they show how time has ambled apace since October, 1907. Said Hector Fuller, the critic:

It may be said that the dramatist wanted to show where his hero's feet strayed; and where he found the girl he was afterwards to make his wife, but if one wants to tell the old, old and beautiful story of redemption of either man or woman through love, it is not necessary to portray the gutters from which they are redeemed. . . .

One week in Washington and one in Baltimore saw on its jolly way to the storehouse the wicked Bull Pup Café and the Hop Fields, etc.

And so back to New York.

In the Sixth Avenue "L" with our little suitcases, we sat, a picture of woe and misery. In the Sixth Avenue "L," for not even a dollar was to be wasted on a taxi. But when the door to our own two rooms was closed, and, alone together, we faced our wrecked hopes, it wasn't so awful. Familiar objects seemed to try and comfort us. After all, it was a little home, and better than a park bench; and the *Century Dictionary*—of which some day we would be complete owners, maybe—and the Underwood, all our own—spoke to us reassuringly.

I do not recall that any job materialized that winter, but something must have happened to sustain us. Perhaps the belated receipt of those few hundred dollars of mine that were on deposit at the German Savings Bank at the time of the Disaster in San Francisco.

To offset what might have been a non-productive winter, Mr. Griffith wrote "War," a pretentious affair of the American Revolution, which Henry Miller would have produced had it been less expensive. "War" had meant a lot of work. For weeks previous to the writing, we had re-

paired daily to the Astor Library where we copied soldiers'
diaries and letters and read histories of the period until
sufficiently imbued with the spirit of 1776. "War" is still
in the manuscript stage with the exception of the Valley
Forge bits which came to life in Mr. Griffith's film
"America"; for Mr. Griffith turned to the spectacle very
early in his career, though he little dreamed then of the
medium in which he was to record the great drama of the
American Revolution.

We met Perriton Maxwell again. Extended and accepted dinner invitations. Our dinner was a near-tragedy.
Before the banquet had advanced to the salad stage, I had
to take my little gold bracelet to a neighboring "Uncle."
The antique furniture necessitated placards which my husband posted conspicuously. For instance, on the sofa—
"Do not sit here; the springs are weak." On a decrepit
gate-legged table—"Don't lean; the legs are loose."

At the Maxwells' dinner our host gathered several
young literati who he thought might become interested in
Mr. Griffith and his literary efforts. Vivian M. Moses,
then editor of *Good Housekeeping* and now Publicity
Manager for The Fox Films, was one, as was Jules E.
Goodman, the playwright. But a "litry" career for Mr.
Griffith seemed foredoomed. A poem now and then, and
an occasional story sold, was too fragile sustenance for
permanency. Some sort of steady job would have to be
found, and the "litry" come in as a side-line.

David Griffith was ready for any line of activity that
would bring in money, so that he could write plays. He always
had some idea in his inventive mind, such as non-puncturable
tires, or harnessing the ocean waves. In the mornings, on wak-

ing, he would lie in bed and work out plots for dramas, scene bits, or even mechanical ideas. After an hour of apparent semi-consciousness, his head motionless on the pillow, he would greet the day with "I hate to see her die in the third act"; or, "I wonder if that meat dish could be canned!" meaning, could a dish he had invented and cooked—a triumph of culinary art—be made a commercial proposition as a tinned food, like Armour's or Van Camp's beans and corned beef.

Pretty good field of activity, canned eats, and might have made David W. Griffith more money than canned drama!

CHAPTER V

THE MOVIES TEMPT

WINTER passed. Spring came.

On the Rialto's hard pavements, day in and day out, Mr. Griffith, his ear to the ground, was wearing out good shoe leather. But nothing like a job materialized, until, meeting up with an old acquaintance, Max Davidson, he heard about moving pictures. Since youthful days in a Louisville stock company these two had not met. And the simple confidences they exchanged this day brought results that were most significant, not only to David Griffith, but to millions of unsuspecting people the world over.

Mr. Davidson had been going down to a place on 11 East Fourteenth Street and doing some kind of weird acting before a camera—little plays, he explained, of which a camera took pictures.

"You've heard of moving pictures, haven't you?"

"Why, I don't know; suppose I have, but I've never seen one. Why?"

"I work in them during the summer; make five dollars some days when I play a leading part, but usually it's three. Keeps you going, and you get time to call on managers too. Now you could write the little stories for the pictures. They pay fifteen dollars sometimes for good ones. Don't feel offended at the suggestion. It's not half bad, really. We spend lots of days working out in the country. Lately we've been doing pictures where they use horses, and it's just like getting paid for enjoying a nice horseback ride. Anybody can ride well enough for the pictures. Just manage to stay on the horse, that's all."

"Ye gods," said the tempted one, "some of my friends might see me. Then I would be done for. Where do they show these pictures? I'll go see one first."

"Oh, nobody'll ever see you—don't worry about that."

"Well, that does make it different. I'll think it over. Where's the place, you said?"

"Eleven East Fourteenth Street."

"Thanks awfully. I'll look in—so long."

The elder Mr. McCutcheon was the director when David applied for a job at the American Mutoscope and Biograph Company and got it.

There were no preliminaries. He was told to go "below" and put on a little make-up. So he went "below" —to the dressing-room, but he didn't put on a "little make-up." He took a great deal of trouble with it although it was largely experimental, being very different from the conventional stage make-up. The only instruction he was given was to leave off the "red" which would photograph black, thus putting hollows in his cheeks. And he didn't need hollows in his cheeks.

When he came up to the studio floor—his dressing and make-up finished—the director, and the actors especially, looked at him as though he were not quite in his right mind. "Poor boob," they thought, to take such trouble with a "make-up" for a moving picture, a moving picture that no one who counted for anything would ever see.

After a short rehearsal, an explanation of "foreground"

and instructions about keeping "inside the lines" and "outside the lines," the camera opened up, ground away for about twenty feet, and the ordeal was over.

When work was finished for the day, Mr. McCutcheon paid his new actor five dollars and told him to call on the morrow. So the next morning there was an early start to the studio. They were to work outside, and there were to be horses!

I shall never forget the sadly amused expression my husband brought home with him, the evening of that second day. Nor his comments: "It's not so bad, you know, five dollars for simply riding a horse in the wilds of Fort Lee on a cool spring day. I think it wouldn't be a bad idea for you to go down and see what you can do. Don't tell them who you are, I mean, don't tell them you're my wife. I think it is better business not to."

So a few days later, I dolled up for a visit to the studio. After I had waited an hour or so, Mr. McCutcheon turned to me and said, "All right, just put a little make-up on; this isn't very important." There was no coaching for the acting; only one thing mattered, and that was, not to appear as though hunting frantically for the lines on the floor that marked your stage, while the scenes were being taken.

Mr. Griffith and I "listened in" on all the stories and experiences the actors at the studio had to tell. We would have all the information we could get on the subject of moving pictures, those tawdry and cheap moving pictures, the existence of which we had hitherto been aware of only through the lurid posters in front of the motion picture places—those terrible moving picture places where we wouldn't be caught dead. But we could find use for as many of those little "fives" as might come our way.

Humiliating as the work was, no one took the interest in it that David Griffith did, or worked as hard. This Mr. McCutcheon must have divined right off, for he used him quite regularly and bought whatever stories he wrote.

Only a few days were needed to get a line on the place. It was a conglomerate mess of people that hung about the studio. Among the flotsam and jetsam appeared occasionally a few real actors and actresses. They would work a few days and disappear. They had found a job on the stage again. The better they were, the quicker they got out. A motion picture surely was something not to be taken seriously.

Those running the place were not a bit annoyed by this attitude. The thing to do was to drop in at about nine in the morning, hang around a while, see if there was anything for you, and if not, to beat it up town quick, to the agents. If you were engaged for a part in a picture and had to see a theatrical agent at eleven and told Mr. McCutcheon so, he would genially say, "That's O. K. I'll fix it so you can get off." You were much more desirable if you made such requests. It meant theatrical agents were seeking you for the legitimate drama, so you must be *good!*

Would it be better to affiliate with only one studio or take them all in? There was Edison, way out in the Bronx; Vitagraph in the wilds of Flatbush; Kalem, like Biograph, was conveniently in town; Lubin was in Philadelphia, and Essanay in Chicago. Melies was out West. It would be much nicer, of course, if one could get in "right" at the Biograph.

Some of the actors did the rounds. Ambitious Florence Auer did and so became identified with a different line of parts at each studio. At Biograph, character comedy; at

Vitagraph, Shakespeare—for "King Lear" and "Richard the Third" with Thomas H. Ince in attendance, were screened as long ago as this; at Edison, religious drama. There she rode the biblical jackass.

The Kalem studio was in the loft of a building on West Twenty-third Street. You took the elevator to where it didn't run any further and then you climbed a ladder up to a place where furniture and household goods were stored.

Bob Vignola could be seen here dusting off a clear place for the camera and another place where the actors could be seated the while they waited until Sidney Olcott, the director, got on the day's job.

Sidney Olcott was an experienced man in the movies even in those early days, for had he not played a star part in the old Biograph in the spring of 1904? As the *Village Cut-up* in the movie of the same name we read this about him in the old Biograph bulletin:

Every country cross-corners has its "Cut-up," the real devilish young man who has been to the "city" at some stage of his career, and having spent thirty cents looking at the Mutoscope, or a dollar on the Bowery at Coney, thinks he is the real thing. The most common evidence of his mental unbalance is the playing of practical jokes, which are usually very disagreeable to the victim. . . .

In a few years Mr. Olcott had evolved from the "village cut-up" at Biograph to director at Kalem.

Here he engaged Miss Auer for society parts and adventuresses. Stopped her on the Rialto one day. "I know you are an actress," said Mr. Olcott, "and that beautiful gray silk dress you have on would photograph so wonderfully, I'll give you ten dollars if you'll wear it in a scene—it's a society part." For a dress that was *gray,* and *silk* too, was a most valuable property and a rare specimen of wardrobe in the movies in those days.

It came as pleasant news that a tabloid version of "When Knighthood Was in Flower" to be called "When Knights Were Bold" was to be screened at Biograph. There were four, or perhaps five, persons in the cast of this première "Knighthood" picture. My husband was one; so was I. The picture commemorates our only joint movie appearance.

I recall only one scene in this movie, a back-drop picturing landscape, with a prop tree, a wooden bench, and a few mangy grass mats, but there was one other set representing an inn. I never saw the picture and couldn't tell much about it from the few scenes in which I played.

A one-reeler, of course—nine hundred and five feet. Now whether the cost of Biograph pictures was then being figured at a dollar a foot, I do not know. But that was the dizzy average a very short time later. Anyhow, our "Flowering Knighthood" was cheap enough compared with what Mr. Hearst spent thirteen years later on his Cosmopolitan production, which cost him $1,221,491.20, and was completed in the remarkably short time of one hundred sixty working days.

Mr. Hearst's "Knighthood" had a remarkable cast of eighteen principal characters representing the biggest names in the theatrical and motion picture world, and the supporting company counted three thousand extra persons and thirty-three horses.

Miss Marion Davies as Princess Mary Tudor was assisted by Lyn Harding, the English actor-manager; Pedro De Cordoba, Arthur Forrest (the original Petronius of "Quo Vadis"), Theresa Maxwell Conover, Ernest Glendenning, (of "Little Old New York"), Ruth Shepley (star of "Adam and Eva"), Johnny Dooley, (celebrated eccentric dancer), George Nash, Gustav von Seyffertitz (for years director and star of the old Irving Place Theatre), Macy Harlam, Arthur Donaldson, Mortimer Snow, William Morris (of "Maytime" fame).

A few other names of world-famous people must be mentioned in connection with this picture, for Joseph Urban was the man of the "sets"; Gidding & Company made the gowns; Sir Joseph Duveen and P. W. French & Company supplied Gothic draperies; and Cartier, antique jewelry.

There were only two old movie pioneers connected with the production: Flora Finch, who back in old Vitagraph days co-starred with John Bunny and after his death held her place alone as an eccentric comedienne; and the director, Robert G. Vignola, who back in the days of our "Knighthood" was the young chap who dusted off the benches and furniture in the old Kalem loft.

But Robert Vignola, who came of humble Italian parentage, had a brain in his young head, and was ambitious. Realizing the limitations of Albany, his home town, he had set out for New York and landed a job in a motion picture studio. Young Vignola represented at the Kalem organization, in the early days, what Bobbie Harron did at Biograph. But the Biograph, from ranking the last in quality of picture production, grew to occupy first place, while Kalem continued on a rather more even way. But Bob Vignola didn't, as the years have shown.

Indeed, many big names have appeared in movies called "When Knighthood Was in Flower," but David Griffith's is not the biggest, nor was it the first, for before the end of the year 1902, in Marienbad, Germany, a film thirty-one feet long was produced and given the title "When Knighthood Was in Flower." The descriptive line in the Biograph catalogue of 1902 (for it was a Biograph production) reads:

Emperor William of Germany and noblemen of the Order of St. John. The Emperor is the last in the procession.

So you see the Ex-Kaiser beat them all to it, even D. W. Griffith and W. R. Hearst, though I'll say that Mr. Hearst's is the best of the "Flowering Knighthoods" to date, and will probably continue so. The story has now been done often enough to be allowed a rest.

But it was Mr. Griffith's big dream, very early in his movie career, along in 1911, to screen some day a great and wonderful movie of the Charles Major play that launched Julia Marlowe on her brilliant career. And in this play which he had decided could be produced nowhere but in England, no less a person than E. H. Sothern was to appear as Charles Brandon, and she who is writing this was to be Mary Tudor.

Dreams and dreams we had long ago, but this was one of the best dreams that did not come true.

CHAPTER VI

MOVIE ACTING DAYS—AND AN "IF"

WE called him "Old Man McCutcheon," the genial, generous person who at this time directed the movies at the American Mutoscope and Biograph Company. Why "Old Man" I do not know, unless it was because he was slightly portly and the father of about eight children, the oldest being Wallace—"Wally" to his intimates. Wally was quite "some pumpkins" around the studio—father's right-hand-man—and then, too, he was a Broadway actor.

It was then the general idea of movie directors to use their families in the pictures. As money was the only thing to be had out of the movies those days, why not get as much as possible while the getting was good? The Mc-Cutcheon kids had just finished working in a Christmas picture, receiving, besides pay checks, the tree and the toys when the picture was finished. So the first bit of gossip wafted about was that the McCutcheons had a pretty good thing of it altogether.

In February, 1908, Wallace McCutcheon was closing an engagement in Augustus Thomas's play, "The Ranger." Appearing in "The Ranger" with young Mr. McCutcheon, were Robert Vignola, John Adolfi, Eddie Dillon, and Florence Auer.

A school picture called "The Snow-man" was to be made which called for eight children—another job for the little

McCutcheons. Grown-up Wally, and mother, were to work too, mother to see that the youngsters were properly dressed and made up.

A tall, slight young woman was needed for the school-mistress and Eddie Dillon, whom Wally had inveigled to the studio, suggested Florence Auer.

The story takes place outside the schoolhouse and a "furious blizzard" is raging, although I would say there was nothing prophetic of the blizzard that raged in D. W. Griffith's famous movie "Way Down East," even though events were so shaping themselves that had Mr. McCutcheon held off a few weeks with his snow story, Mr. Griffith would have arrived in time to offer suggestions. And he would have had something to say, had he been so privileged, for "The Snow-man's" raging "blizzard" was made up of generous quantities of *sawdust!*

The legs, arms, torso, and head of the *Snow-man* were fashioned of fluffy, white cotton, each a separate part, and were hidden under the drifts of sawdust, to be found later by the children who came to romp in the snow and make a snow-man. The places where the *Snow-man's* fragments were buried were marked so that the children could easily find them. One youngster pretends to mold of sawdust an imaginary leg, but in reality is hunting the buried finished one, on locating which, she surreptitiously pulls it from beneath the sawdust. In this way, finally, all the parts of the Snow-man are dug out of the sawdust snow, and put together, revealing a beautiful Snow-man.

Then the Good Fairy of the Snows who all this time has been dreaming in the silver crescent of the moon, looking for all the world like the charming lady of the *Cascarets* ads, is given a tip that the children have finished their

Biograph Mutoscope of the murder of Stanford White by Harry Thaw on Madison Square Garden roof, made shortly after the tragedy. (*See p. 69*)

The first Biograph Girl, Florence Lawrence, in "The Barbarian," otherwise known as "Ingomar, the Barbarian." Filmed at the home of Ernest Thompson Seton at Cos Cob, Conn. (*See p. 59*)

From "The Politician's Love Story." Left to right: Linda A. Griffith, Arthur Johnson, Mack Sennett. A beautiful sleet had covered the trees and foliage of Central Park and this scenario was hurriedly gotten up so as to photograph a wonderful winter fairyland. (*See p. 80*)

Snow-man. So it is time for her to wake up and come out of the moon. From her stellar heights, by means of a clumsy iron apparatus, she is lowered to earth. Sadly crude it all was, but it thrilled the fans of the day, nevertheless. With her magic wand the Good Fairy touches the *Snow-man* and he comes to life. Predatory Pete now comes along, sees Mr. *Snow-man,* and feeling rather jolly from the consumption of bottled goods, he puts his pipe in the *Snow-man's* mouth, and when he sees the *Snow-man* calmly puff it, in great fright he rushes off the scene, dropping his bottle, the contents of which the *Snow-man* drains. In the resultant intoxication the *Snow-man* finds his way into the schoolhouse. Finding the schoolhouse too warm, he throws the stove out of the window. Then he throws himself out of the window and lies down in the snow to "sleep it off."

When the children return the following morning, the *Snow-man,* who is still sleeping, frightens them almost into convulsions. Then the picture really got started—the "chase" began. Sufficiently primitive it was, to have been the first "chase"; but it wasn't—for almost at the movie's inception the chase was a part of them. This *Snow-man* chase takes place in front of a stationary back-drop, that pictures a snowdrift. The actors standing off-stage ready for the excitement, come on through the sawdust snow, kicking it up in clouds, eating it, choking on it, hair, eyes, and throat getting full of it. Back and forth against this one "drop," the actors chase. On one run across, a prop tree would be set up. Then as the actors were supposed to have run some hundred yards at least, on the next time across, the prop tree would be taken away and a big *papier maché* rock put in its place. That scene being photographed, the rock would give way to a telegraph pole, and so on until half a dozen chases had been staged before the one "drop."

Thus far advanced, artistically and otherwise, was the motion picture this spring of 1908 when "Lawrence" Griffith found himself astride a horse, taking the air in the wide stretches of Coytesville, New Jersey, and getting five dollars to boot. Also found himself so exhilarated, mentally and otherwise, that in the evening he turned author, not of poorly paid poems, but of the more profitable movies. Wrote a number which he sold for fifteen dollars each, a very decent price considering that this sort of authorship meant a spot-cash transaction.

The first little cinema drama of which he was the author and which was immediately put into the works was "Old Isaacs, the Pawnbroker." Very bitter in feeling against the Amalgamated Association of Charities was this story of a kind-hearted Hebraic money-lender.

On May 6th, with "Lawrence" Griffith the star, was released "The Music Master," but not David Belasco's. Then came "Ostler Joe" of Mrs. James Brown Potter fame, scenario-ized by Mr. Griffith. He also played the part of the priest in the scene where the child dies. In early July came "At The Crossroads of Life" and "The Stage Rustler."

Biograph's sole advertising campaign at this time consisted of illustrated bulletins—single sheets six to ten inches, carrying a two by three inch "cut" from the film and descriptive matter averaging about three hundred and fifty words. They were gotten up in florid style by a doughty Irishman by the name of Lee Dougherty who was the "man in the front office." He was what is now known as "advertising manager," but the publicity part of his job not taking all his time, he also gave scripts the "once over" and still had moments for a friendly chat with the waiting actor.

Although every day was not a busy day at the Biograph for David Griffith, he felt the best policy would be to keep in close touch with whatever was going on there. So he did that, but he also looked in at other studios during any lull in activities. Looked in up at Edison and was engaged for a leading part in quite a thriller, "The Eagle's Nest." Lovely studio, the Edison, but not so much chance to get in right, David felt—it was too well organized. Looked in at Kalem too, but Frank J. Marion, who was the presiding chief there, could not be bothered. Entirely too many of these down-on-their-luck actors taking up his time.

There were whispers about that Lubin in Philadelphia needed a director. So David wrote them a letter telling of all his varied experiences, which brought an answer with an offer of sixty dollars a week for directing and a request that he run over to Philadelphia for an interview.

Now one had to look like something when on that sort of errand bent. I had to get our little man all dressed up. Could afford only a new shirt and tie. This, with polished boots and suit freshly pressed, would have to do. But, even so, he looked quite radiant as he set forth for the Pennsylvania Station to catch his Every-hour-on-the-hour.

But nothing came of it. Lubin decided not to put on another director or make a change—whichever it was. The husband of Mrs. Mary Carr, the Mrs. Carr of William Fox's "Over the Hill" fame, continued there, directing the movies which he himself wrote. After dinner each night he would roll back the table-cloth, reach for pad and pencil, and work out a story for his next movie.

Back to the dingy "A. B." for us. Strange, even from the beginning we felt a sort of at-home feeling there. The casualness of the place made a strong appeal. What would happen if some one really got on the job down there some day?

And so it came about shortly after "The Snow-man" that the elder Mr. McCutcheon fell ill, and his son Wallace took over his job. He directed "When Knights Were Bold"; directed Mr. Griffith in several pictures. But Wally was not ambitious to make the movies his life job. He soon made a successful début in musical comedy. Some years later he married Pearl White, the popular movie star.

It began to look as though there soon might be a new director about the place. And there was. There were several.

No offer of theatrical jobs came to disrupt the even tenor of the first two months at Biograph. It was too late for winter productions and too early for summer stock, so there was nothing to worry about, until with the first hint of summer in the air, my husband received an offer to go to Peake's Island, Maine, and play villains in a summer stock company there.

Forty per, the salary would be, sometimes more and sometimes less than our combined earnings at the studio. To go or not to go? Summer stock might last the summer and might not. Three months was the most to expect. The Biograph might do as much for us.

How trivial it all sounds now! Ah, but believe me, it was nothing to be taken lightly then. For a decision that affects one's very bread and butter, when bread and butter has been so uncertain, one doesn't make without heart searchings and long councils of war.

So we argued, in a friendly way. Said he: "If I turn this job down, and appear to be so busy, they soon won't send for me at all. Of course, if this movie thing is going to last and amount to anything, if anybody could tell you anything about it, we could afford to take chances. In one way it is very nice. You can stay in New York, and *if* I can find time to write too—fine! But you know you can't go on forever and not tell your friends and relatives how you are earning your living."

Then said she: "How long is Peake's Island going to last? What's sure about summer stock? What does Peake's Island mean to David Belasco or Charles Frohman? We've got this little flat here, with our very own twenty dollars' worth of second-hand furniture, and the rent's so low— twenty. You don't know what's going to happen down at the Biograph, you might get to direct some day. Let's stick the summer out anyhow, and when fall comes and productions open up again, we'll see, huh?"

So we put Peake's Island behind us.

Now it is as sure as shooting, *if* "Lawrence" Griffith had accepted the offer to play stock that summer he never would have become the David W. Griffith of the movies. Had he stepped out then, some one else surely would have stepped in and filled his little place; and the chances are he would never have gone back to those queer movies.

Of course, now we know that even in so short a time this movie business had gotten under his skin. David Griffith had tasted blood—cinema blood. And the call to stay, that was heard and obeyed when Peake's Island threatened to disrupt the scheme of things, was the same sort of call that made those other pioneers trek across the plains with their prairie schooners in the days of forty-nine. With Peake's Island settled, we hoped there would be no more theatrical temptations, for we wanted to take further chances with the movies.

CHAPTER VII

D. W. GRIFFITH DIRECTS HIS FIRST MOVIE

CONSIDERING the chaotic condition of things in the studio as a result of Mr. McCutcheon's illness, it was a propitious time to take heed and get on to the tricks of this movie business. To David Griffith the direction was insufferably careless, the acting the same, and in the lingering bitterness over his play's failure he gritted his teeth and decided that if he ever got a chance he certainly could direct these dinky movies.

The studio was so without a head these days that even Henry Norton Marvin, our vice-president and general manager, occasionally helped out in the directing. He had directed a mutoscope called "A Studio Party" in which my husband and I had made a joint appearance.

With the place now "runnin' wild," Mr. Marvin wondered whom he'd better take a chance on next.

He put the odds on Mr. Stanner E. V. Taylor.

In the studio, one day shortly after my initiation, Mr. Taylor approached me and asked if I could play a lead in a melodrama he was to direct. A lead in a melodrama— with a brief stage career that had been confined to winsome ingénues! But I bravely said, "Oh, yes, yes, indeed I can."

What I suffered! I had a husband who beat and deserted me; I had to appear against him in court, and I fainted and did a beautiful fall on the court-room floor. After my acquittal I took my two babies and deposited them on a wealthy doorstep; wandered off to the New Jersey Palisades; took a flying leap and landed a mass of broken bones at the bottom of the cliff.

Selected for the fall was a beautiful smooth boulder which had a sheer drop on the side the camera did not get of possibly some fifteen feet to a ledge about six feet wide, from which ledge, to the bottom of the Palisades, was a precipitous descent of some hundred feet.

There were so many rehearsals of this scene of self-destruction that the rock acquired a fine polish as "mother" slipped and slid about. That the camera man's assistant might try the stunt for at least the initial attempts at getting the focus, never occurred to a soul. But a suggestion was made that if "mother" removed her shoes she might not slide off so easily. Which she did for the remaining rehearsals. Then finally as the sun sank behind the Palisades, "mother" in her last emotional moments, sank behind the boulder.

On that picture I made twenty-eight dollars; oh, what a lot of money! The most to date. If pictures kept up like that! And the whole twenty-eight was mine, all mine, and I invested it at Hackett, Carhart on Broadway and Thirteenth in a spring outfit—suit, shoes, hat, oh, everything.

The picture—the only one Mr. Taylor directed—lacked continuity. Upstairs in his executive office, Mr. Henry Norton Marvin was walking the floor and wondering what about it. Why couldn't they get somewhere with these movies? Another man fallen down on the job. Genial Arthur Marvin, H. N.'s brother, and Billy Bitzer's assistant at the camera, was being catechized as to whether he had noticed any promising material about the studio.

"Well," drawled the genial Arthur, "I don't know. They're a funny lot, these actors, but there's one young man, there's one actor seems to have ideas. You might try him."

"You think he might get by, eh?"

"Well, I don't think you'd lose much by trying him."

"What's his name? I'll send for him."

"Griffith. Lawrence Griffith."

Later that day a cadaverous-looking young man was closeted with the vice-president in the vice-president's dignified quarters.

"My brother tells me you appear to be rather interested in the pictures, Mr. Griffith; how would you like to direct one?"

Mr. Griffith rose from his chair, took three steps to the window, and gazed out into space.

"Think you'd like to try it, Mr. Griffith?"

No response—only more gazing into space.

"We'll make it as easy as we can for you, Mr. Griffith, if you decide you'd like to try."

More gazing into space. And finally this: "I appreciate your confidence in me, Mr. Marvin, but there is just this to it. I've had rather rough sledding the last few years and you see I'm married; I have responsibilities and I cannot afford to take chances; I think they rather like me around here as an actor. Now if I take this picture-directing over and fall down, then you see I'll be out my acting job, and you know I wouldn't like that; I don't want to lose my job as an actor down here."

"Otherwise you'd be willing to direct a picture for us?"

"Oh, yes, indeed I would."

"Then if I promise that if you fall down as a director, you can have your acting job back, you will put on a moving picture for us?"

"Yes, then I'd be willing."

It was called "The Adventures of Dolly."

Gossip around the studio had it that the story was a "lemon." Preceding directors at the studio had sidestepped it. *Dolly,* in the course of the story, is nailed into a barrel by the gypsies who steal her; the barrel secreted in the gypsy wagon; the horses start off at breakneck speed; the barrel falls off the wagon, rolls into the stream, floats over a waterfall, shoots the rapids, and finally emerges into a quiet pool where some boys, fishing, haul it ashore, hear the child's cries, open the barrel, and rescue *Dolly.*

Not a very simple job for an amateur. But David Griffith wasn't worried. He could go back to acting were the picture no good. Mr. Arthur Marvin was assigned as camera man. There were needed for the cast: *Dolly,* her mother and father, the gypsy man, the gypsy man's wife, and two small boys.

Upstairs in the tiny projection room pictures were being run for Mr. Griffith's enlightenment. He was seeing what Biograph movies looked like. Saw some of old man McCutcheon's, and some of Wally McCutcheon's, and Stanner E. V. Taylor's one and only.

That evening he said to me: "You'll play the lead in my first picture—not because you're my wife—but because you're a good actress."

"Oh, did you see Mr. Taylor's picture?"

"Yes."

"How was it?"

"Not bad, but it don't hang together. Good acting; you're good, quite surprised me. No one I can use for a husband though. I must have some one who *looks* like a 'husband'—who looks as though he owned more than a cigarette. I heard around the studio that they were going to hand me a bunch of lemons for actors."

So, dashing madly here and there for a father for little *Dolly*, Mr. Griffith saw coming down Broadway a young man of smiling countenance—just the man—his very ideal. Of course, he must be an actor. There was no time for hesitation.

"Pardon me, but would you care to act in a moving picture? I am going to direct a moving picture, and I have a part that suits you exactly."

"Moving pictures, did you say? Picture acting? I am sure I don't know what you are talking about. I don't know anything about picture acting."

"You don't need to know—just meet me at the Grand Central Depot at nine o'clock to-morrow morning."

And so Arthur Johnson became a movie actor.

To my mind no personality has since flickered upon the screen with quite the charm, lovableness, and magnetic humor that were his. He never acquired affectations, which made him a rare person indeed, considering the tremendous popularity that became his and the world of affectation in which he lived.

For the gypsy man Mr. Griffith selected Charles Inslee, an excellent actor whom he had known on the Coast. Mr. Inslee was a temperamental sort, but Mr. Griffith knew how to handle him. So with Mrs. Gebhardt for the gypsy wife, Mr. Griffith completed his cast without using a single one of the "lemons" that were to have been wished upon him;

and as there were only outdoor sets in "The Adventures" he did not have any of the "lemons" around to make comments.

Even the business of the barrel proved to be no insurmountable difficulty. Yards and yards of piano-wire were attached, which, manipulated from the shore, kept the barrel somewhat in focus. The one perturbed person was our camera man, who even though middle-aged and heavy, time and time again had to jump about, in and out of the stream, grabbing tripod and clumsy camera, trying to keep up with the floating barrel.

We went to Sound Beach, Connecticut, to take "The Adventures."

It was a lovely place, I thought. The Black-eyed Susans were all a-bloom, and everywhere was green grass although it was nearly midsummer. We spent almost a week working on "The Adventures," for the mechanical scenes took time, and—joy!—between us we were making ten dollars a day as long as the picture lasted.

And then who could tell!

"If the photography is there, the picture will be all right; if it looks as good on the negative as it looked while we were taking it, it ought to get by," opined the director.

From out of the secrecy of the dark room came Arthur Marvin, nonchalantly swinging a short strip of film.

"How is it?"

"Looks pretty good, nice and sharp."

"Think it's all right?"

"Yeh, think it is."

Hopeful hours interspersed with anxious moments crowded the succeeding days. By the time the picture was developed, printed, and titled, we were well-nigh emotionally exhausted. What would they say upstairs? What *would* they say?

In the darkened little projection room they sat.

On the screen was being shown "The Adventures of Dolly."

No sound but the buzz and whir of the projection machine. The seven hundred and thirteen feet of the "Adventures" were reeled off. Silence. Then Mr. Marvin spoke:

"That's it—that's something like it—at last!"

Afterwards, upstairs in the executive offices, Mr. Marvin and Mr. Dougherty talked it over, and they concluded that if the next picture were half as good, Lawrence Griffith was the man they wanted.

The next picture really turned out better.

The world's première of "The Adventures of Dolly" was held at Keith and Proctor's Theatre, Union Square, July 14, 1908.

What a day it was at the studio! However did we work, thinking of what the night held. But as the longest day ends, so did this one. No time to get home and pretty-up for the party. With what meager facilities the porcelain basin and make-up shelf in the dressing-room offered, we managed; rubbed off the grease paint and slapped on some powder; gave the hair a pat and a twist; at Silsbee's on Sixth Avenue and Fourteenth Street, we picked up nourishment; and then we beat it to Union Square.

A world's première indeed—a tremendously important night to so many people who didn't know it. No taxis— not one private car drew up at the curb. The house filled up from passers-by—frequenters of Union Square—lured by a ten-cent entertainment. These were the people to be pleased—they who had paid out their little nickels and dimes. So when they sat through Dolly's seven hundred feet, interested, and not a snore was to be heard, we concluded we'd had a successful opening night.

The contract was drawn for one year. It called for forty-five dollars per week with a royalty of a mill a foot on all film sold. Mr. Marvin thought it rather foolish to accept so small a salary and assured my husband the percentage would amount to nothing whatever right off. But David was willing—rather more than willing—to gamble on himself. And he gambled rather well this time. For, the first year his royalty check went from practically nothing to four and five hundred dollars a month—before the end of the year.

Wonderful it was—too good to be true. Although, had he known then that for evermore, through weeks and months and years, it was to be movies, movies, nothing but movies, David Griffith would probably then and there have chucked the job, or, keeping it, would have wept bitter, bitter tears.

CHAPTER VIII

DIGGING IN

"WELL, we're in the movies—we're working in the moving pictures."

"Moving pictures? You're working in moving pictures? What do you mean, you're working in moving pictures?"

"We're working at a place—they call it a studio—acting in little plays—dramas, and comedies—a camera takes pictures while we act, and the pictures are shown in those five- and ten-cent theatres that are all around the town, mostly on Third and Ninth Avenues and Fourteenth Street —such high-class neighborhoods."

"Those dreadful places? I wouldn't be seen going into one of them."

Yes, that was the attitude in those dark and dismal days when David signed that contract with the Biograph Company. For one year now, those movies so covered with slime and so degraded would have to come first in his thoughts and affections. That was only fair to the job. But only one who had loved the theater as he had, and had dreamed as he had of achieving success therein, could know what heartaches this strange new affiliation was to bring to him. Times came, agonizing days, when he would have given his life to be able to chuck the job. Mornings when on arising he would gaze long, long moments out

53

the window, apparently seeing nothing—then the barely audible remark, "I think I'll 'phone and say I cannot come." On such days he dragged heavy, leaden feet to 11 East Fourteenth Street.

And there was an evening when, returning home after a drab day at the studio, and finding his modest ménage festive with ferns and wild flowers, he became so annoyed that with one swoop he gathered up nature and roughly jammed her into the waste paper basket. A visiting relative who'd helped gather the flowers worried so over the strange procedure that I had to explain—"It's those pictures; you know they're just the fringe of acting."

The emotions that would sweep over us at times! How our pride was hurt! How lacking in delicacy people could be! With what a patronizing air the successful and prosperous actor-friend would burst into the studio! Mr. Griffith would say, "Well, how about it? If you're hanging around this summer, how would you like to work with me a bit?" Polite and evasive the reply, "Well, you see, I'm awfully busy just now, have several offers and—well—when I'm signed up I'll drop around again." But we, in the know, understood that all the King's horses and all the King's men could not induce such to join our little band of movie actors. We were always conscious of the fact that we were in this messy business because everything else had failed— because nobody had seemed to want us, and we just hadn't been able to hang on any longer.

But David buckled to the job like a true sport. It was *his job* and he would dignify it. The leaden mornings came to be quite the exception to the rule. Many days were greeted with bright and merry song. And so, firm and unshakeable in our determination to do the most with what

Jeanie Macpherson, Marion Sunshine, Edwin August, Alfred Paget, Blanche Sweet and Charles West in a scene from "From Out the Shadow." The brilliant social world of early movie days. (See p. 71)

"Murphy's," where members of Biograph's original stock company consumed hearty breakfasts when Jersey bound. (*See p. 83*)

we had, we dismissed the silly sensitive business and set to work.

What we had to work with was this: a little studio where interior scenes were taken, and exteriors also, for there was little money for traveling expenses—Fort Lee, Greenwich, and the Atlantic Highlands comprised our early geographical horizon. A few actors, a willing and clever camera man, a stage carpenter, and a scenic artist, comprised the working force. Funny studio! Interesting old workshop! "The Last Leaf's" ballroom!

The outer doors of the building opened into a broad hall from which on the left as one entered, a door gave into Mr. Dougherty's office; on the right was another door—the entrance to the bookkeeping department. An old colonial stairway on this same side led up to the projection room and other offices. The spacious hall of the main floor ended with double doors opening into the studio.

There, first to meet the eye—unless one stumbled on it before seeing it—for it completely blocked the entrance—was a heavy rolling platform on which the camera, poised atop of its tripod, was set. So if the studio doors chanced to invite you during the taking of a scene, you would have to remain put in the few feet of space between the platform and the doors until the scene was finished. Usually there would be some one to keep you company in your little niche.

It was an easy matter in those days to get into the studio. No cards of announcement were needed—no office boy insulted you, no humiliation of waiting, as to-day. A ring of the bell and in you'd go, and Bobbie Harron would greet you if he chanced to be near by. Otherwise, any one of the actors would pass you the glad word.

On an ordinary kitchen chair a bit to one side of the

camera, Mr. Griffith usually sat when directing. The actors when not working lingered about, either standing or enjoying the few other kitchen chairs. During rehearsals actors sat all over the camera stand—it was at least six feet square —and as the actors were a rather chummy lot, the close and informal intimacy disturbed them not the least.

A "scene" was set back center, just allowing passage room. What little light came through the few windows was soon blocked by dusty old scenery. On the side spaces of the room and on the small gallery above, the carpenters made scenery and the scene painters painted it—scenery, paint pots, and actors were all huddled together in one friendly chaos. We always had to be mindful of our costumes. To the smell of fresh paint and the noise of the carpenters' hammers, we rehearsed our first crude little movies and in due time many an old literary classic.

Rolls of old carpet and bundles of canvas had to be climbed over in wending one's way about. To the right of the camera a stairway led to the basement where there were three small dressing-rooms; and no matter how many actors were working in a picture those three dark little closets had to take care of them all. The developing or "dark" room adjoined the last dressing-room, and all opened into a cavernous cellar where the stage properties were kept. Here at the foot of the stairs and always in every one's way, the large wardrobe baskets would be deposited. And what a scramble for something that would half-way fit us when the costumes arrived!

We ate our lunches in the dingy basement, usually seated on the wardrobe baskets. Squatted there, tailor-fashion, on their strong covers, we made out pretty well. On days when we had numbers of extra people, our lunch

boy, little Bobbie Harron, would arrange boards on wooden
horses, and spread a white cloth, banquet fashion. Especially effective this, when doing society drama, and there
would be grand dames, financiers, and magnates, to grace
the festive board.

In a back corner of the studio reposed a small, oak,
roll-top desk, which the new director graced in the early
morning hours when getting things in shape, and again
in the evening when he made out the actors' pay checks.
When the welcome words came from the dark room, "All
right, everybody; strike!" the actors rushed to the roll-top,
and clamored for vouchers—we received our "pay" daily.
Then the actor rushed his "make-up" off, dressed, passed
to the bookkeeper's window in the outer office, presented
his voucher, and Herman Bruenner gave him his money.
And then to eat, and put away a dollar towards the week's
rent, and to see a movie for ten cents!

A little group of serious actors soon began to report
daily for work. As yet no one had a regular salary except
the director and camera man. "Principal part" actors received five and "extras" three dollars.

In August this first year Mr. Griffith began turning
out two releases a week, usually one long picture, eight
to eleven hundred feet, and one short picture, four to five
hundred feet. The actors who played the principal parts
in these pictures were Eddie Dillon, Harry Salter, Charles
Inslee, Frank Gebhardt, Arthur Johnson, Wilfred Lucas,
George Nichols, John Compson, Owen Moore, Mack Sennett, Herbert Pryor, David Miles, Herbert Yost, Tony
O'Sullivan, and Daddy Butler. Of the women Marion
Leonard, Florence Lawrence, and myself played most of
the leading parts, while Mabel Stoughton, Florence Auer,

Ruth Hart, Jeanie Macpherson, Flora Finch, Anita Hendry, Dorothy West, Eleanor Kershaw (Mrs. Tom Ince), and Violet Mersereau helped out occasionally. Gladys Egan, Adele de Garde, and Johnny Tansy played the important child parts.

Though I speak of playing "principal parts," no one had much chance to get puffed up, for an actor having finished three days of importance usually found himself on the fourth day playing "atmosphere," the while he decorated the back drop. But no one minded. They were a good-natured lot of troupers and most of them were sincerely concerned in what they were doing. David had a happy way of working. He invited confidence and asked and took suggestions from any one sufficiently interested to make them. His enthusiasm became quite infectious.

In the beginning Marion Leonard and I alternated playing "leads." She played the worldly woman, the adventuress, and the melodramatic parts, while I did the sympathetic, the wronged wife, the too-trusting maid, waiting, always waiting, for the lover who never came back. But mostly I died.

Our director, already on the lookout for a new type, heard of a clever girl out at the Vitagraph, who rode a horse like a western cowboy and who had had good movie training under Mr. Rainous. He wanted to see her on the screen before an audience. Set up in a store on Amsterdam Avenue and 160th Street was a little motion picture place. It had a rough wooden floor, common kitchen chairs, and the reels unwound to the tin-panny shriek of a pianola. After some watchful waiting, the stand outside the theatre —the sort of thing sandwich men carry—finally announced "The Dispatch Bearer," a Vitagraph with Florence Lawrence. So, living near by, after dinner one night we rushed over to see it.

It was a good picture. Mr. Griffith concluded he would like to work with Mr. Rainous for a while and learn about the movies. For one could easily see that besides having ability Florence Lawrence had had excellent direction.

Well, David stole little Florrie, he did. With Harry Salter as support in his nefarious errand, he called on Miss Lawrence and her mother, and offered the Vitagraph girl twenty-five dollars a week, regular. She had been receiving fifteen at Vitagraph playing leading parts, sewing costumes, and mending scenery canvas. She was quite overcome with Mr. Griffith's spectacular offer, readily accepted, and by way of celebrating her new prosperity, she drew forth from under the bed in the little boarding-house room, her trombone—or was it a violin?—and played several selections. As a child, Miss Lawrence, managed by her mother, and starred as "Baby Flo, the child wonder-whistler" had toured the country, playing even the "tanks."

Immediately she joined the Biograph, Florence Lawrence was given a grand rush. But she never minded work. The movies were as the breath of life to her. When she wasn't working in a picture, she was in some movie theater seeing a picture. After the hardest day, she was never too tired to see the new release and if work ran into the night hours, between scenes she'd wipe off the make-up and slip out to a movie show.

Her pictures became tremendously popular, and soon all over the country Miss Lawrence was known as "The Biograph Girl." It was some years before the company allowed the names of actors to be given out, hence "Biograph Girl" was the only intelligent appellation. After

Miss Lawrence left Biograph, Mary Pickford fell heir to the title.

Miss Lawrence's early releases show her versatility. Two every week for a time: "Betrayed by a Handprint," "The Girl and the Outlaw," "Behind the Scenes," "The Heart of Oyama," "Concealing a Burglar," "Romance of a Jewess," "The Planter's Wife," "The Vaquero's Vow," "The Call of the Wild," "The Zulu's Heart," "The Song of the Shirt," "Taming of the Shrew," "The Ingrate," "A Woman's Way."

Like Mary Pickford, Miss Lawrence was an awfully good sport about doing stunts. One day a scene was being filmed with Miss Lawrence thrown tummy-wise across a horse's saddled back. As the horse dashed down the roadway he came so close to the camera that we who were watching breathlessly, for one moment closed our eyes, for Miss Lawrence's blond head just missed the camera by a few inches.

Rainy August days forced us to work in the studio. Mr. Griffith had read a story by Jack London called "Just Meat." He changed the name to "For Love of Gold" and let it go at that. We had no fear of lawsuits from fractious authors those days.

The story was about two thieves, who returned home with the latest spoils, get suspicious of each other and each, unknown to the other, poisons the other's coffee and both die. The big scenes which were at the table when the men become distrustful of each other could be told only through facial expression. "Ah," puzzled Mr. Director, "how can I show what these two men are thinking? I must have the camera closer to the actors—that's what I must do—and having only two actors in these scenes, I can."

Up to this time, every scene had been a long shot—that is, the floor—the carpet—the greensward—showed yards in front of the actors' feet. But Mr. Griffith knew he couldn't show nine feet of floor and at the same time register expression. So to his camera man he said: "Now don't get excited, but listen. I'm going to move the camera up, I'm going to show very little floor, but I'm going to show a large, full-length figure; just get in the actors' feet —get the toes—one foot of foreground will do.

"Well, we've never done anything like that—how do you think that's going to look?—a table with a man on each side filling up the whole screen, nearly."

"We'll do it—we'll never get anywhere if we don't begin to try new things."

The burglars were screened so big that every wicked thought each entertained was plainly revealed. Everybody came to like the idea afterwards, especially the actors.

Along in November, Mr. Griffith began work on a series of domestic comedies—the "Jones Pictures." Florence Lawrence played Mrs. Jones, and John Compson, Mr. Jones. Their movie marital début was in "A Smoked Husband." The Jones movies were probably the first to achieve success as a series.

CHAPTER IX

FIRST PUBLICITY AND EARLY SCENARIOS

IN Biograph's story, quite a few who stuck to the ship in these first days are big names in the movies to-day.

In the town of Erie, Pa., in the early nineteen hundreds flourished a little newspaper, on the staff of which was Frank Woods. Besides reporting "news," Frank Woods sold advertising. Erie, Pa., not long satisfying his ambitions, Mr. Woods set out for the journalistic marts of New York City, and shortly after found himself selling advertising for the *New York Dramatic Mirror*. The idea of getting ads from the picture people came to him when he noticed that pictures were not mentioned in the *Dramatic Mirror*. Writers on the paper were told that any reference to the movies would be promptly blue-penciled.

Mr. Woods figured that if he could interest the movie people he might get ads from them and the *Dramatic Mirror* wouldn't mind that. But the picture people turned deaf ears. Why pay money for an ad in a paper that was all too ready to crush them? Besides, the *Mirror* didn't circulate among the exhibitors and those interested in the movies. The movie people would stick to the more friendly *Billboard*—thank you kindly—it could have their ads.

Another idea came to Frank Woods. How about pictures being reviewed? He put the plan before Lee Dougherty, for Lee was always genial and had time to listen. Lee said: "Fine, give us real serious reviews—tell us where we are wrong—but don't expect an ad for your effort."

The result of this conversation was that three reviews appeared in the *New York Dramatic Mirror*, June, 1908. On a rear end page captioned "The Spectator," Frank E. Woods dissertated through some columns on the merits and demerits of the movies, and thus became their first real critic. We were very grateful for the few paragraphs. It meant recognition—the beginning. How gladly we parted with our ten cents weekly to see what "Spec" had to say about us.

But Mr. Woods didn't get an ad from the Biograph. So he had another heart-to-heart talk with Mr. Dougherty, and Doc said: "Never mind, keep it up—but as I told you, the reviews aren't going to influence us about ads."

But in August the Company came across and bought a quarter-page ad for the Biograph movies.

The active mind of Frank Woods was not going to stop with critical comments on moving pictures. His new duties necessitated his seeing pictures; and, looking them over and analyzing them for his reviews, he said to himself; "Oh, they're terrible—I could do better myself—such stories!" So he wrote three "suggestions" that's all they were—and that's what they were then called. With great aplomb, he took them to Mr. Dougherty, and to his amazement Mr. Dougherty turned the whole three down. Sorry, but he didn't think them up to scratch. But Mr. Woods would not be fazed by a turn-down like that. He wrote three more "suggestions."

The studio had a sort of nominal supervisor, a Mr. Wake, whose job was to O. K. little expenditures in the studio and to pass on the purchase of scenarios. One day, not long after our A. B. affiliation, just as I was entering the main foyer, Mr. Griffith coming from the projection room seemed more than usually light-hearted. So I said, "You're feeling good—picture nice?"

"Oh, yes, all right, but"—this in a whisper—"Wake's been fired."

I wondered how I could wait all that day, until evening, to hear what had happened. But I did, and learned that Mr. Wake with Biograph money had purchased silk stockings for Mutoscope girls, and then had given the girls the stockings for their own.

However, during a temporary absence from the studio before Mr. Wake's dismissal, Frank Woods came down with three more suggestions which were shown to Mr. Griffith direct. He bought the whole bunch, three at fifteen dollars apiece, *nine five-dollar bills, forty-five dollars.*

Around the *Dramatic Mirror* offices Mr. Woods was already jocularly being called "M. P. Woods." And this day that he disposed of his three "suggestions," Moving Picture Woods with much bravado entered the *Mirror's* office, went over to the desk, brushed aside some papers, cleared a place on the counter, and in a row laid his nine five-dollar bills.

In the office at the time were George Terwilliger (how many scenarios he afterwards wrote), Al Trahern (Al continued with his stock companies and featuring his wife Jessie Mae Hall), and Jake Gerhardt, now in the business end of the movies. The trio looked—and gasped—and looked—and in unison spoke:

"*Where* did you get all that?"

"Moving Pictures!"

"Moving Pictures? For heaven's sake, tell us about it."

"How did you do it?" queried George Terwilliger. "Forty-five dollars for three stories, good Lord, and they gave you the money right off, like that."

So Mr. Woods told his little story, and as the conversation ended, George Terwilliger reached for paper and pencil, for five-dollar bills were beckoning from every direction. Maybe he could put it over, too. He did—he sold lots and lots of "suggestions." Frank Woods wrote thirty movies for Biograph.

Frank Woods now set about to criticise the pictures with the same seriousness with which he would have criticised the theater. He bought books about Indians and let the producers know there was a difference between the Hopi and the Apache and the Navajo. With a critical eye, he picked out errors and wrote of them frankly, and his influence in the betterment of the movies has been a bigger one than is generally known outside the movie world. Mr. Woods is really responsible for research. And Mr. Dougherty gives him credit for turning in the first "continuity." The picture that has that honor is a version of Tennyson's "Enoch Arden," called "After Many Years."

Scenarios that reached the Biograph offices, due to lack of organization, were sometimes weeks in reaching the proper department, but Mr. Griffith got first chance at "After Many Years." Both he and Mr. Dougherty thought it pretty good stuff, but the obvious emotional acting that had prevailed somewhere in every picture so far, was here entirely lacking. Quiet suppressed emotion only, this one had. But Doc said he'd eat the positive if it wouldn't make a good picture. So it was purchased.

But "After Many Years," although it had no "action," and some of us sat in the projection room at its first showing with heavy hearts, proved to write more history than any picture ever filmed and it brought an entirely new technique to the making of films.

It was the first movie without a chase. That was something, for those days, a movie without a chase was not a movie. How could a movie be made without a chase? How could there be suspense? How action? "After Many Years" was also the first picture to have a *dramatic* close-up —the first picture to have a cut-back. When Mr. Griffith suggested a scene showing Annie Lee waiting for her husband's return to be followed by a scene of Enoch cast away on a desert island, it was altogether too distracting. "How can you tell a story jumping about like that? The people won't know what it's about."

"Well," said Mr. Griffith, "doesn't Dickens write that way?"

"Yes, but that's Dickens; that's novel writing; that's different."

"Oh, not so much, these are picture stories: not so different."

So he went his lonely way and did it; did "After Many Years" contrary to all the old established rules of the game. The Biograph Company was very much worried—the picture was so unusual—how could it succeed?

It was the first picture to be recognized by foreign markets. When one recalls the high class of moving pictures that Pathé and Gaumont were then putting out, such as "The Assassination of the Duc de Guise," this foreign recognition meant something.

"After Many Years" made a change in the studio. All "suggestions" now came directly to Mr. Dougherty's office. He selected the doubtful ones and the sure bets and with

Mr. Griffith read them over the second time. They threshed out their differences in friendly argument. So Lee Dougherty became the first scenario editor.

And of the sad letters and grateful ones his editing jobs brought him, this letter from a newspaper man on a Dayton, Ohio, paper, now dead, he prizes most highly:

L. E. DOUGHERTY, EDITOR,
 KINEMACOLOR COMPANY,
  LOS ANGELES, CALIF.

DEAR SIR:

Excuse me, but I can't help it. When I cashed the $25 check for "Too Much Susette," the scenario of mine which you accepted, I took $5 of the money and put it on "Just Red" who won at Louisville at the juicy price of 30 to 1. I hope the film will bring your company as much luck as the script has brought me.

Yours very truly,

GEORGE GROEBER.

"Doc" was Mr. Griffith's friendly appellation for "the man in the front office," Lee Dougherty. It was going some for Mr. Griffith to give any one a nickname. He never was a "hail fellow well met." It was Mr. So-and-so from Mr. Griffith and to Mr. Griffith with very few exceptions. Never once during all the Biograph years did he ever publicly call even his own wife by any other name than "Miss Arvidson." Only in general conversation about the movies, and in his absence, was he familiarly referred to as "Griff," or "D. W.," or the "Governor."

Mr. Dougherty was the one man at 11 East Fourteenth Street before the Griffith régime who had more than a speaking acquaintance with the movies. In the summer of 1896 as stage manager of the old Boston Museum, he installed there the first projection machine of American manufacture, the Eidoloscope. When the season at the Boston Museum was over, Mr. Dougherty, who had become quite fascinated with this new idea in entertainment, went to New York City. The Biograph Company along about 1897 had just finished a moving picture of Pope Leo XIII taken at the Vatican. Pictures of the late Pope Benedict XV were announced as the first pictures made of a Pope, "approved by His Holiness." While they may be the first approved ones, Captain Varges of the International News Reel, who claims the honor, brought the third motion picture camera into the Vatican grounds. The second film—Pope Pius X in the Vatican, and gardens, and the Eucharistic Congress, was released in 1912.

Well, anyhow, Mr. Dougherty took a set of Biograph's Pope Leo XIII pictures to exhibit in the towns and cities of New Jersey and Pennsylvania on the old Biograph projection machine—one vastly superior to the Eidoloscope. The company exhibiting the picture consisted of an operator on the machine and Mr. Dougherty who lectured. And when he began his little talk (there was no titling or printed matter in the picture), the small boys in the gallery would yell "spit it out, we want to see the picture." Numbers of motion picture directors to-day might well heed the sentiments of those small boys.

From exhibiting Pope Leo XIII's picture, Mr. Dougherty became stage director of One Minute Comedies for the Biograph which at this time had a stage on the roof of a building at 841 Broadway. And sometimes in the midst of a scene the weather would pick up scenery and props and deposit them in Broadway. So came about experiments with electric lights, satisfactory results first being obtained with the Jeffries-Sharkey prize fight.

The One Minute Comedies finally were given up, but the Mutoscopes, being Biograph's biggest source of revenue, were continued. The Mutoscopes were brief film playlets that were viewed in the penny-in-the-slot machines.

One day, before Mutoscopes ended, my husband asked me to run over to Wanamaker's with him and help choose some pretty undies for the Mutoscope girls—photographically effective stuff—so we selected some very elegant heavy black silk embroidered stockings and embroidered pink Italian silk vests and knickers—last-word lingeries for that time.

I felt rather ill about it. "Oh dear," I thought, "this is *some* business, but I'll be brave, I will, even though I die." Well, the parcel being wrapped, David took it and then handed it to me, and I thought, "Why should I carry the bundle?" So we reached Fourteenth Street. David started to the left without his parcel; I was continuing up Broadway, so handed it to him. But the lingerie wasn't for Mutoscopes at all—but for me—just a little surprise. So then with a light and happy heart, I took my way home to admire my beautiful present.

After the Biograph had engaged David, Mr. Dougherty did not want them to make any more Mutoscopes. Mr. Griffith directed possibly six. In order to influence Biograph to cut out the Mutoscopes, Doc got very cocky, and he said to Mr. Kennedy and Mr. Marvin, "You wait, you'll see pictures on Broadway some day, like you do plays." But they gave him the laugh. "Yes," Doc added, "and they will accord them the same dignified attention that John

Drew receives." They laughed some more at this, and said, "Pictures will always be a mountebank form of amusement."

But Doc's prophesy came true.

And David did no more Mutoscopes.

From "Edgar Allan Poe," with Barry O'Moore (Herbert Yost) and Linda Griffith. (*See p. 90*)

Herbert Pryor, Linda Griffith, Violet Mersereau and Owen Moore in "The Cricket on the Hearth." (*See p. 92*)

"Little Mary," portraying the type of heroine that won her a legion of admirers. (See p. 104)

Register of Caudebec Inn at Cuddebackville. (See p. 119)

CHAPTER X

WARDROBE—AND A FEW PERSONALITIES

THE "Jones" pictures became very popular. Many persons well known in the movies to-day, played "bits" in them. Jeanie Macpherson, author of "The Ten Commandments" was "principal guest" in "Mr. Jones at the Ball." Miss Macpherson, who for many years has been and still is chief scenario writer and assistant to Cecil B. DeMille, got her first movie job on the strength of a pale blue crepe-de-chine evening gown.

How funny we were when we moved in the world of brilliant men and beautiful women only we, who represented them, knew. Dress suits of all vintages appeared. Any one with "clothes" had a wonderful open sesame. A young chap whom we dubbed "the shoe clerk"—who never played a thing but "atmosphere"—got many a pay-check on the strength of his neat, tan, covert cloth spring overcoat—the only spring overcoat that ever honored the studio. (An actor could get along in the spring with his winter suit and no overcoat!)

Clothes soon became a desperate matter, so Biograph consented to spend fifty dollars for wearing apparel for the women. Harry Salter and I were entrusted with the funds and told to hunt bargains. We needed negligees, dinner dresses, ball gowns, and semi-tailored effects. The clothes were to be bought in sizes to fit, as well as could be, the three principal women.

In that day, on Sixth Avenue in the Twenties, were numbers of shops dealing in second-hand clothing, and Mr. Salter and I wandered among them and finally at a little place called "Simone," we closed a deal. We got a good batch of stuff for the fifty—at least a dozen pieces—bizarre effects for the sophisticated lady, dignified accoutrements for the conventional matron, and simple softness for young innocence.

How those garments worked! I have forgotten many, but one—a brown silk and velvet affair—I never can forget. It was the first to be grabbed off the hook—it was forever doing duty. For it was unfailing in its effect. Arrayed in the brown silk and velvet, there could be no doubt as to one's moral status—the maiden lady it made obviously pure; the wife, faithful; the mother, self-sacrificing.

Deciding, impromptu, to elaborate on a social affair, Mr. Griffith would call out: "I can use you in this scene, Miss Bierman, if you can find a dress to fit you." The tall, lean actresses, and the short ones found that difficult, and thus, unfortunately, often lost a day's work. Spotting a new piece of millinery in the studio, our director would thus approach the wearer: "I have no part for you, Miss Hart, but I can use your hat. I'll give you five dollars if you will let Miss Pickford wear your hat for this picture." Two days of work would pay for your hat, so you were glad to sit around while the leading lady sported your new headpiece. You received more on a loan of your clothes, sometimes, than you did on a loan of yourself. Clothes got five dollars always, but laughter and merry-making upstage went for three.

Jeanie Macpherson had recently returned from Europe

with clothes the like of which had never been seen at Biograph. From the chorus of "Hello People" at the Casino Theatre little Jeanie entered the movies and even though she had a snub nose and did not photograph well, what could Mr. Griffith do but use her?

Jeanie proved to be a good trouper; she was conscientious and ambitious. Though only extras and bits came her way, David encouraged her. She was rather frail, and one time after remaining ill some days when on a picture up in the country, Mr. Griffith thought he should give her good advice. So he told her to live on a farm for some months, and drink milk and get strong, there being no future without health; he certainly could not use her in parts were she to faint on him thus. But Jeanie confided she'd have to overcome fainting without "months on a farm"—that luxury she couldn't afford.

Since Biograph Miss Macpherson has carried on in every department of picture making except the acting. She early took stock of herself and recognized that her future would not be in the ranks of the movie stars. Just where it would be she did not then know—nor did any one else.

On a day in this slightly remote period Jesse Lasky and Cecil DeMille were lunching at Rector's in New York —music, luscious tidbits, and Mr. Lasky casually remarking: "Let's go into the moving picture business."

"All right, let's," answered Mr. DeMille with not the slightest hesitation.

Mr. Lasky, thus encouraged, suggested more "Let's," to each of which Mr. DeMille as promptly agreed "Let's."

Along came brother-in-law Sam Goldfish, married to Blanche Lasky, sister to Jesse. Mr. Goldfish (now Goldwyn) was in the glove business up in Gloversville, New

York, and he was very grouchy this day because the Government had taken the duty off gloves, and he was eager to listen in on this new idea of Mr. Lasky's.

By the time that lunch was finished this is what had happened: Mr. Goldfish had put up $5,000, Mr. Lasky $5,000, and Arthur Friend $5,000, and with the $15,000 Cecil DeMille was to go out to California to make movies. He begged his brother William to put up $5,000 and become a partner but William said: "No, one of us had better be conservative and keep the home fires burning." So when William later went into the movies, he went to work for his brother Cecil, and he has been doing so up to this time.

Mr. Cecil DeMille became Director General of the new Jesse Lasky Pictures, and Mr. Oscar Apfel, General Manager. Out on Vine Street, Hollywood, Mr. DeMille took over a stable, and began to make movies. It was a crude equipment, but the company fell heir to some beer kegs from which they viewed their first picture "The Squaw Man" released sometime in 1913. The stable is still a part of the Hollywood Famous Players-Lasky modern studio, but the beer kegs have vanished.

Pictures kept on radiating from the stable with quite gratifying success. In time along came Jeanie Macpherson intent on an interview with Mr. C. B. DeMille. Jeanie now knew so much about the movies and C. B. so little, he just naturally felt the Lord had sent her. Miss Macpherson's presentation of ideas always got over to Cecil. So Jeanie signed up with the new firm on that rather long ago day and now she gets one thousand a week, I understand, for writing Mr. DeMille's big pictures.

We must go back now and rescue Jeanie from Mr. Jones's Ball, for in "Mrs. Jones Entertains," she has duties to perform. In that picture she was not "principal guest" but the "maid." Flora Finch was a guest. Miss Finch in another Jones movie becomes a book agent soliciting Mr. Jones in his office. In "Mr. Jones has a Card Party," Mack Sennett appears as one of husband's rummies, and in yet another "Jones," Owen Moore, first husband of Mary Pickford, is seen as "atmosphere" escorting a lady from a smart café. So chameleon-like were our social relations in the "Jones Comedy Series."

A Flora Finch tidbit here comes to light. Though fifteen years have elapsed, they have not dimmed the memory of the one hundred and eighty-five feet of "Those Awful Hats." The exhibitor was told: "It will make a splendid subject to start a show with instead of the customary slides."

The "set" represented the interior of a moving picture theatre. The company was audience. Miss Finch was also "audience," only arriving late she had a separate entrance. Miss Finch wore an enormous hat. When she was seated, no one at the back or side of her could see a thing. But out of the unseen ceiling, soon there dropped an enormous pair of iron claws (supposedly iron) that closed tightly on the hat and head of the shrieking Miss Finch, lifting her bodily out of her seat and holding her suspended aloft in the studio heaven.

How many times that scene was rehearsed and taken! It grew so late and we were all so sleepy that we stopped counting. But pay for overtime evolved from this picture.

The members of the stock company that had grown up worked on a guaranty of so many days a week. Now with so much night work our director felt that the actors not on "guaranties" should be recompensed and it was ruled that after 7 P.M. they would receive three extra dollars. So when 6 P.M. would arrive with yet another scene to be taken, the non-guaranty actors became very cheery. More money loomed, and more sandwiches, pie, coffee, or milk, on the company. Frequently those not on the guaranteed list made more than those on it, which peeved the favored ones.

Along about now Mr. Herbert Yost contributed some artistic bits. Once he was Edgar Allan Poe and he wrote "The Raven" while his sick wife, poor little Virginia, died. We were a bit afraid of being too classic. The public might not understand—we must go slowly yet awhile, but not all our days.

Mr. Yost was one actor who used a different name for his picture work. He called himself "Barry O'Moore" in the movies. Not that he felt the movies beneath him, but he was nervous about the future reaction. He showed good foresight. For as soon as the big theatrical producers got wind of the fact that their actors were working in moving picture studios, they decided to put a crimp in the idea. The Charles Frohman office issued an edict that any actor who worked in moving pictures could not work for them. But the edict was shortly revoked. Even so long ago had the power of the little motion picture begun to be felt.

CHAPTER XI

MACK SENNETT GETS STARTED

ONE of our regular "extra" people was Mack Sennett. He quietly dubbed along like the rest, only he grouched. He never approved whole-heartedly of anything we did, nor how we did it, nor who did it. There was something wrong about all of us—even Mary Pickford! Said the coming King of Comedy productions: "I don't see what they're all so crazy about her for—I think she's affected." Florence Lawrence didn't suit him either—"she talks baby-talk." And to Sennett "baby-talk" was the limit! Of myself he said: "Sometimes she talks to you and sometimes she doesn't." Good-looking Frank Grandin he called "Inflated Grandin."

But beneath all this discontent was the feeling that he wasn't being given a fair chance; which, along with a smoldering ambition, was the reason for the grouch.

When work was over, Sennett would hang around the studio watching for the opportune moment when his director would leave. Mr. Griffith often walked home wanting to get a bit of fresh air. This Sennett had discovered. So in front of the studio or at the corner of Broadway and Fourteenth Street he'd pull off the "accidental" meeting. Then for twenty-three blocks he would have the boss all to himself and wholly at his mercy. Twenty-three blocks of uninterrupted conversation. "Well now, what do you really think about these moving pictures? What do you

77

think there is in them? Do you think they are going to last? What's in them for the actor? What do you think of my chances?"

To all of which Mr. Griffith would reply: "Well, not much for the actor, if you're thinking of staying. The only thing is to become a director. I can't see that there's anything much for the actor as far as the future is concerned."

Mr. Sennett had come to the movies via the chorus of musical comedy. It also was understood he had had a previous career as a trainer for lightweight boxers. If there was one person in the studio that never would be heard from—well, we figured that person would be Mack Sennett. He played policemen mostly—and what future for a movie policeman? His other supernumerary part was a French dude. But he was very serious about his policeman and his French dude. From persistent study of Max Linder—the popular Pathé comique of this day—and adoption of his style of boulevardier dressing, spats, boutonniére, and cane, Mr. Sennett evolved a French type that for an Irishman wasn't so bad. But even so, to all of us, it seemed hopeless. Why did he take so much pains?

He got by pretty well when any social flair was unnecessary; when Mary Pickford and I played peasants, tenement ladies, and washwomen, Mack occasionally loved, honored, and cherished us in the guise of a laborer or peddler. He had a muscle-bound way about him in these serious rôles— perhaps he was made self-conscious by the sudden prominence. But Mary and I never minded. The extra girls, however, made an awful fuss when they had to work in a comedy with Sennett, for he clowned so. They would rather not work than work with Sennett. How peeved they'd get! "Oh, dear," they'd howl, "do I have to work with Sennett?"

Now 'tis said he is worth five millions!

In "Father Gets in the Game," an early release, Sennett is seen as the gay Parisian papa, the Linder influence plainly in evidence.

Mr. Griffith was more than willing, if he could find a good story with a leading comedy part suitable to Mr. Sennett, to let him have his fling. Finally, one such came along —quite legitimate, with plenty of action, called "The Curtain Pole"—venturesome for a comedy, for it was apparent it would exceed the five-hundred-foot limit. It took seven hundred and sixty-five feet of film to put the story over.

Released in February, 1909, it created quite a sensation.

The natives of Fort Lee, where "The Curtain Pole" was taken, were all worked up over it. Carpenters had been sent over a few days in advance, to erect, in a clearing in the wooded part of Fort Lee, stalls for fruits, vegetables, and other foodstuffs. The wreckage of these booths by M. Sennett in the guise of *M. Dupont* was to be the big climax of the picture. The "set" when finished was of such ambitious proportions—and for a comedy, mind you —that we were all terribly excited, and we concluded that while it had taken Mr. Sennett a long time and much coaxing to get himself "starred," it was no slouch of a part he had eventually obtained for himself.

I know I was all stirred up, for I was a market woman giving the green cabbages the thrifty stare, when the cab with the curtain pole sticking out four or five feet either side, entered the market-place. M. Dupont, fortified with a couple of absinthe frappés, was trying to manipulate the pole with sufficient abandon to effect the general destruction of the booths. He succeeded very well, for before I had paid for my cabbage something hit me and I was knocked not only flat but considerably out, and left genuinely unconscious in the center of the stage. While I was satisfied he should have them, I wasn't so keen just then about Mack Sennett's starring ventures. But he gave a classic and noble performance, albeit a hard-working one.

One other picture was released this same year with Mack Sennett in a prominent part—"The Politician's Love Story."

New York's Central Park awoke one February morning to find her leafless trees and brush all a-glisten with a sleet that made them look like fantastic crystal branches. When the actors reported at the studio that morning, they found Mr. Griffith in consultation with himself. He did not want to waste that fairyland just a few blocks away.

A hurried look through pigeon-holed scripts unearthed no winter story. "Well," announced our director, "make up everybody, straight make-up. Bobby, pack up the one top hat, the one fur coat and cap, I'll call a couple of taxis, and on the way we'll change this summer story into a winter one."

So was evolved "The Politician's Love Story" in which were scenes where lovers strolled all wrapped up in each other and cuddled down on tucked-away benches. Well, lovers can cuddle in winter as well as summer, and we were crazy to get the silver thaw in the picture; and we got it, though we nearly froze. But we had luxurious taxis to sit in when not needed, and afterwards we were taken to the Casino to thaw out, and were fed hot coffee and sandwiches in little private rooms.

"The Curtain Pole" and "The Politician's Love Story" started the grumbling young Mack Sennett on the road to fame and fortune. Like the grouchy poker player who kicks himself into financial recuperation, Mack Sennett grouched himself into success.

CHAPTER XII

ON LOCATION—EXPERIENCES PLEASANT AND OTHERWISE

BEFORE the first winter drove us indoors there had been screened a number of Mexican and Indian pictures. There was one thriller, "The Greaser's Gauntlet," in which Wilfred Lucas, recruited from Kirke La Shelle's "Heir to the Hoorah" played the daring, handsome, and righteous José. And Wilfred Lucas, by the way, was the first real g-r-a-n-d actor, democratic enough to work in our movies. That had happened through friendship for Mr. Griffith. They had been in a production together.

For a mountain fastness of arid Mexico, we journeyed not far from Edgewater, New Jersey. No need to go further. Up the Hudson along the Palisades was sufficiently Mexico-ish for our needs. There were many choice boulders for abductors to hide behind and lonely roads for hold-ups. New Jersey near by was a fruitful land for movie landscape; it didn't take long to get there, and transportation was cheap. Small wonder Fort Lee shortly grew to be the popular studio town it did.

In those days, movie conveyance for both actors and cargo was a bit crude. We had no automobiles. When Jersey-bound, we'd dash from wherever we lived to the nearest subway, never dreaming of spending fifty cents on a taxi. We left our subway at the 125th Street station. Down the escalator, three steps at a bound, we flew, and took up another hike to the ferry building. And while we hiked this stretch we wondered—for so far we had come breakfastless—if we would have time for some nourishment before the 8:45 boat.

A block this side of the ferry building was "Murphy's," a nice clean saloon with a family restaurant in the back, where members of the company often gathered for an early morning bite. We stuffed ourselves until the clock told us to be getting to our little ferry-boat. Who knew when or where we might eat again that day?

"Ham," Mr. Murphy's best waiter, took care of us. As the hungry breakfasters grew in number and regularity Mr. Murphy became inquisitive. Mr. Murphy was right, we didn't work on the railroad and we didn't drive trucks. So, who, inquired Mr. Murphy of Ham, might these strange people be who ate so much and were so jolly in the early morning?

And Ham answered, "Them is moving picture people."

And Mr. Murphy replied, "Well, give them the best and lots of it."

We needed "the best and lots of it." We needed regular longshoremen's meals. Outdoor picture work with its long hours meant physical endurance in equal measure with artistic outpourings.

Ham is still in Mr. Murphy's service, but his job has grown rather dull with the years. No more picture people to start the day off bright and snappy. Now he only turns on the tap to draw a glass of Mr. Volstead's less than half of one per cent.

"But I want to ask you something," said Ham as I started to leave.

"Yes?"

"Would you tell me"—hushed and awed the tone—"did Mary Pickford ever come in here?"

"Oh, yes, Ham, she came sometimes."

"I told the boss so, I told him Mary Pickford had come here with them picture people."

Whether Mary had or hadn't, I didn't remember, but I couldn't deny Ham that little bit of romance to cheer along his colorless to-days.

Ham's breakfast disposed of, we would rush to the ferry, seek our nook in the boat, and enjoy a short laze before reaching the Jersey side. At one of the little inns along the Hudson we rented a couple of rooms where we made up and dressed. Soon would appear old man Brown and his son, each driving a two-seated buggy. And according to what scenes we were slated for, we would be told to pile in, and off we would be driven to "location."

"Old Man Brown" was a garrulous, good-natured Irishman who regaled us with tales of prominent persons who, in his younger days, had been his patrons. How proud he was to tell of Lillian Russell's weekly visit to her daughter Dorothy who was attending a convent school up the Hudson!

Speaking of "Old Man Brown" brings to mind "Hughie." Hughie's job was to drive the express wagon which transported costumes, properties, cameras, and tripods. In the studio, on the night preceding a day in the country, each actor packed his costume and make-up box and got it ready for Hughie. For sometimes in the early morning darkness of 4 A.M. Hughie would have to whip up his horses in front of 11 East Fourteenth Street so as to be on the spot in Jersey when the actors arrived via their speedier locomotion.

Arrived on location, Johnny Mahr and Bobbie Harron would climb the wagon, get out the costumes, and bring them to the actor. And if your particular bundle did not arrive in double-quick time and you were in the first or second scene, out you dashed and did a mad scramble on to the wagon where you frantically searched. Suppose it had been left behind!

Hughie had a tough time of it trucking by two horse-power when winter came along. So I was very happy some few years later, when calling on Mr. Hugh Ford at the Famous Players' old studio in West Fifty-sixth Street, N. Y., now torn down, to find Hughie there with a comfortable job "on the door."

David Griffith was always overly fastidious about "location." His feeling for charming landscapes and his use of them in the movies was a significant factor in the success of his early pictures. So we had a "location" woman, Gene Gauntier, who dug up "locations" and wrote scenarios for the princely wage of twenty-five dollars weekly. Miss Gauntier will be eternally remembered as the discoverer of Shadyside. Shades of Shadyside! with never a tree, a spot of green grass, or a clinging vine; only sand, rocks, and quarries from which the baked heat oozed unmercifully.

Miss Gauntier's aptitude along the location line, however, did not satisfy her soaring ambition, so she left Biograph for Kalem. Under Sidney Olcott's direction, she played *Mary* in his important production "From the Manger to the Cross," and was the heroine of some charming Irish stories he produced in Ireland.

"The Redman and the Child" was the second picture

Biograph's new director produced, and his first Indian picture. Charles Inslee was the big-hearted Indian chief in the story and little Johnny Tansy played the child. The picture made little Johnny famous. He had as much honor as the movies of those days could give a child. Jackie Coogan was the lucky kid to arrive in the world when he did.

When the New Theatre (now the Century), sponsoring high-class uncommercial drama opened, Johnny Tansy was the child wonder of the company. Here he fell under the observant eye of George Foster Platt and became his protégé. And so our Johnny was lost to the movies.

We went to Little Falls, New Jersey, for "The Redman and the Child," which, at the time, was claimed to be "the very acme of photographic art." I'll say we worked over that Passaic River. Mr. Griffith made it yield its utmost. As there was so little money for anything pretentious in the way of a studio set, we became a bit intoxicated with the rivers, flowers, fields, and rocks that a munificent nature spread before us, asking no price.

My memories of working outdoors that first summer are not so pleasant. We thought we were going to get cool, fresh air in the country, but the muggy atmosphere that hung over the Hudson on humid August days didn't thrill us much. I could have survived the day better in the studio with the breeze from our one electric fan.

On Jersey days, work finished, back to our little Inn in a mad rush to remove make-up, dress, and catch the next ferry. Our toilet was often no more than a lick and a promise with finishing touches added as we journeyed ferrywards along the river road in old man Brown's buggy.

Were we ever going anywhere but Fort Lee and Edge-

Caudebec Inn at Cuddebackville.   *(See p. 119)*

From "The Mended Lute," made at Cuddebackville, with Florence Lawrence, Owen Moore and Jim Kirkwood.
(See p. 116)

Frank Powell, Mr. Griffith's first $10-a-day actor, with Marion Leonard in "Fools of Fate," made at Cuddebackville.
(See p. 108)

Richard Barthelmess as *Arno*, the youngest son, with Nazimova in "War Brides," a Herbert Brennon production. The part that put Dicky over.

(See p. 136)

water and Shadyside? I do believe that first summer I was made love to on every rock and boulder for twenty miles up and down the Hudson.

Well, we did branch out a bit. We did a picture in Greenwich, Connecticut. Driving to the station, our picture day finished, we passed a magnificent property, hemmed in by high fences and protected with beautiful iron gates. Signs read "Private Property. Keep Out." We heeded them not. In our nervous excitement (we were not calm about this deed of valor) we kept away from the residence proper, and drove to the outbuildings and the Superintendent's office. Told him we'd been working in the country near by and would appreciate it much if we could come on the morrow and take some scenes; slipped him a twenty, and that did the trick.

There was nothing we had missed driving around Millbank, which, we learned later, was the home of Mrs. A. A. Anderson, the well-known philanthropist who passed away some few years ago. So on the morrow, bright and early, we dropped anchor there, made up in one of the barns, and were rehearsing nicely, being very quiet and circumspect, when down the pathway coming directly toward us, with blood in her eye, marched the irate Mrs. Anderson. Trembling and weak-kneed we looked about us. Could we be hearing aright? Was she really saying those dreadful things to us? Weakly we protested our innocence. Vain our explanation. And so we folded our tents and meekly and shamefacedly slunk away.

Before the summer was over we went to Seagate and Atlantic Highlands. It wasn't very pleasant at Atlantic Highlands, for here we encountered the summer boarder. As they had nothing better to do, they would see what we were going to do. We were generally being lovers, of course, and strolling in pairs beneath a sunshade until we reached the foreground, where we were to make a graceful flop onto the sandy beach and play our parts beneath the flirtatious parasol. Before we were ready to take the scene we had to put ropes up to keep back the uninvited audience which giggled and tee-heed and commented loudly throughout. We felt like monkeys in a zoo—as if we'd gone back to the day when the populace jeered the old strolling players of Stratford town.

Mr. Griffith got badly annoyed when we had such experiences. His job worried him, the nasty publicity of doing our work in the street, like ditch diggers. So he had to pick on some one and I was handy. How could *I* stand for it? Why was *I* willing to endure it? He *had* to, of course. So thinking to frighten me and make me a good girl who'd stay home, he said: "Something has occurred to me; it's probable this business might get kind of public—some day, you know, you may get in the subway and have all the people stare at you while they whisper to each other, 'That's that girl we saw in the movie the other night.' *And how would you like that?*"

One saving grace the Highlands had for us. We could get a swim sometimes. And we discovered Galilee, a fishing village about twenty miles down the coast, the locale of that first version of Enoch Arden—"After Many Years."

But when winter came, though we lost the spectators we acquired other discomforts. Our make-up would be frozen, and the dreary, cold, damp rooms in the country hotels made us shivery and miserable. We'd hurriedly climb into our costumes, drag on our coats, and then light our little alcohol stove or candle to get the make-up sufficiently smeary. When made up, out into the cold, crisp day. One of the men would have a camp-fire going where we'd huddle between scenes and keep limber enough to act. Then when ready for the scene Billy Bitzer would have to light the little lamp that he attached to the camera on cold days to warm the film so it wouldn't be streaked with "lightning." While that was going on we stood at attention, ready to do our bit when the film was.

We weren't so keen on playing leads on such days as those, for when you are half frozen it isn't so easy to look as if you were calmly dying of joy, for which emotional state the script might be asking. What we liked best in the winter was to follow Mack Sennett in the chases which he always led, and which he made so much of, later, when he became the big man in Keystone films. The chase warmed us up, for Mack Sennett led us on some merry jaunts, over stone walls, down gulleys, a-top of fences—whatever looked good and hard to do.

Somehow we found it difficult to be always working with the weather. Though we watched carefully it seemed there always were "summer" stories to be finished, almost up to snow time; and "winter" stories in the works when June roses were in bud. Pink swiss on a bleak November day 'neath the leafless maple didn't feel so good; nor did velvet and fur and heavy wool in the studio in humid August.

But such were the things that happened. We accepted them with a good grace.

CHAPTER XIII

AT THE STUDIO

THIS story must now take itself indoors. We are terribly excited over Tolstoy's "Resurrection." So even though it be May, we must to the studio where the carpenters and scene painters are fixing us a Siberia.

As the days went by we produced many works of literary masters—Dickens, Scott, Shakespeare, Bret Harte, O. Henry, and Frank Norris. We never bothered about "rights" for the little one-reel versions of five-act plays and eight hundred page novels. Authors and publishers were quite unaware of our existence.

Arthur Johnson, Owen Moore, and Florence Lawrence played the leading parts in our "free adaptation of Leo Tolstoy's Powerful Novel." And it so happened that just as Prince Demetri was ready to don his fur robes, and the poor exiles their woolen slips, for the trudge over the snow-clad steppes, a nice hot spell came our way, and we must have been the hottest Russians that ever endured Siberia.

Owen Moore got so querulous with the heat—he was playing one of those handsome, cruel officers who poke bayonets at the innocent and well-behaved exiles—that he nearly killed us throwing tables and heavy furniture at us. I objected to the realism. We were all a bit peevish, what with the unseasonable heat and the last moment discovery that the costumer had sent our wrapper-like dresses in sizes miles too large.

The scene being set and rehearsals finished, there were left just the few moments while the property man added the finishing touches to the salt and flour snow (we had graduated from sawdust), to make the costumes wearable. So another girl and I grabbed the lot and rushed into a little Polish tailor shop in the basement next door and borrowed the Polish tailor's sewing machines so that we could put in the necessary hems and pleats. Zip went the sewing machines—there was no time to lose—for we could not afford two days of Russian exiles at three dollars per day.

Nine o'clock was the morning hour of bustle and busyness at 11 East Fourteenth Street. But the actors in their eagerness to work were on the job long before nine sometimes. They straggled along from all directions. They even came by the horse-drawn surface car whose obliging and curious conductors stopped directly in front of No. 11.

And so curious became one conductor that he was not able to stand the strain, and he quit his job of jerking Bessie's reins, and got himself a job as "extra." Although the conductor's identity was never fully established, we had strong suspicions that it was Henry Lehrman, an extra who had managed in a very short time to get himself called *Pathé*, which was good for an Austrian.

"Actors"—graduates from various trades and professions of uncertain standing, and actors without acting jobs, lounged all over the place, from the street steps where they basked on mild, sunny days, into the shady hall where they kept cool on hot days; and had they made acquaintance with studio life, they could be found in the privacy of the men's one dressing-room shooting craps—the pastime during the waiting hours.

An especially busy hour 9 A.M. when we were to start on a new picture. What kind of a picture was it to be? The air was full of expectancy. Who would be cast for the leads? How keen we were to work! How we hoped for a good part—then for any kind of a part—then for only a chance to rehearse a part. In their eagerness to get a good part in a movie, the actors behaved like hungry chickens being fed nice, yellow corn, knocking and trampling each other in their mad scramble for the best bits.

This Mr. Griffith did enjoy. He would draw his chair up center, and leisurely, and in a rather teasing way, look the company over. And when you were being looked at you thought, "Ah, it's going to be me." But in a few minutes some one else would be looked at. "No, it was going to be he." A long look at Owen, a long look at Charlie, a long look at Arthur, and then the director would speak: "Arthur, I'll try you first." One by one, in the same way the company would be picked. There would be a few rough rehearsals; some one wouldn't suit; the chief would decide the part was more in Owen's line. Such nervousness until we got all set!

Indeed, we put forth our best efforts. There was too much competition and no one had a cinch on a line of good parts. When we did "The Cricket on the Hearth," Mr. Griffith rehearsed all his women in the part of *Dot*, Marion Leonard, Florence Lawrence, Violet Mersereau and then he was nice to me. Miss Mersereau however, portrayed *May Plummer*—making her movie début. Herbert Pryor played *John Perrybingle,* and Owen Moore, *Edward Plummer.*

Sometimes after rehearsing a story all day our director would chuck it as "no good" and begin on another. He never used a script and he rehearsed in sequence the scenes of every story until each scene dovetailed smoothly, and the acting was O. K. He worked out his story using his actors as chessmen. He knew what he wanted and the camera never began to grind until every little detail satisfied him.

There was some incentive for an actor to do his best. More was asked of us than to be just a "type," and the women couldn't get by with just "pretty looks." We worked hard, but we liked it. With equal grace we all played leads one day and decorated the back drop the next. On a day when there would be no work whatever for you, you'd reluctantly depart. Sometimes Mr. Griffith almost had to drive the non-working actors out of the studio. The place was small and he needed room.

Sometimes when rehearsing a picture he liked a lot, it would be as late as 3 P.M. before a fainting, lunchless lot of actors would hear those welcome words, "All right, everybody, get your lunches and make up." Then Bobbie Harron would circulate the Childs' menu card and the thirty-cent allotment would be checked off. Roast beef or a ham-and-egg sandwich, pie, tea, coffee, or milk usually nourished us. And it was a funny thing, that no matter how rich one was, or how one might have longed for something different, even might have been ill and needed something special, none of us ever dreamed of spending a nickel of his own.

While the actors ate and made up, and the carpenters were getting the set ready, Mr. Griffith, accompanied by three or four or five or six actors not on the working list that afternoon, would depart for a restaurant near by. But no woman was ever invited to these parties. This social arrangement obtained only on days when a new picture was to be got under way. David Griffith was a generous host, but he always got a good return on his investment. For while being strengthened on luscious steak, steins of Pilsener, and fluffy German pancakes all done up in gobs of melted butter, lemon juice, and powdered sugar, ideas would sprout, and comments and suggestions come freely from the Knights of Lüchow's Round Table, and when the party was over they returned to the studio all happy, and the director ready for a big day's work.

But the other actors, now made up and costumed but fed only on sandwiches, were wearing expressions of envy and reproach which made the returning jolly dogs feel a trifle uncomfortable.

"Well, let's get busy around here—wasting a hell of a lot of time—six o'clock already—have to work all night now—now come on, we'll run through it—show me what you can do—Bitzer, where do you want them? Come in and watch this, Doc." Mr. Griffith was back on the job all right.

One such rehearsal usually sufficed. Then Johnny Mahr with his five-foot board would get the focus and mark little chalk crosses on the floor, usually four, two for the foreground and two for the background. Then Johnny would hammer a nail into each cross and with his ball of twine, tying it from nail to nail, enclose the set. Now a rehearsal for "lines." And when Bitzer would say it was O. K. and Doc beamed his round Irish smile, we would take the picture, and God help the actor who looked at the camera or at the director when he was shouting instructions while the scene was being photographed.

The old ways of doing were being revolutionized day by day with the introduction of the close-up, switchback,

light effects, and screen acting that could be recognized
as a portrayal of human conduct. Exhibitors soon began
clamoring for A. B. pictures, not only for the U. S. A. but
for foreign countries as well; and as Mr. Griffith had a
commission on every foot of film sold, it was an easy matter
for us to judge our ever-increasing popularity.

The Biograph Company readily acknowledged its young
director's achievements, and the other companies soon took
cognizance of a new and keen competitor. The first
metropolitan showings began a rivalry with the other companies. Once in the race, we were there to win—and we
did. Biograph pictures came to mean something just a
little different from what had been. There was a sure
artistic touch to them; the fine shadings were there that
mark the line between talent and genius.

David Griffith had found his place; found it long before
he knew it. In ways, it was a congenial berth. Mr. Marvin,
once he saw how the wind blew, seldom came into the studio.
He was willing to let the new producer work things out
his own way. An occasional conference there was, neces-
sarily—a friendly chat as to how things were coming along.

Mr. Marvin was tall and dark, quite a handsome man
—so approachable. The actors felt quite at ease with him.
Had he not been one of us? Had he not directed even
Mr. Griffith in a penny-in-the-slot movie? Years later I
recalled the incident to Mr. Marvin. He had forgotten it
completely, but with a hearty laugh said: "No did I really?
Well, God forgive me."

"God forgive us all," I answered.

Liking Mr. Marvin as we did, we did not quite understand or approve the sudden, unexpected intrusion of Mr.
J. J. Kennedy, one day.

"Oh, our *president?* Why, do you suppose," the anxious actors queried, "he's become suddenly so interested?" What could poor movie actors be expected to know of politics and high finance? Everything had been so pleasant, we couldn't understand it. We were rather awed by Mr. Kennedy at first. Red-headed, pugnacious Irish Jeremiah—why, he never gave an actor a smile or the faintest recognition, and feeling ourselves such poor worms, as a result, we became nothing less than Sphinxes whenever his rare but awe-inspiring presence graced the studio.

But we soon learned that "fighting J. J." was of some importance in this movie business. And other things about him we learned: that he was a big man in the world of engineering—a millionaire who lived in a lovely brownstone in Brooklyn. We soon discovered he was human, too.

It seemed Mr. Kennedy had had his affairs all settled to retire from the world of business activities, when, in the critical days resulting from the 1907 panic, he stepped into the breach and saved from impending disaster the American Mutoscope and Biograph Company.

The little A. M. and B. Co. would have been terribly surprised had she been told that she was to become the organization that would develop some of the greatest of motion picture directors and stars—the Augustin Daly stock company of the movies. For while there is never the grind of its preposterous old camera to be heard in the length of the land to-day, while for years (at the time of writing this, nearly ten) all its wheels of activity have been silent, "The Old Biograph" remains as the most romantic memory, the most vital force in the early history of the American motion picture.

The association with these two scholarly gentlemen

Messrs. Kennedy and Marvin, unusual then as to-day in the picture business, helped to soften the crudities of the work, and tone down the apparent rough edges of our job. So considerate of our tender feelings were both Mr. Marvin and Mr. Kennedy, that when either desired to visit or bring interested friends into the studio, they would ask Mr. Griffith for a propitious moment, and then stand off in the background as though apologizing for the intrusion.

Mr. Griffith, but not by way of retaliation, had reason to make intrusions on his bosses. He went pleading the cause of better screen stories. For that was the ticklish point—to raise our artistic standard—not to depart too rapidly from the accepted—and to keep our product commercial.

David Griffith began feeling his wings. He dared to consider a production of Browning's "Pippa Passes." If just once he could do something radical to make the indifferent legitimate actors, critics, writers, and a better class of public take cognizance of us! So there resulted long discussions with the Biograph executives as to the advisability of Browning in moving pictures, and after much persuasion consent was eventually granted.

There was no question in our minds as to whether "Pippa Passes" would be an artistic success. Had this classic writer fashioned his famous poem directly for the movies he couldn't have turned out a better screen subject. But might not the bare idea of the high-brow Robert scare away the moving picture public?

In those days there were several kinds of motion picture publics. In sections of New York City, there was the dirty, dark little store, a sheet at one end and the projection machine at the other. It took courage to sit through a show in such a place, for one seldom escaped without some weary soul finding a shoulder the while he indulged in forty winks. Besides this there were the better-known Keith and Proctor Theatres on Fourteenth Street, Twenty-third, and 125th Street, the Fourteenth Street Theatre, and the old Academy of Music.

In the smaller American cities, the motion picture public was of middle-class homey folks who washed their own supper dishes in a hurry so as to see the new movie, and to meet their neighbors who, like themselves, dashed hatless to the nickelodeon, dragging along with them the children and the dog.

Things like this happened, when dinner hour was approaching, and mother was anxiously awaiting her child: the neighborhood policeman would casually saunter over to the picture house, poke his head in at the door, spy the wanted child, tap her little shoulder, gently reproving: "Jennie, your mother wants you"—whereupon Jennie would reluctantly tear herself away so that the family could all sit down together to their pot-roast and noodles.

Yes, Browning would need courage.

"Pippa Passes" being ever in Mr. Griffith's mind these days, he scanned each new face in the studio as he mulled over the needed characters. The cast would be the best possible one he could get together.

CHAPTER XIV

MARY PICKFORD HAPPENS ALONG

IT was a bright May morning in 1909. When I came off the scene, I noticed a little girl sitting quietly in a corner near the door. She looked about fourteen. I afterwards learned she was nearing seventeen. She wore a plain navy-blue serge suit, a blue-and-white striped lawn shirt-waist, a rolled brim Tuscan straw sailor hat with a dark blue ribbon bow. About her face, so fresh, so pretty, and so gentle, bobbed a dozen or more short golden curls—such perfect little curls as I had never seen.

A timid applicant usually hugged the background. Bold ones would press forward to the camera and stand there, obtruding themselves, in the hope that the director would see them, like their look, and engage them for a day's work.

But Mary Pickford tucked herself away in a niche, while she quietly gave us "the once over." The boss's eagle eye had been roving her way at intervals, the while he directed, for here was something "different"—a maid so fair and an actress to boot! Pausing a moment in his work, he came over to me and said, "Don't you think she would be good for Pippa?"

"Ideal," I answered.

Before we closed shop that day, he had Mary make up —gave her a violin, and told her to walk across the stage while playing it so that Billy Bitzer could make a test.

Before she left the studio that day, every actor there

99

had a "line" on Mary.   In the dressing-room, the word went around:

"There's a cute kid outside; have you seen her?"

"No, where is she?"

"She's been sitting out there in a corner by herself."

"Guess I'll take a look."

"She's cute all right; they're taking a test."

Something was impending.   There was excitement and expectancy in the air.   America's Sweetheart was soon to make her first screen appearance.

The test was O. K. and Mary was told to come to the studio on the morrow.   David promised her five dollars a day for her first picture, and were her work good, he'd talk business with her.   That satisfied Mary.

As "Giannina," the pretty daughter of Taddeo Ferrari, in "The Violin Maker of Cremona" Mary Pickford made her motion picture début.   She was ideally suited to the part, and had good support from David Miles as the cripple Filippo.

The studio bunch was all agog over the picture and the new girl, long before the quiet word was passed to the regulars a few days later: "Projection room, they're going to run 'The Violin Maker.' "   After the showing, Mr. Griffith had a serious conversation with Mary and offered her twenty-five dollars a week for three days' work.   This Mary accepted.   She felt she might stay through the summer.

Her second picture was "The Lonely Villa," the brain child of Mack Sennett, gleaned from a newspaper—good old-fashioned melodrama.   Mary played a child of twelve with two younger sisters and a mother.   They were nice people, and wealthy.   Miss Leonard, playing the mother, would be beautifully arrayed in the brown-silk-and-velvet. But what could be done for Mary? She had no clothes fit for the wealthy little aristocrat she was to portray and there was nothing in the meager stock wardrobe for her. "Oh, she's so pretty," I said to my husband, "can't we dress her up? She'll just be darling in the right kind of clothes." So he parted with twenty dollars from the cash register and trusted me to dispose of it at Best's—then on Twenty-third Street—for a proper wardrobe. Off I went on my joyful errand, and brought back to the studio a smart pale blue linen frock, blue silk stockings to match, and nifty patent leather pumps. What a dainty little miss she looked, her fluffy curls a-bobbing, when she had donned the new pretties!

During the dreary waits between scenes, there being no private dressing-rooms, actors would be falling all over each other, and they could find seclusion only by digging themselves in behind old and unused scenery. Owen Moore was especially apt in hiding himself. He had an unfriendly way of disappearing. None of the herd instinct in him. At times we had quite a job locating him. Cruising along the back drop of a Coney Island Police Court, or perhaps a section of the Chinese wall, we'd innocently stumble upon him. But we didn't need to hunt him the day that Mary Pickford was all dressed up in Best & Company's best. That day he never left the camera stand, and his face was all one generous Irish smile. (How little we know when our troubles are going to begin!)

Following "The Lonely Villa" came "The Way of Man" and then a series of comedies in which Mary was teamed with Billy Quirk, "Sweet and Twenty," "They Would Elope," "His Wife's Visitors."

Though Mary Pickford affiliated with the movies for twenty-five dollars weekly with the understanding that she would work three days a week and play "parts" only, she was a good sport and would come in as an "extra" in a scene if we needed her. So occasionally in a courtroom scene, or a church wedding where the camera was set up to get the congregation or spectators from the rear, Mary could attend with perfect safety as the Pickford curls, from the back of her head, would never have been recognized by the most enthusiastic fan of that day. Mr. Griffith would not have his "Mary" a "super."

Considering the stellar position she has held for years, and her present-day affluence, many movie fans may think that Mary Pickford was kissed by the fairies when she was born. Not so. Life's hard realities—the understanding of her little family's struggles to make both ends meet when she was even as young as Jackie Coogan at the time of his first appearance with Charlie Chaplin in "The Kid"—that was her fairy's kiss—that and her mother's great love for her.

Of course, such idolatry as Mrs. Smith gave her first-born might have made of her a simpering silly, or worse. But Gladys Smith (as Mary Pickford was born) was pretty —and she had talent and brains. So what wonder if Mother Smith often sat all through the night at her child's bedside, not wanting to sleep, but only to worship her beautiful daughter?

Mary told me her story in our early intimate days together in the movies. With her little gang she was playing in the streets of Toronto where she was born, perhaps playing "bean bag"—she was indeed young enough for that.

In frock coat and silk hat an advance agent was looking

Biograph's one automobile (note D. W. G. on door), in front of Old Redonda Hotel. (See p. 185)

From "Wark" to "work," with only the difference of a vowel. (See p. 185)

Jeanie Macpherson, Frank Grandin, Linda Griffith and Wilfred Lucas, in "Enoch Arden."

The Norwegian's shack, the scene of Enoch's departure. From "Enoch Arden."

Annie Lee. From "Enoch Arden," the first two-reel picture. (See p. 195)

The vessel that was towed from San Pedro. From "Enoch Arden."

over the prospects for business in the town, and at the same time looking for a few kids needed in his show. His eye caught pretty little Gladys Smith. Would Mama let her play at the opera house?

"Let's ask Mama."

Mama, the young Mrs. Smith, consented. Seeing that, a very few years afterwards, through an accident on the St. Lawrence River boat on which her husband worked, Mama was suddenly left a young widow with three tiny youngsters to support, her consent that day proved to be one of those things just meant to be.

With the Valentine Stock Company in her home town when only five, Mary played her first part, *Cissy* in "The Silver King." In 1902, Mary was already a "star," playing *Jessie* in "The Fatal Wedding." The season of 1904 found Gladys Smith, then twelve years old, playing leading parts, such as *Dolly* in "The Child Wife," a play written by Charles Taylor, first husband to Laurette and the father of her two children. The following season Gladys Smith created the part of *Freckles* in "The Gypsy Girl," written by Hal Reid, father of the popular and much loved Wallace Reid. Gladys Smith's salary was then forty dollars per week and she sent her mother, who was living in Brooklyn, fifteen dollars weekly for her support. In 1906 the Smith family toured with Chauncey Olcott in "Edmund Burke." But it was as the little boy *Patsy Poor* in "New York Life" that Mary's chance came for better things.

David Belasco had told Gladys he would give her a hearing. And so the day came when on the dark and empty stage of the Republic Theatre, a chair her only "support," Gladys did Patsy's death scene for Mr. Belasco and he thought so well of it that she was engaged for Charlotte

Walker's younger sister *Betty* in "The Warrens of Virginia."

So "The Warrens of Virginia" with Gladys Smith, rechristened by Mr. Belasco "Mary Pickford" (a family name) came and went. The magic wand of Belasco had touched Mary, but magic wands mean little when one needs to eat. "The Warrens of Virginia" finished its run, and Mary, her seventeen years resting heavily upon her, was confronted with the long idle summer and the nearly depleted family exchequer. So arrived the day in the late spring, when from the weary round of agencies and with faint hope of signing early for next season little Mary wandered to the old Biograph studio at 11 East Fourteenth Street.

Such a freshly sweet and pretty little thing she was, that her chances of not being engaged were meagre. Since that day when she first cast her lot with the movies—that day in June, 1909, when the Pickford releases so inauspiciously started, they have continued with only one interruption. That was in January, 1913, when in David Belasco's production of "The Good Little Devil," she co-starred with Ernest Truex. What an exciting day at the studio it was when it was discovered that Mr. Belasco was up in the projection room seeing some of Mary's pictures!

Mary's return to the legitimate was a clever move. It made for publicity and afterward served her, despite the shortness of the engagement, as a qualification for becoming an Adolph Zukor-Famous Player.

Mr. Zukor established his "Famous Players" through the production of "Queen Elizabeth," the first feature picture with a famous player, the player being no less a personage than the divine Sarah Bernhardt. This was in 1912. So when Mary Pickford became a Famous Player, it caused considerable comment. However, she has become the most famous of all the Famous Players engaged by Mr. Zukor.

And as for Famous Players, long before Adolph Zukor's day, they had been appearing before a movie camera. As far back as 1903 Joseph Jefferson played in his famous "Rip Van Winkle" for the American Mutoscope and Biograph Company. And Sarah Bernhardt appeared as *Camille*, in the Eclair Company's two-reel production of the Dumas play in 1911.

Mary Pickford did not reach the peak of fame and affluence without her "ifs." When the first fall came, and little Mary had not connected up with a legitimate job, she said to me one day: "Miss Arvidson, we have just fifty dollars in the bank for all of us, and I'm worried to death. I want to get back on the stage. Of course, the pictures are regular, but if I had enough put away, I'd get out."

Another day: "If I stay in the movies I know I will just be ruined for the stage—the acting is so different—and I never use my voice. Do you think it will hurt me if I stay in the pictures any longer?"

"Well, Mary," I answered, "I cannot advise you. We all just have to take our chances."

Good fortune it was for the movies, for her family and for her, that she stayed. In the beginning she encountered practically no competition. Not until dainty Marguerite Clark left the field of the legitimate in 1913 and appeared in her first charming photoplay "Wildflower" did Miss Pickford ever need to bother her little head over anything as improbable as a legitimate competitor in a field where she had reigned as queen undisputed and unchallenged.

It is often asked whether Mary Pickford is a good business woman. My opinion is that she's a very good business woman. And I am told that she had a head for business as far back as the days of *Patsy Poor*. She must have an understudy and no one but sister Lottie was going to be that understudy. Lottie stayed the season even though no emergency where she could have officiated, presented itself.

I know Mary brought a business head with her to Biograph. Mr. Griffith had told her if she'd be a good sport about doing what little unpleasant stunts the stories might call for, he would raise her salary. The first came in "They Would Elope," some two months after her initiation.

The scene called for the overturning of the canoe in which the elopers were escaping down the muddy Passaic. Not a second did Mary demur, but obediently flopped into the river. The scene over, wet and dirty, the boys fished her out and rushed her, wrapped in a warm blanket, to the waiting automobile.

It was the last scene of the day—we reserved the nasty ones for the finish. Mary's place in the car was between my husband and myself. Hardly were we comfortably settled, hardly had the chauffeur time to put the car in "high," before Mary with all the evidence of her good sportsmanship so plainly visible, naïvely looked up into her director's face and sweetly reminded him of his promise. She got her raise. And I got the shock of my young life. That pretty little thing with yellow curls thinking of money like that!

Later, when Carl Laemmle had bucked the General Film Company with the organization of his independent company, the "Imp," he enticed Mary away from the Biograph by an offer of twenty-five dollars a week over her then one hundred weekly salary. Mary was still under legal age, so Owen Moore, to whom Mary had been secretly married, had to sign the contract. He with several other "Biographers" had gone over to the "Imp." Mrs. Smith with Lottie and Jack still clung to the Biograph. Mid anguished tears Mrs. Smith showed me the contract, and in a broken voice said: "What's to become of Mary at that awful 'Imp' with no one to direct her? How could she have been influenced to leave Mr. Griffith for only twenty-five dollars extra and not even consult her mother? What good will the twenty-five dollars do with her career ruined?"

But the break did not hurt Mary. It helped her. She soon sued the "Imp," claiming that her artistic career was being ruined as she was being forced to act with carpenters. That was the story according to the dailies. Shortly afterward she was back at Biograph with another twenty-five dollar weekly advance in her salary.

CHAPTER XV

ACQUIRING ACTORS AND STYLE

THROUGH conflicting emotions and varying decisions and an ever-increasing interest and faith in the new work, Biograph's first movie actors stuck. With Mary Pickford pictures winning favor, David Griffith became ambitious for new talent, and as the right sort didn't come seeking, *he* decided to go seeking. He'd dash out of the studio while the carpenters were putting up a new set, jump into a taxi, call at the different dramatic agencies, and ask had they any actors who might like to work in moving pictures at ten dollars a day!

At one of these agencies—Paul Scott's—he arrived just as a good-looking manly sort of chap was about to leave.

"That's the type I want."

Mr. Scott replied, "Well, I'll introduce you."

Mr. Griffith lost no time in telling the personable Frank Powell about the movies, and offering the new salary, secured his services.

With his fair bride, Eleanor Hicks, who had been playing "leads" with Ellen Terry, while he stage managed, Mr. Powell had just returned from England. But Miss Terry and London triumphs were now of the past, and Mr. Powell was glad enough to end the tiresome hunt for a job, and his temporary money worries by becoming the first actor to be engaged by Mr. Griffith at the fancy price of ten dollars a day. Mr. Powell was well worth the ten for he had good presence, clean-cut features, and wore good clothes. He became our leading aristocrat, specializing in brokers, bankers, and doctors—the cultured professional man. David soon saw that he could take over little responsibilities and relieve him of many irksome details not concerned with the dramatic end. So he became the first assistant, and then a director of comedies—the first—under Mr. Griffith's supervision.

In time he went with William Fox as director. He discovered the screen's first famous vamp, Theda Bara. Against Mr. Fox's protests—for Mr. Fox wanted a well-known movie player—Frank Powell selected the unknown Theda from among the extras to play Mr. Kipling's famous lady in "A Fool There Was," because she was a strange-looking person who wore queer earrings and dresses made of odd tapestry cloths. The picture made William Fox his first big money in the movies, and established his place in the motion picture world.

"His Duty" was Frank Powell's first picture. In the cast were Owen Moore and Kate Bruce. "The Cardinal's Conspiracy"—the name we gave to "Richelieu"—marked Mr. Powell's first important screen characterization. It was taken at Greenwich, Connecticut, on Commodore Benedict's magnificent estate, *Indian Harbor*. Soon came "The Broken Locket" which had a nice part for Kate Bruce.

Fortunate "Brucie," as her confrères call her! She seems never to have had to hunt a job since that long ago day when D. W. Griffith picked her as a member of the old Biograph Stock Company. Little bits or big parts mattered nothing to "Brucie" as long as she was working with us.

David hunted movie recruits not only at the dramatic agencies, but also at the Lambs and Players Clubs of New York City. It was at the Lambs he found James Kirkwood, and determined right off to get him down to the studio. He had to be subtle. He never knew what mighty indignation might be hurled at him for simply suggesting "movie acting" to a legitimate actor. But Jim Kirkwood made good his promise to come, and no effort was spared to make the visit both pleasant and impressive.

I always thought we were a rather well-behaved lot— there was rather strict discipline maintained at all times. But on this occasion we old troupers were told to "sit pretty," to be quiet and stay in the dressing-room if there were no scenes being taken in which we were working, and if we were called upon to work, to please just "work" and not be sociable. Our director seemed to be somewhat ashamed of his faithful old crew. So the studio remained hushed and awed—a solemn dignity pervaded it. In the dressing-room, those who didn't know what was going on said, "Why are you all so quiet?"

"Oh, don't you know?" we sang in unison. "There's a Broadway actor out there, from the *Henry Miller Company.*"

"Oh, you don't say so!"

The effect was funniest on Mack Sennett. He wore a satirical smile that spoke volumes. For he had divined that these "up-stage" new actors were to get more than five per day; besides, he was getting few enough parts as things were, now where *would* he be?

"Lord Jim" was certainly treated with great deference. He was shown several scenes "in the taking," and then escorted upstairs to see some of Mary Pickford's pictures. The Cook's tour over, Mr. Kirkwood agreed to appear in the movies.

A slow, easy manner had Jim Kirkwood, which with

underlying strength made for good screen technique. Early June was the time of his first release, "The Message," in which picture as *David Williams* he portrayed the honest, big-hearted farmer. Mr. Kirkwood, the diamond-in-the-rough type, was honest and big-hearted through all his movie career. He was the heroic Indian, as in "Comata, the Sioux"; the brave fisherman as in "Lines of White on a Sullen Sea"—the latter one of Stanner E. V. Taylor's early classic efforts which was taken in the little fishing village of Galilee in October, 1909.

Harriet Quimby, now established as a journalist, came down to visit. Thought it would be good fun to act in a scene, so she played a village fishermaiden and thus qualified as a picture actress for her other more thrilling performance two years later. I was with her that time, on the flying field at Dover, where Bleriot had landed on the very first Channel crossing, and where she was to "take off" for France. Gaumont took a five-hundred-foot picture of the flight, titling it "The English Channel Flown by a LADY AVIATOR for the First Time."

The day Harriet Quimby flew the English Channel brought sad news to the world, for that appalling disaster —the sinking of the *Titanic*—occurred. It also brought a personal sadness to the Biograph, for Mr. Marvin's youngest son, who was returning from his honeymoon, was lost. Before the happy couple had sailed, a moving picture of the wedding had been taken in the studio.

It was not long after his initiation that Mr. Kirkwood brought a fellow Lamb, Mr. Walthall, to the studio. He had been one of the three "bad men" with Mr. Kirkwood in "The Great Divide," which play had just finished its New York run.

Mr. Griffith, an Italian costume picture on the ways, was snooping around for an actor who not only could look but also act an Italian troubadour. When he met Henry Walthall of the dark, curly hair, the brown eyes, the graceful carriage, he rested content. "The Sealed Room" was the name of the screened emotion that put Mr. Walthall over in the movies. Wally's acting proved to be the most convincing of its type so far. He was very handsome in his silk and velvet, and gold trappings, with a bejeweled chain around his neck, and a most adorable little mustache.

It was foreordained that the Civil War should have a hearing very soon. There was Kentucky, David Griffith's birth state, calling, and there in our midst was the ideal southerner, Henry Walthall. And so after a few weeks the first "Stirring Episode of the Civil War"—a little movie named "In Old Kentucky"—was rushed along. In the picture were Mary Pickford, Owen Moore, Kate Bruce, and many lesser lights. It was a long time back that Mr. Walthall started on his career of "Little Colonels." He portrayed many before he climaxed them with his great "Little Colonel" in "The Birth of a Nation!"

A remarkable trio—Frank Powell, Jim Kirkwood, and Henry Walthall—such distinct types. Though they all owned well-tailored dress suits, Frank Powell's was featured most often. Henry Walthall, suggestive of romance, had fewer opportunities; and rugged Jim Kirkwood only occasionally was permitted to don his own soup-and-fish and look distingué.

With the acquisition of the ten-dollar-a-day actor, we seemed to acquire a new dignity. No doubt about recruits fresh from Broadway lending tone—although the original five-per-day actors, who were still getting the same old five, looked with varying feelings of resentment and delight at their entrance. We old ones figured that for all our faithfulness and hard work, we might have been raised right off to ten dollars, too. But at least there was hope in that ten per—the proposition looked better now with salaries going up, and actors coming to stay, and willing to forego the dazzling footlights and the sweet applause of the audience.

Having reached ten-dollars-a-day, it didn't take so long to climb to twenty—undreamed extravagance—but good advertising along the Rialto and at the Lambs Club. "Twenty dollars a day? It listens well—the movies must have financial standing, anyway," the legitimate concluded.

Occasionally, Frank Craven, since famous as the author of many successful Broadway plays, came down and watched pictures being made. While he personally didn't care about the movies, through him Jack Standing came down and jobbed at twenty per. Through friendship for Mr. and Mrs. Frank Powell, with whom he had acted in Ellen Terry's company, David Powell entered the fold for twenty per. Even though money tempted, the high-class actor came more readily through friendship for some one already "in" than as a cold business proposition. Our movie money was talking just the same.

But hard as it was to get men, it was much harder to get women. They would not leave that "drammer" (how they loved it!) to work in a dingy studio with no footlights, no admiring audience to applaud them, and no pretty make-ups.

Only occasionally did I accompany my husband on a tour of the dramatic agencies, for our manner to each other was still a most unmarried one. I'd wait in the taxi while he went up to the different offices to see if he could entice some fair feminine. But, after each visit, back he'd plump into the taxi so distressed, "I can get men, but I cannot get women; they simply won't come."

Well, if he couldn't lure ladies from the agencies, he'd grab them off the street. With Austin Webb, an actor friend who has since left the stage for promotion of oil and skyscrapers, he was strolling along Broadway one day when a little black-haired girl passed by accompanied by her mother.

"Now that's the kind of girl I'm looking for," said Mr. Griffith.

Mr. Webb answered: "Well, why not speak to her? She's an actress, you can bet your hat on that."

But the movie director having a certain position to maintain, and not wanting to be misunderstood, hesitated. Mr. Webb volunteered, stepped up to and asked the girl would she like to work in a moving picture. Prompt her reply, "Oh, I'd love to, I just love pictures." The "girl" was Marion Sunshine of the then vaudeville team of Sunshine and Tempest. She was quite a famous personality to be in Biograph movies at this time.

Now Austin Webb, who during David Griffith's movie acting days had loaned him his own grand wardrobe, was one who might have become a big movie star. David implored him to try it, but he was skeptical. It took sporting blood to plunge moviewards in the crude days of our beginnings. Who could tell which way the thing would flop?

CHAPTER XVI

CUDDEBACKVILLE

I WAS not one of the select few who made the first trip to Cuddebackville, New York. I had been slated for a visit to my husband's folks in Louisville, Kentucky, and while there this alluring adventure was slipped over on me.

A new picture was being started out at Greenwich, Connecticut, at Commodore Benedict's, the day I was leaving, and as I was taking a late train, I was invited out on a farewell visit, as it were.

The picture was "The Golden Supper," taken from Tennyson's "Lover's Tale." I arrived just in time for the Princess's royal funeral. Down the majestic stairway of the Commodore's palatial home, the cortège took its way, escorting on a flower-bedecked stretcher, in all her pallid beauty, the earthly remains of the dead little princess.

Now in the movies, if anywhere, a princess must be beautiful. I knew not who was playing this fair royal child until the actors put the bier down, and the princess sat up, when I was quite dumbfounded to see our own little Dorothy West come to life.

Dorothy had done nicely times before as a little child of the ghetto and as frail Italian maids of the peasant class, and now here she was a full-fledged princess. So, in my amazement, I said to my husband, for it was a sincere, impersonal interest in the matter that I felt: "Is Dorothy West playing the Princess? Aren't you taking a chance?"

With great assurance he answered, "Oh, with the photography we now have, I can make them all beautiful."

Next day, as the lovely Shenandoah Valley spread out before me, I kept hearing those startling words, "Oh, with the photography we now have, I can make them all beautiful."

"The Mended Lute" was perhaps the first picture produced with the inspiring background of Cuddebackville scenery. Florence Lawrence, Owen Moore, and Jim Kirkwood the leading actors. David wrote me to Louisville on his return to New York:

DEAR LINDA:

Well, I am back in New York. Got back at twelve o'clock last night. . . . I have accounts to make out for eight days, imagine that job, can you?

Haven't had my talk with Mr. Kennedy as yet, as I have been away, but expect to on Tuesday or Wednesday as soon as I can see him. Lost six pounds up in the country, hard work, if you please. . . .

And then I want to go back to that place again and take you this time because it's very fine up there. I am saving a great automobile ride for you—if I stay. . . .

"If I stay"—always that "if." A year had now rolled by and in August Mr. Griffith would sign his second contract—*if* he stayed.

The hegira to Cuddebackville had been undertaken to show Biograph officials what could be done by just forgetting the old stamping grounds adjacent to Fort Lee. Contract-signing time approaching, Mr. Griffith wanted to splurge. A number of scripts had collected that called for wild mountainous country, among them "The Mended Lute." Mr. Kennedy and our secretary, Mr. R. H. Hammer; Mr.

Griffith and his photographer, Mr. Bitzer, sitting in conference had decided upon a place up in the Orange Mountains called Cuddebackville. It had scenic possibilities, housing facilities, and lacked summer boarders. Through an engineering job—the construction of a dam at one end of the old D. L. and W. Canal, on whose placid waters in days gone by the elder Vanderbilt had towed coal to New York—Mr. Kennedy had become acquainted with Cuddebackville.

Unsuspecting sleepy little village, with your one small inn, your general store, and your few stray farms! How famous on the map of movie locations you were to become! How famous in many lands your soft, green mountains, your gently purling streams, your fields of corn!

"The Mended Lute" would be Mr. Griffith's catchpenny. The beauties he had crowded in the little one-reeler should suffice to bowl over any unsuspecting President. So this "Cuddebackville Special," along with several others that had collected awaiting Mr. Kennedy's pleasure, was projected for the authorities. And David signed up for another year at an increase in salary and a doubling of his percentage. And he could go to Cuddebackville whenever he so desired.

Of course, the next time *she* went, and she had that "great automobile ride" that he was saving for her.

Joy, but didn't they become delirious, the actors slated for a Cuddebackville week. A week in the mountains in August, with no hotel bill, and pay checks every day! Few there were so ultra modern that they would take no joy in the bleating of the lambs but would prefer their city third floor back.

Much preparation for such a week. We had to see

that our best blouse was back from the laundry and our dotted swiss in order for evening, our costumes right, and grease-paint complete, for any of us might be asked to double up for Indians before the week was over.

It was a five-hour trip—a pretty one along the Hudson to West Point—then through the Orange Mountains. Our journey ended at a little station set in a valley sweet with tasseled corn and blossoming white buckwheat. In the distance—mountains; near by—beckoning roads lined with maples. It was the longest stop that an Ontario and Western train had ever made at Cuddebackville. Such excitement and such a jam on the little platform! No chance to slink in unnoticed as on the first unpretentious visit.

"Were we sure it was the right place?" the conductor kept asking.

"Oh, yes, quite so."

Damned if he could make it out. For we didn't look like farmers come to settle in the country; nor like fishermen come to cast for trout in the Neversink—we had nothing with us that resembled expensive fishing rods and boots; nor did we look like a strange religious sect come to worship in our own way. No, nor might we have been one of a lost tribe of Cuddebacks who after years of vain searching had at last discovered the remote little spot where the first Monsieur Caudebec had pitched his tent so far from his own dear France. As the train steamed on its way, from the rear platform the conductor was still gazing, and I thought he threw us a rather dirty look.

An express wagon was waiting for our load of stuff— big wads of canvas for the teepees, cameras, and costume baskets. A man in a red automobile was also waiting— Mr. Predmore, who owned Caudebec Inn where we were

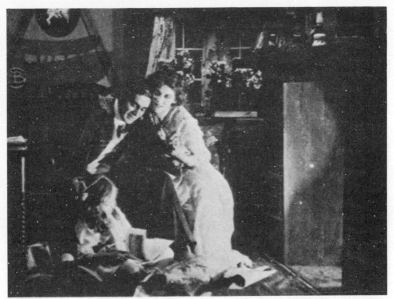

The most artistic fireside glow of the early days. From "The Drunkard's Reformation," with Linda Griffith, Arthur Johnson and Adele de Garde.

(*See p. 128*)

The famous "light effect." From "Pippa Passes," with Gertrude Robinson.

(*See p. 97*)

From "The Mills of the Gods," with Linda Griffith and Arthur Johnson. (*See p. 49*)

Biograph's first Western studio. Scene from "The Converts," with Linda Griffith, Arthur Johnson and Marion Leonard. (*See p. 150*)

to stop. Mr. Griffith and Mr. Bitzer and a few other of the important personages took their places in the automobile—the second in the county—the "Red Devil" we afterwards called it. The actors straggled along.

Caudebec Inn was no towering edifice—just a comfy place three stories high, with one bathroom, a tiny parlor, rag-rugged, and a generously sized dining-room whose cheerful windows looked upon apple orchards. It was neat and spotlessly clean. On two sides were broad piazzas. The inn faced the basin at the head of the old D. L. and W. Canal, and the canal took its pretty way alongside for a mile or more until it spilled itself over a busted dam (Mr. Kennedy's I opined—it was the only one about), making lovely rapids which later we used in many a thriller.

It was extremely fortunate that we were the only guests. We filled the place. Such a thing as an actor having a room to himself, let alone a bed, was as yet unheard of in those vagrant days. Mr. Powell doubled and sometimes tripled them. Some actors got awfully Ritzy, resenting especially the tripling, and at night would sneak downstairs hoping to find a nice vacant hammock on the porch. But that had all been looked into. The hammock would be occupied by some lucky devil whose snores were being gently wafted on the soft summer breezes. Three in a bed, two in a cot, or two in a hammock—the stringy old-fashioned kind of hammock—which would offer the better comfort?

Immediately after lunch, the boss and Billy Bitzer, with Mr. Predmore at the wheel, would depart in "The Red Devil" on a location hunt. The carpenters must get right to work on their stockade. The actors were soon busy digging out costumes and grease paint boxes, and getting made up and costumed; for as soon as the chief returned, he would want to grab a couple of scenes if the light still held. The making up was not a quiet process. As the actors acquired brown grease paint and leather trappings, animal skins and tomahawks—what a pow-wow!

When the Cuddeback farmer first met the Biograph Indian, "Gad," thought he, "what was the world coming to anyhow? Moving picture people? Smart folks to have found their Cuddebackville. Who'd have believed it? New York City actors riding up and down their roads, and stopping off to do wicked stage acting right in front of their best apple tree."

"Hey there, Hiram, how'll five bucks suit you?"

Hiram was a bit deaf.

"No? Ten? All right, here she is."

Hiram we won completely. He hoped we'd come often. And the Big Farmer's "help" were with us heart and soul. We sometimes used them for "extras" and paid them five dollars. Back to the farm at five per week after that? No, they'd wait and loaf until the "picture people" came again. The picture people nearly demoralized the farming business in Cuddebackville and environs—got the labor situation in a terrible mess.

There was need for a stone house in "1776" or "The Hessian Renegades," and for "Leather Stocking"—a genuine pre-revolutionary stone house. Three saddle horses were also needed. For the moment we were stumped.

Toward late afternoon when the light began to fail us, we would utilize the time hunting the morrow's locations. This fading hour found Billy Bitzer, David, and myself (myself still in Janice Meredith costume and curls of "1776") enjoying the physical luxury of the "Red Devil," but mentally disturbed over the stone house and horses. We happened to turn into a pretty road; we spied a beautiful gateway and beyond the gateway, grassy slopes and wonderful trees and pools of quiet water.

"Let's stop here a minute," said Mr. Griffith. "Whose place is this?"

"I'd never go in there, if I were you," answered Mr. Predmore. "That place belongs to Mr. Goddefroy, he's the wealthiest man around here; won't have an automobile on his place and is down on anybody who rides in one; has fine stables and the automobiles are just beginning to interfere with his horseback rides. I don't know just how he'd receive you. Anyhow I can't drive you in in this car of mine." So we parked outside in the roadway.

"We've got to work in here, that's all there is to it," said David, looking about. But where did anybody live? The road wound up and up. Sheep nibbling on the velvet grass were mixed in with a few prize pigs taking their siestas beneath beautiful copper beeches. "Certainly is some place," he continued. We had sauntered up the gravel road quite to the hilltop before we saw coming towards us across the lawn, a bright-eyed, pink-cheeked woman in simple gingham dress. She greeted us pleasantly. The situation was explained and the lady replied, "Well, that is very interesting, and as far as I am concerned you are quite welcome to take some pictures here, but you must ask the boss first."

Over by his stables we found the "Boss."

"We'd like to take some pictures, please, on your beautiful place." Stone houses and horses we had quite forgotten for the moment in the wealth of moving picture backgrounds the estate provided. "We're stopping up at the Inn for a week—doing some Fenimore Cooper stories, and we are looking primarily for a stone house and some horses."

"Have you seen the old stone house down below?"

"Stone house?" I repeated to myself; then to be sure, whispered to Bitzer, "Did he say a *stone* house?"

Bitzer replied, "Yes, he said a stone house." Mr. Griffith managed to pull himself together, but his answer came rather halting, "Why, why, no."

"Come along and I'll show you. Maybe you can use it."

Weak-kneed and still struggling for breath we trailed along—and when we saw it—

Just built for us was the old stone house that had been on the place so long that no one knew when it had been built. But we hesitated. "We'll have to bring horses, because the party leaves on horseback, and that would mess up your place too much."

"Oh, yes, I forgot, you haven't your horses yet. I wonder if some of ours would do," said Mrs. Goddefroy, who was none other than the gingham-clad lady.

Back to the stable we went, emotionally upset by now, but trying to appear calm. We'd been quite reconciled to take a stab at it with the rough work-horses of the Cuddebackville farmer; had thought to groom them up a bit and let it go at that. But here were gentlemen's horses. Yes, gentlemen's horses, but neither Miss Leonard nor myself rode, and these spirited prancing creatures of the Goddefroy stables filled us with alarm. I would look for something "gentle," and not too young and peppy, but with the characteristics of good breeding and training.

And that is how "Mother" and I met.

"Mother" is one of the treasured memories of my

motion picture life. What a gentle old mother she was! healthy, so lazy, and so safe. How relieved I was—how at ease on her broad back. "Mother" ambled on the scene and "Mother" ambled off; she ate the grasses and the flowers on the canal bank; she was not a bit concerned over having her picture taken. I have always felt the credit was wholly hers that my uncle, my sister, and I made our journey safely until the bad Indians surprised us going through the woods.

It was lots of fun being invited on these location-hunting expeditions. An automobile ride was luxury. These were the first and we were getting them for nothing. No, the picture business was not so bad after all.

Back at the Inn the Indians would be changing from leather fringes and feathered head dresses to their bathing suits. And when the location party returned, they'd have reached the green slopes of the Big Basin where, soap in hand, they would be sudsing off the brown bolamenia from legs and arms before the plunge into the cool waters of the Big Basin—a rinse and a swim "to onct."

The girls who "did" Indians had the privacy of the one bathroom for their cleaning up. So they were usually "pretty" again, lounging in the hammocks or enjoying the porch rockers; a few would be over in the spring house freshening up on healthful spring water; a few at the General Store buying picture post-cards.

And then came dinner and in ones, twos, and threes, the company strolled in—a hungry lot. Frail little Mrs. Predmore wondered would she ever get the actors fed up. It took her the week usually, she afterwards confided. When the cook would let her, she'd go into the kitchen and make us lemon meringue pies. The actors were always hoping the cook would leave, or get sick, or die, so Mrs. Predmore could cook all the dinner.

Sometimes we were very merry at dinner. When Arthur Johnson would arrive bowing himself gallantly in, in a manner bred of youthful days as a Shakespearean actor with the Owen Dramatic Company, loud and hearty applause would greet him, which he'd accept with all the smiling, gracious salaams of the old-time ten, twenty, and thirty tragedian.

Evening at Cuddebackville!

The biggest thrill would be an automobile ride to Middletown, nine miles away. If Mr. Predmore weren't busy after dinner, he'd take us. It was a joyful ride over the mountains to Middletown, quite the most priceless fun of an evening. Every one was eager for it except the little groups of twos, who, sentimentally inclined, were paddling a canoe out on the basin or down the canal. There would be Mary Pickford and Owen Moore, and James Kirkwood and Gertrude Robinson, and Stanner E. V. Taylor and Marion Leonard, experiencing tense moments in the silence broken only by the drip, drip of the paddle beneath the mellow moon. Romance got well under way at Cuddebackville.

The evening divertisements became more complex as we became better acquainted. "Wally" Walthall, Arthur Johnson, and Mack Sennett became our principal parlor entertainers. "Wally" rendered old southern ditties as only a true southern gentleman from Alabama could.

Arthur Johnson and Mack Sennett did good team-work; they were our Van and Schenck. Arthur, who presided at the piano, had a sentimental turn; he liked "The Little Grey Home in the West" kind of song, but the future producer of movie comedies was not so sentimentally disposed. As long as harmony reigned in the camp of Johnson and Sennett, there were tuneful evenings for the musically inclined. But every now and then Sennett would get miffed about something and never a do-re-mi would be got out of him, and when Arthur's nerves could stand the strain no longer, he'd burst forth to the assemblage, "I wouldn't mind if he'd fuss with me, but this silence thing gets my goat."

Those who cared not for the Song Festival could join Jeanie Macpherson who, out in the dining-room, would be supervising stunts in the world of black magic. Here Tony O'Sullivan could always be found. He told hair-raising ghost stories and wound up the evening's fun by personally conducting a tour through the cemetery. The cemetery lay just beyond the apple orchard, and along the canal bank to the back of the Inn.

Now were the moon bright, the touring party might get a glint of lovers paddling by. Arrived back at the Inn, they might greet the "Red Devil" returning with a small exclusive party from the Goddefroys—Mr. Griffith and Miss Arvidson, Mr. Powell and Miss Hicks.

There was just one little touch of sin. Secluded in an outbuilding some of the boys played craps, sometimes losing all their salary before they got it. One of the men finally brought this wicked state of affairs to Mr. Griffith's attention, and there were no more crap games.

In front of Caudebec Inn the "Red Devil" is snorting and getting impatient to be started on her way to the station, for the actors are strolling down the road ahead of her.

Mr. Griffith and Mr. Predmore are just finishing the final "settling up" of the board bill. Little Mrs. Predmore looking tinier than ever—she seemed to shrivel during our strenuous weeks—is gratefully sighing as she bids us farewell. She was glad to see us come, and she was glad to see us go.

Meanwhile, out in Hollywood, the Japs are still raising carnations, and a few bungalow apartment houses are just beginning to sprout on the Boulevard; but otherwise the foothills continue their, as yet, undisturbed sleep beneath the California sunshine.

CHAPTER XVII

"PIPPA PASSES" FILMED

THERE was a frictional feeling in our return to prosaic studio life after the glorious freedom of the country. But the new "projections"—the pictures that had been printed and assembled in our absence—would take the edge off and cheer us up some; we were all a-thrill about seeing the first run of the pictures we had taken in the country; and we were eager about the picture we were to do next.

During our absence we would have missed seeing not only our own releases but those of the other companies, which, our day's work finished, we used to try to catch up on. Mondays and Thursdays had come to be release days for Biograph pictures. Then at some theatres, came whole evenings devoted to them. On these occasions exhibitors would put a stand outside saying "Biograph Night." After the first showing it was a difficult job to locate a picture. From Tenth Avenue to Avenue A, we'd roam, and no matter how hot, stuffy, or dirty the place might be, we'd make the grade in time.

"Pippa Passes," which was to make or unmake us, was all this time hanging fire. Mr. Griffith was getting an all star cast intact. The newly recruited James Kirkwood and Henry Walthall gave us two good men who, with Owen Moore and Arthur Johnson, were all the actors needed. For the women, there were Marion Leonard, Gertrude

Robinson, and myself. And little Mary Pickford whom our director had engaged with Pippa in mind (?). When the day came to shoot Browning for the first time, it was winsome Gertrude Robinson with black curls and dark blue eyes who was chosen for the rôle of the spiritual Pippa. David thought Mary had grown a bit plump; she no longer filled his mental image of the type.

When at last we started on "Pippa Passes," things went off with a bang. Each of the four themes—Morn, Noon, Evening, Night—would be followed by a flash of Pippa singing her little song.

It was "Morn" that intrigued. To show "daybreak" in Pippa's little room would mean trying out a new light effect. The only light effect so far experimented with had been the "fireside glow." The opportunity to try a different kind so interested Mr. Griffith that before he began to "shoot" Pippa, he had a scheme all worked out.

He figured on cutting a little rectangular place in the back wall of Pippa's room, about three feet by one, and arranging a sliding board to fit the aperture much like the cover of a box sliding in and out of grooves. The board was to be gradually lowered and beams of light from a powerful Kleig shining through would thus appear as the first rays of the rising sun striking the wall of the room. Other lights stationed outside Pippa's window would give the effect of soft morning light. Then the lights full up, the mercury tubes a-sizzling, the room fully lighted, the back wall would have become a regular back wall again, with no little hole in it.

All this was explained to the camera men Billy Bitzer and Arthur Marvin, for the whole technical staff was in attendance on the production of this one thousand foot feature—one thousand feet being the length of our features at this time. Bitzer didn't think much of the idea, but Arthur Marvin, who had seen his chief's radical ideas worked out successfully before, was less inclined to skepticism. But response, on the whole, was rather snippy. While David would have preferred a heartier appreciation, he would not be deterred, and he spoke in rather plain words: "Well, come on, let's do it anyhow; I don't give a damn what anybody thinks about it."

Pippa is asleep in her little bed. The dawn is coming—a tense moment—for Pippa must wake, sit up in her little bed, rise, cross to the window, and greet the dawn in perfect harmony with the mechanical force operating the sliding board and the Kleigs. All was manipulated in perfect tempo.

The skeptical studio bunch remained stubborn until the first projection of the picture upstairs. At first the comments came in hushed and awed tones, and then when the showing was over, the little experiment in light effects was greeted with uncontrolled enthusiasm.

"Pippa Passes" was released on October 4, 1909, a day of great anxiety. We felt pretty sure it was good stuff, but we were wholly unprepared for what was to happen. On the morning of October 10th, while we were scanning the news items in the columns of the *New York Times,* the while we imbibed our breakfast coffee, our unbelieving eyes were greeted with a column headlined thus:

BROWNING NOW GIVEN IN MOVING PICTURES

"Pippa Passes" the Lastest Play
Without Words to be Seen
In the Nickelodeons

THE CLASSICS DRAWN UPON

Even Biblical Stories Portrayed For
Critical Audiences—Improvement
Due to Board of Censors

It was all too much—much too much. The newspapers were writing about us. A conservative New York daily was taking us seriously. It seemed incredible, but there it was before our eyes. It looked wonderful! Oh, so wonderful we nearly wept. Suddenly everything was changed. Now we could begin to lift up our heads, and perhaps invite our lit'ry friends to our movies!

This is what the *New York Times* man had to say:

"Pippa Passes" is being given in the nickelodeons and Browning is being presented to the average motion picture audiences, who have received it with applause and are asking for more.

This achievement is the present nearest-Boston record of the reformed motion picture play producing, but from all accounts there seems to be no reason why one may not expect to see soon the intellectual aristocracy of the nickelodeon demanding Kant's Prolegomena to Metaphysics with the "Kritik of Pure Reason" for a curtain raiser.

Since popular opinion has been expressing itself through the Board of Censors of the People's Institute, such material as "The Odyssey," the Old Testament, Tolstoy, George Eliot, De Maupassant and Hugo has been drawn upon to furnish the films, in place of the sensational blood-and-thunder variety which brought down public indignation upon the manufacturers six months ago. Browning, however, seems to be the most rarefied dramatic stuff up to date.

As for Pippa without words, the first films show the sunlight waking Pippa for her holiday with light and shade effects like those obtained by the Secessionist Photographers.

Then Pippa goes on her way dancing and singing. The quarreling family hears her, and forgets its dissension. The taproom brawlers cease their carouse and so on, with the pictures alternately showing Pippa on her way, and then the effect of her "passing" on the various groups in the Browning poem. The contrast between the tired business man at a roof garden and the sweatshop worker applauding Pippa is certainly striking. That this demand for the classics is genuine is indicated by the fact that the adventurous producers who inaugurated these expensive departures from cheap melodrama are being overwhelmed by offers from renting agents. Not only the nickelodeons of New York but those of many less pretentious cities and towns are demanding Browning and the other "high-brow" effects.

There certainly was a decided change in the general attitude toward us after this wonderful publicity. Directly we had 'phone calls from friends saying they would like to go to the movies with us; and they would just love to come down to the studio and watch a picture being made. Even our one erudite friend, a Greek scholar, inquired where he could see "Pippa Passes." As the picture was shown for only one night, we thought it might be rather nice to invite the dead-language person and his wife to the studio. They came and found it intensely interesting: met Mary Pickford and thought her "sweet."

Besides the Greek professor, another friend, one of the big men of the Old Guard—an old newspaper man, and president and editor of *Leslie's Weekly* and *Judge* at this time—began making inquiries.

The night the Ritz-Carlton Hotel in New York City opened, David thought it wouldn't be a bad idea to splurge a bit and invite Mr. Sleicher to dinner, he being the editor who had paid him six dollars for his poem, "The Wild Duck." He'd surely think we had come a long pace ahead in the movies, dining at the Ritz, and doing it so casual-like.

Talk there was at the dinner about newspapers and magazines, and then we got around to the movies, and the money they were making. Mr. Sleicher said: "Well, there's more money in them than in my business, but I like my business better. Now in my game, twenty-four hours or even less, after a thing happens you can see a picture of it and read about it in the paper, and you can't do that in your movies." (I understand that even before the time of this dinner, events of special interest occasionally found their way to the screen on the day they happened. In London, in 1906, the Urbanora people showed the boat race between Cambridge and Harvard Universities on the evening of the day they were held, but we did not know about that.)

Mr. Griffith was not going to be outdone; so, with much bravado, for he was quite convinced of its truth, he said: "Well, we are not doing it now, but the time will come when the day's news events will be regularly pictured on the screen with the same speed the ambitious young reporter gets his scoop on the front page of his newspaper. We'll have all the daily news told in moving pictures the same as it is told in words on the printed page. Now, I'm willing to bet you."

But John Sleicher was skeptical. Had he not been, he would then and there have invested some of his pennies in the movies. He regretted the opportunity many times afterward, for while the prediction has not been fulfilled exactly, the News Reel of to-day gives promise that it will be. However, Mr. Sleicher lived to enjoy the News Reel quite as much as he did his newspaper, and that meant a great deal for him.

These little happenings were encouraging. Intelligent

persons on the outside were taking interest. So again we'd
buck up and go at the movie job with renewed vigor.

For a time we lived in the clouds—our habitat a mountain peak. But that couldn't last. No kind of mountain
peak existence could. We should have known. Even after
all the encouragement, down off our peak we'd slip into the
deep dark valley again.

We tried to keep an unswerving faith, but who could
have visioned the great things that were to come? Doubts
still persisted. Yes, even after the Browning triumph, longings came over us to return to former ambitions. They
had not been buried so deeply after all. We'd see a fine
play and get the blue devils. In this mood my husband
would do the rounds of the movie houses and chancing upon
a lot of bad pictures, come back utterly discouraged.

"They can't last. I give them a few years. Where's
my play? Since I went into these movies I haven't had
a minute to look at a thing I ever wrote. And I went into
them because I thought surely I'd get time to write or do
something with what I had." (Monetary needs so soon
forgotten!) "Well, anyhow, nobody's going to know I
ever did this sort of thing when I'm a famous playwright.
Nobody's ever going to know that David W. Griffith, the
playwright, was once the Lawrence Griffith of the movies."

So "Lawrence" continued on the next Biograph contract. The two names would get all balled up sometimes
and I'd get peeved and say: "Why don't you use your right
name? I think you're so silly."

But David remained obdurate until he signed his third
Biograph contract.

CHAPTER XVIII

GETTING ON

O NE thing was sure—the pictures were making money. The percentage told that story. What a thrill we got at the first peek at the royalty check each month. Made us nervous. Where were we headed? Sometimes we almost wished that financially we were not succeeding so well, for then we would have quitted the movies. But wouldn't that have been a crazy thing to do? A year of fifty-two working weeks? At the rate we were going, we could keep at it for three years, and quit with twelve thousand in the bank, then David could write plays and realize his youthful ambition.

We lived simply. When the royalty check before the end of the second year amounted to nine hundred and a thousand a month, we still maintained a thirty-five-dollar-a-month apartment. Never dreamed of getting stylish. No time for it. So each month there was a nice little roll to bank, and it was put right into the Bowery Savings Bank. The only trouble with a savings bank was they wouldn't accept more than three thousand dollars, so we secured a list of them and I went the rounds depositing honest movie money with a rapidity quite unbelievable.

The Griffiths were not the only thrifty ones. When Mary Pickford was getting one hundred a week, her mother wept because she wouldn't buy pretty clothes. At Mount Beacon this happened. One of the perky little ingénue-ish

A desert caravan of the early days. (*See p. 197*)

From "The Last Drop of Water," one of the first two-reelers, produced in San Fernando desert, with Jeanie Macpherson (seated, front row).
(*See p. 197*)

Mabel Normand with Lee Dougherty, Jr., "off duty."

(*See p. 204*)

extra girls appeared in a frock decidedly not home-made. You could count on it that it had come either from Macy's or Siegel-Cooper's Eighteenth Street store, and that it had cost a whole week's wages. Not much escaped Ma Smith's eagle eye, and so she wailed: "I wish Mary would buy clothes like the other girls." But Mary, the same simple, unaffected Mary that a year since had said "thank you" for her twenty-five, was quite contented to continue wearing the clothes her mama made her, and at that a few would do.

A few years after this time I met Mary in Macy's one summer day and hardly recognized her. She had grown thin and had acquired style. I admired her smart costume and said: "Nice suit, Mary, I'm looking for one. Mind telling me where you found it?" But Mary, with a note of boredom, so unlike the Mary I'd known, answered: "Oh, my aunt brought me six from Paris."

"Mary, you haven't forgotten how we used to strike bargains with the salesman at Hearn's on Fourteenth Street, have you?"

"Oh," said Mary, quickly coming back to earth and proving greatness but a dream, "wasn't it fun? Let's go over to the Astor and have tea."

Across from Macy's, Mary's first bus was parked and young brother Jack was chauffing. When we hopped into the car, we found a very disgruntled youth who, having waited longer than he thought he ought to have, gave me a stony stare and never spoke a word. As far as young Jack Smith was concerned, I'd never been on earth before.

We wondered about Mack Sennett. Would he ever buy a girl an ice cream soda? Marion Leonard said it would be his birthday if he ever did. But the day arrived when Mack Sennett did open up. He bought a seventy-five-dollar diamond necklace for Mabel Normand, and then after some misunderstanding between himself and Mabel, proving he had a head for business, he offered it to different members of the company for eighty-five dollars.

Spike Robinson, who used to box with Mr. Griffith and who now boxes with Douglas Fairbanks, looms up as the one generous member of the company, being willing always to buy the girls ice cream sodas or lemonade or sarsaparilla —the refreshments of our age of innocence.

The fall of 1909 brought to the studio a number of new women who proved valuable additions to our company. Stephanie Longfellow, who was a *bona fide* niece of the poet Henry, was one of them. Her first pictures were released in August. They were "The Better Way" and "A Strange Meeting." Miss Longfellow was quite a different type from her predecessors and her work was delightful. She was a refreshing personality with unusual mental attainments. *"She's* a lady," said the director. Some ten years ago Miss Longfellow retired to domestic life via a happy marriage outside the profession.

Handsome Mrs. Grace Henderson became our grande dame of quality, breezing in from past glories of "Peter Pan" (having played *Peter's* Mother) and of the famous old Daly Stock Company.

Another grande dame of appearance distinguished, drawing modest pay checks occasionally, and with a cultural family background most unusual for a stage mother, was Caroline Harris. Miss Harris, otherwise Mrs. Barthelmess, and mother of ten-year-old Dicky Barthelmess, was one stage mother not supported by her child. Only when home on a vacation from military school did Dicky work in a picture. He made his début with Mrs. Tom Ince, and his little heart was quite broken when he discovered his only scene had been cut out.

Miss Harris's first stage appearance had been with Benjamin Chapin playing *Mrs. Lincoln* in "Lincoln at the White House," afterwards called "Honest Abe." Her first part in the movies was in DeMaupassant's "The Necklace," in which Rose King played the lead. Miss Harris had learned of the Biograph through a girl who jobbed at the studio, Helen Ormsby, the daughter of a Brooklyn newspaper man.

Mabel Trunelle had a rather crowded hour at the Biograph. She had had considerable experience at the Edison studio and was well equipped in movie technique. She had come on recommendation of her husband, Herbert Pryor, and she succeeded, even though a wife—which was unusual, for wives of the good actors were not popular around the studio. If an actor wanted to keep on the right side of the director, he left his wife at home; that meant a sacrifice often enough, for there were times without number when women were needed and a wife could have been used and the five dollars kept in the family, but the majority preferred not to risk it. Dell Henderson and George Nichols succeeded quite well with this "wife" business, but they seem to have been the only ones besides Mr. Pryor.

Florence Barker, a good trouper who had had stock experience in Los Angeles, her home town, now happened along to enjoy popularity, and to become Frank Powell's leading woman. Through her Eleanor Kershaw, sister to Willette, and wife to the late Thomas H. Ince, happened to come to the Biograph.

Quite the most pathetic figure at the studio was Eleanor

Kershaw Ince. In deep mourning for her mother who had just been killed in an accident, and all alone, with a tiny baby at home, she put in brave hours for her little five-dollar bills. When six o'clock came and her work was not finished, how she fretted about her little one. That baby, Tom Ince's eldest child "Billy," is now a husky lad and he probably doesn't know how we all worried over him then. Miss Kershaw played sad little persons such as the maid in "The Course of True Love," flower girls, and match girls, in wispy clothes, on cold November days, offering their wares on the streets of Coytesville and Fort Lee.

There was the blond and lily-like Blanche Sweet, an undeveloped child too young to play sweethearts and wives, but a good type for the more insignificant parts, such as maids and daughters. David wanted to use her this first winter in a picture called "Choosing a Husband," so he tried her out, but finding her so utterly unemotional, he dismissed her saying, "Oh, she's terrible." Then he tried Miss Barker and had her play the part. But he directed Miss Sweet in her first picture, "All on Account of a Cold."

Mr. Powell liked Miss Sweet's work, and so did Doc, and so Mr. Powell used her in the first picture he directed, "All on Account of the Milk." Mr. Powell was rehearsing in the basement of No. 11 while Mr. Griffith was doing the same upstairs. Mary Pickford played the daughter and Blanche Sweet, the maid, and in the picture they change places.

On the back porch of a little farmhouse a rendezvous takes place with the milkman. It was bitterly cold, and even though the girls wore woolen dresses under their cotton aprons, they looked like frozen turnips. The scenes being

of tense love, the girls were supposed to be divinely rap-
turous and to show no discomfort—not even know it was
winter. But the breathing was a different matter, for as
young Blanche uttered endearing words to her lover, a
white cloud issued from her mouth. Now that would look
dreadful on the screen. So in the nervousness of the situation Mr. Powell yelled at her, "Stop talking, just *look* at
him, this is supposed to be summer." She obeyed, when
from her delicate nostrils came a similar white line of
frosted breath at which the director, now wholly beside himself, yelled, "Stop breathing, what kind of a picture do you
think this will be, anyhow." So little Blanche proceeded
to strangle for a few moments while we secured a few feet
of summer.

In "The Day After"—four hundred and sixty feet of
a New Year's party picture, showing what a youngster she
was, Blanche Sweet played *Cupid*.

Kate Bruce had become the leading character woman.
Little Christie Miller, frail, white, and bent, played the
kindly old men, while Vernon Clarges interpreted the more
pompous, distinguished elderly ones. Daddy Butler was
mostly just a nice kind papa, and George Nichols played
a diversified range of parts—monks, rugged Westerners,
and such. George Nichols had been a member of the old
Alcazar and Central Theatres in San Francisco, where Mr.
Griffith in his stranded actor days had worked.

Of the children, little Gladys Egan did remarkable work
playing many dramatic leading parts. Her performance in
"The Broken Doll" should be recorded here. Adele de
Garde was another nine-year-old child wonder. These
children were not comiques. They were tragediennes and
how they could tear a passion to tatters! The Wolff children

sufficed well in infantile rôles. Their mother kept a dramatic agency for children.

Boys were little in demand, and as Mary Pickford usually had her family handy, we came to use little Jack—he was at this time nine years old. He created quite a stir about the old A. B. He even managed to make himself the topic of conversation at lunch time and other off-duty hours. "Had he a future like sister Mary?" We were even then ready to grant Mary a future.

Lottie was discussed too, but in a more casual way. No one was especially interested in Lottie. Mary was very hesitant in bringing her to the studio; she confided that Lottie was not pretty and she didn't think she'd be good in the movies. She was the tomboy of the family and she loved nothing better than to play baseball with the boys, and when later she did become a Biograph player she had her innings at many a game.

For a year and a half that had winged its way, my husband and I had kept our secret well, although a something was looming that might make us spill it. There had been nervous moments. Only three people at the studio knew the facts of the case, Wilfred Lucas, Paul Scardon, and Harry Salter. But Wilfred Lucas, whose hospitality we'd frequently enjoyed, never betrayed us.

Nor did Paul Scardon. I don't remember Mr. Scardon doing any work of consequence at the Biograph, but he eventually connected up with the Vitagraph, becoming one of its directors. He discovered Betty Blythe, developed her from an unknown extra girl to a leading woman of prominence. After the death of his first wife, he married her. Miss Blythe has been a big star for some years now and while Mr. Scardon has not been directing her, he travels with her to distant enchanting lands, to Egypt, the Riviera, and such places where Miss Blythe has been working on big feature pictures. It was under William Fox's banner that Miss Blythe first came into prominence. The picture was "The Queen of Sheba."

Lucas and Scardon were friends of ours before our marriage, but Harry Salter was the only person about the studio in whom David had confided. And I wasn't told a thing about it. Helping to purloin Florence Lawrence from the Vitagraph, Mr. Salter had just naturally fallen in love with her and they had been secretly married, and no one knew it but Mr. Griffith. A fellow-feeling probably had made David a bit confidential—an unusual thing for him. It was one day, on a little launch going to Navesink. My husband was in the front of the boat, his back to us. Harry and Florence and I were seated aft. We were quietly enjoying the ride, not a word being spoken, when Harry Salter, pointing to a hole in the heel of David's stocking, at the same time turned to me and with a knowing smile said, "Miss Arvidson, look!"

The something that was looming that would make us reveal our well-concealed secret, was a trip to California to escape the bad eastern weather of January, February and March.

Now I did not intend to spend three nights on the Santa Fé Limited in a Lower Eight, or an Upper Three, when there was the luxury of a drawing-room at hand. Nor was it my husband's wish either. I felt I had earned every little five-per-day I'd had from the Biograph and had minded my own business sufficiently well to share comfort with the director. Yes, I would take my place as that most unwelcome person—the director's wife. So when the tickets were being made up, Mr. Hammer was brought into the secret, but he just couldn't believe it. But Mr. Dougherty said: "Well, that is bringing coal to Newcastle." Nobody could understand what he meant by this, but that is what he said.

CHAPTER XIX

TO THE WEST COAST

AFTER shivering through one Eastern winter, trying to get the necessary outdoor scenes for our pictures, we concluded that it would be to our advantage to pack up the wardrobe, the cameras, and other paraphernalia, get a little organization together, and with a portmanteau of Western scripts hie ourselves to the city of Los Angeles.

We weren't the first to go there. Selig already had a studio there. Frank Boggs had brought a little company of Selig players to Los Angeles in the early days of 1908. The next company that reached the coast was that of the New York Motion Picture Patents Corporation, making the Bison brand of pictures. They had arrived in Los Angeles about Thanksgiving, 1909—seventeen players under the command of Fred Balshofer.

Kalem was taking pictures in Los Angeles, too. I felt very much annoyed one night, shortly before we left New York, to see a Kalem picture with Carlyle Blackwell and Alice Joyce having a petting party in Westlake Park.

How we did buzz around, those last weeks in New York! Mr. Powell's company worked nights to keep up the two one-thousand-foot releases per week.

News was already being broadcast that it was quite O. K. down at the Biograph if you got in right—that they were doing good things and were going to send a company to California for the winter, which would mean a regular salary for the time away.

And so arrived Mr. Dell Henderson, who became leading man for the night company at five per night. The demands for physical beauty that he had to fulfil certainly should have earned more than the ordinary five. He had to be so handsome that his jealous wife prevails upon thugs to waylay him and scar for life his manly beauty so that the admiring women will let him alone.

This movie, "The Love of Lady Irma," was one of the first pictures Mr. Powell directed. Florence Barker, who became the leading woman for the No. 2 California Comedy Company, played *Lady Irma,* the jealous wife. She had joined the company in December, her first picture being "The Dancing Girl of Butte," in which she was cast with Owen Moore and Mack Sennett.

It was in these days that Eleanor Kershaw did her bit; also Dorothy West and Ruth Hart. Miss Hart, now Mrs. Victor Moore and the mother of two children, played the sweet domestic wife, a rôle Mr. Griffith felt she was a good exponent of, and which she has successfully continued in her private life.

Frank Grandin appears in his first leading part, playing *The Duke* in "The Duke's Plan"; and our atmospheric genial Englishman, Charles Craig, affiliated the same month, playing opposite Mary Pickford in "The Englishman and the Girl."

The studio was now a busy place. A Civil War picture had to be rushed through before we could get away. Mr. Powell was busy engaging actors for it and had just completed his cast of principals when he bumped into an actor friend, Tommy Ince. It seems Mr. Ince at the moment was "broke." Apologetically, Mr. Powell said he couldn't offer anything much, but if Mr. Ince didn't mind coming in as an "extra" he would give him ten dollars for the day. This quite overcame Tom Ince and he stammered forth, "Glory be"—or words to that effect—"I'd be glad to get five." Only one part did Tom Ince play with Biograph and that was in "The New Lid" with Lucille Lee Stewart, Ralph Ince's wife and sister of Anita Stewart.

I happened to call on Eleanor Hicks Powell one evening in the summer of 1912 when our only Biograph baby, Baden Powell, had reached the creeping age. During the evening Mr. and Mrs. Tom Ince dropped in. Of course, we talked "movies." Mr. Ince was worrying about an offer he'd had to go to California as manager and leading director of the 101 Ranch, Kaybee Company, for one hundred and twenty-five dollars per week, as I remember. He offered me forty dollars to go out as leading woman, but I couldn't see the Indians. Mr. Ince couldn't see them either—but it was the best offer that had come his way.

Mr. Ince made a great success out of the 101 Ranch, but having ambitions to do the "high-class," he moved on in quest of it. Took to developing stars like Charles Ray, Enid Markey, and Dorothy Dalton; became one of the Triangle outfit with David Griffith and Mack Sennett; exploited dramatic stars like George Beban, Billie Burke, and Enid Bennett; did "Civilization"—but *after* "The Birth of a Nation."

Who was to go to California and who wasn't? Ah, that was the question! Some husbands didn't care to leave their wives, and as they couldn't afford to take them, they were out. Some didn't mind the separation. Some of the women had ties; if not husbands, mothers; and the California salary would not be big enough to keep up two homes. Some didn't want to leave New York; and some who should have known they didn't have a ghost of a chance wept sad and plentiful tears whenever the director looked their way. One of these was Jeanie Macpherson. Jeanie didn't go along this first time.

A few days after Christmas was the time of the first hegira to the land of the eucalyptus and the pepper tree. It was a big day.

We were going to Los Angeles to take moving pictures, and Hollywood didn't mean a thing. Pasadena the company knew about. Like Palm Beach, it was where millionaires sojourned for two months during the Eastern winter. San Gabriel Mission they'd seen photos of, and counted on using it in pictures. They understood there were many beaches accessible by trolley; and residential districts like West Adams; even Figueroa, the home of Los Angeles's first millionaires, was a fine avenue then; and Westlake and Eastlake Parks which were quite in town. But they didn't know Edendale from the Old Soldiers' Home at Sawtelle. San Pedro? Yes, that was where the steamers arrived from San Francisco. San Fernando? Well, yes, there was a Mission there too, but it was rather far away, and right in the heart of a parched and cactus-covered desert. Mt. Lowe was easy—there was the incline railway to help us to the top.

Four luxurious days on luxurious trains before we would sight the palms and poinsettias that were gaily beckoning to us across the distances.

Let us away!

The company departed via the Black Diamond Express on the Lehigh Valley, which route meant ferry to Jersey City. A late arrival in Chicago allowed just comfortable time to make the California Limited leaving at 8 P.M.

The company was luxurious for but three days.

It was only Mr. R. H. Hammer, my husband, and myself who had been allotted four full days of elegance. We *de luxe'd* out of New York via the Twentieth Century Limited. I had come into my own.

Mr. Powell was in charge of the company and so he checked them off on arrival at the ferry—Marion Leonard, Florence Barker, Mary Pickford, Dorothy West, Kate Bruce, the women; George Nichols, Henry Walthall, Billy Quirk, Frank Grandin, Charlie West, Mack Sennett, Dell Henderson, Arthur Johnson, Daddy Butler, Christie Miller, Tony O'Sullivan, and Alfred Paget, the men. There were three wives who were actresses also, Eleanor Hicks, Florence Lee (Mrs. Dell Henderson), and Mrs. George Nichols. And there were two camera men, Billy Bitzer and Arthur Marvin; a scenic artist, Eddie Shelter; a carpenter or two, and two property boys, Bobbie Harron and Johnny Mahr.

No theatrical job had come along for Mary Pickford, and the few summer months she had intended spending in "the pictures" would lengthen into a full year now that she had decided to go with us to California. Her salary was still small: it was about forty dollars a week at this time.

Frank Powell had a busy hour at the Ferry Building although Mr. Griffith was there also to see that all the company got on board. He had not anticipated too smooth an exit. Nor did he get it, even though he had taken well into account his temperamentalists. And sure enough, Arthur Johnson and Charlie West arrived breathless and hatless, fresh from an all-night party, just as the last gong rang.

And while David was nervously awaiting them and while dear relatives were weeping their fond farewells, the Pickford family chose the opportune moment to put on a little play of their own.

Ma Smith, it seems, had made up her mind that a last minute hold-up might succeed in forcing Mr. Griffith to raise Mary's salary—I'm not sure whether it was five or ten dollars a week. So they held a little pow-wow on the subject, right on the dock, in the midst of all the excitement; and Jack began to cry because he wasn't going along with his big sister; and Owen Moore between saying sad good-byes to Mary, hoped the boss might relent and give him the ten extra he had held out for, for Los Angeles.

For, much as Owen loved Mary and Mary loved Owen, he let a few dollars part them for the glorious season out in California.

Well, anyhow, little Jack's tears and Mother Smith's talk and pretty Mary's gentle but persistent implorations did not get her the ten dollars extra. David had something up his sleeve he knew would calm the Smith family, and make them listen to reason, and he delivered it with a firm finality.

"Now I've got little Gertie Robinson all ready to come on at a moment's notice. Mary goes without the five (or ten) or not at all."

Mary went. Then Jack began to bawl. It was a terrible family parting. So Mr. Griffith compromised and said he'd take Jack and give him three checks a week, fifteen dollars. The company paid his fare, of course, for we had extra tickets and plenty of room for one small boy in the coaches at our disposal.

It was a pleasant trip, especially for those who had not been to California before. Some found card games so engrossing that they never took a peek at the scenery. Some, especially Mary and Dorothy West, oh'd and ah'd so that Arthur Johnson, thinking the enthusiasm a bit overdone, began kidding the scenery lovers. "Oh, lookit, lookit," Arthur would exclaim when the gushing was at its height.

The "Biograph Special" we were. We had rare service on the train. We had every attention from the dining-car steward. Had we not been allowed three dollars per day for meals on the train? And didn't we spend it? For the invigorating air breathed from the observation platform gave us healthy appetites.

At San Bernardino (perhaps the custom still survives, I don't know, for now when I go to Los Angeles, I go via the Overland Limited to San Francisco instead) we each received a dainty bouquet of pretty, fragrant carnations. Flowers for nothing! We could hardly believe our eyes.

At last we were there! Mr. Hammer gallantly suggested, although it was afternoon, that the women of the company go to a hotel at the Biograph's expense, until they located permanent quarters. So the ladies were registered at the Alexandria, then but lately opened, and shining and grand it was. Although they made but a short stay there, they attracted considerable attention. One day Mary Pickford stepped out of the Alexandria's elevator just as William Randolph Hearst was entering. Seeing Mary, he said, "I wonder who that pretty girl is." And one night at dinner, between sips of his ale, indicating our table which was but one removed from his, Mr. Hearst wondered some more as to who the people were.

The players were quite overcome at the company's hospitality. It was quite different from traveling with a theatrical road show where you had to pay for sleepers and meals, and where you might be dumped out at a railroad station at any hour of the cold gray dawn, with a Miners' Convention occupying every bed and couch in the town, and be left entirely to your own resources.

I may be wrong, but I think Mr. Grey of the office force (but not the Mr. Grey of the present Griffith organization; it was years before his movie affiliation, and the Biograph's Mr. Grey has been dead some years now) went out to California ahead of the company to make banking arrangements and look around for a location for the studio.

On Grand Avenue and Washington Street, hardly ten minutes by trolley from Broadway and Fifth, and seven by motor from our hotel, mixed in with a lumber yard and a baseball park, was a nice vacant lot. It was surrounded by a board fence six feet or so in height, high enough to prevent passers-by from looking in on us. Just an ordinary dirt lot, it was. In the corners and along the fence-edges the coarse-bladed grass, the kind that grows only in California, had already sprouted, and otherwise it looked just like a small boy's happy baseball ground. It was selected for the studio.

A stage had to be rigged up where we could take "interiors," for while we intended doing most of our work "on location," there would have to be a place where we could lay a carpet and place pieces of furniture about for parlor, bedroom—but not bath. As yet modesty had de-

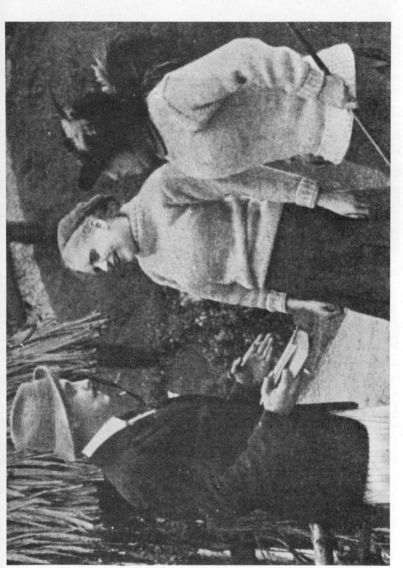

Joe Graybill, Blanche Sweet and Vivian Prescott, in "How She Triumphed." (*See p. 184*)

Mack Sennett, Mabel Normand and Fred Mace, in a "Keystone Comedy."
(*See p. 204*)

Lunch on the "lot," Biograph's "last word" studio, the second year. Left to right: Mack Sennett, William Beaudine, Eddie Dillon, Vivian Prescott.
(*See p. 202*)

terred us from entering that sanctum of tiles, porcelain, cold cream, and rose-water jars. Mr. C. B. DeMille was as yet a bit away in the offing, and Milady's ablutions and Milord's Gilette were still matters of a private nature—to the movies.

A load of wood was ordered from our neighbor, and the carpenters set about to fix up a stage and some dressing-rooms: we couldn't dress and make up in our hotels, that was sure, nor could we do so in the open spaces of our "lot."

Our stage, erected in the center of the lot, was merely a wooden floor raised a few feet off the ground and about fifty feet square, of rough splintery wood, and when we "did" Western bar-rooms—*au naturel*—it was just the thing.

Two small adjoining dressing-rooms for the men soon came into being; then similar ones for the women. They looked like tiny bath-houses as they faced each other across the lot. They sufficed, however. There were no quarrels as to where the star should dress. When there were extras, they dressed in relays, and sometimes a tent was put up.

Telegraph poles ran alongside the studio and after our business became known in the neighborhood, and especially on days when we were portraying strenuous drama and got noisy, up these poles the small boys would clamber and have a big time watching the proceedings and throwing us friendly salutations which didn't always help along the "action."

A place had to be found where our camera men could develop the film and we could see the results of our work, for when a picture left Los Angeles it must be complete and ready for release, so down on Spring Street and Second, a loft was rented for a few dollars a month. It was a roomy, though dingy, barn of a place, but it served our purpose well. A tiny dark room was boarded off and fixed up for the developing, and a place set apart for the printing. The huge wheels on which the prints were dried stood boldly apart in the room. There was a little desk for cutting and splicing. At the head of the room furthest from the windows a screen was set, and a sort of low partition about midway the length of the loft hemmed in the projection room.

When things had settled into a routine, and on rainy days, we rehearsed and worked out scenarios up in our loft. We also had the costumes delivered there. The loft was always accessible, and we spent many evenings seeing projections and getting our things together for an early morning start.

Across the street from the loft was a famous old eating place, Hoffman's, where my husband and I dined when we returned late or too weary to dress for the more pretentious hotel dining-room. It was a bit expensive for some of the company, but convenient to our headquarters was one of those market places, indigenous to Los Angeles, where violets and hams commingled on neighborly counters, that served good and inexpensive food on a long white enameled table where guests sat only on one side, on high, spindly stools. It was patronized generously by the actors for breakfast and lunch, when we were working in the downtown studio. Here Mary Pickford and brother Jack and Dorothy West were regular patrons.

While the studio was being put in shape, the members of the company had been scooting about looking for suitable places to live. Salaries were not so large, but that economy had to be practiced, even with the fourteen dollars a week expense money allowed every member of the company.

Mary Pickford had brother Jack to look after, and she decided that if she clubbed in with some of the girls and they all found a place together it would be cheaper, and also not so lonely for her. So Mary, with Jack, and two of the young girls—Dorothy West and Effie Johnson—thirty-dollar-a-weekers, found shelter in a rooming house called "The Lille." It was on South Olive and Fifth Streets, but it is there no more. The four had rooms here for three and a half per week per person.

But the quartette didn't stay long at "The Lille"—decided they needed hotel conveniences. So they scurried about and located finally for the winter at the New Broadway Hotel on North Broadway and Second Streets. Here they lived in comfort, if not in style, with two rooms and a connecting bath, for five fifty per week per person.

When we got going, Mr. Griffith was rather glad Jack Smith was along, for with the two companies working we found we could use a small boy quite often. So Jack earned his fifteen a week regularly that first California winter.

The men of the company were all devoted to little Jack. He would sit around nights watching them play poker, sometimes until 3 A.M.; he didn't want to be forever at the movies with his big sister. Mary allowed Jack fifty cents a night for his dinner; he'd connect up somewhere or other with his pals, in any event with his big brother Dell Henderson, and they would make a night of it.

We were to be no proud owners of an automobile, but rented one by the hour at four dollars for car and chauffeur. The director and his camera man and persons playing leads would travel by motor to location while the others would trolley. As Los Angeles had, even then, the most wonderful system of trolleys in the world, there were few places, no matter how remote, that could not be reached by electric car.

Sunday came to be a big day for the automobile, for on that day we scouted for the week's locations—that is, after David had made out his weekly expenses, his Sunday morning job.

Here is a sample, recorded in almost illegible pen-and-ink longhand:

Luncheon (30 actors)............................ $ 7.50
Carfare (30 actors, location both ways) 15.00
Automobile (so many hours $4. per) 100.00
Locations (gratuities for using people's places) .. 20.00
Incidentals 17.00
Extras (not actors, not incidentals either) 11.00

Those sufficiently interested may add.

CHAPTER XX

WE would not have been true to the traditions of the Golden State had we not used a Mission in our first picture. We meant to do our very best right off and send back a knock-out.

So to San Gabriel we went to get the lovely old Mission atmosphere in a picture called "Threads of Destiny."

We spread ourselves; we took the Mission front, back and sideways, inside and out; we used the worn old stairway, shaded by a fragrant pepper tree, that led to the choir loft: we even planted lilies—or rather, Mary Pickford as *Myrtle*, the orphan girl of San Gabriel, planted lilies—along the adobe wall of the old cemetery where slept baptized Indians and Mexicans.

It was pleasant sprawling about in the lazy sunshine. We who were "atmosphere" wandered about the cemetery, reading the old tombstones, and had the priest guide us through the Mission showing us its three-hundred-year-old treasures. And across the way we visited the curio shop where we bought pretty post-cards and ate *tamales*, real Mexican *tamales*.

We would experiment on this Mission picture. We wanted a dim, religious light, and here it was, and we wanted to get it on the screen as it looked to us, the real thing. One little window let in an afternoon slant of soft sunshine that fell directly upon the pulpit where Christie Miller, playing an old priest, was to stand and bless the congregation. If we could light up Christie, the devout worshipers could be mere shadows and it would look fine— just what we wanted. Billy Bitzer would "get" it if it could be got, that we knew. So while Billy was tuning up his camera, Bobby Harron came and gathered in the congregation from the curio shop and cemetery, and we quietly took our places in the chapel and did our atmospheric bit. We did pray—we prayed that it would be a good effect.

We rather held our breath at the picture's first showing until his tricky scene was flashed on the screen. Then we relaxed; it was all there!

Spanish California was not to be neglected this trip, and our next picture, a romance of the Spanish dominion, called "In Old California" is historical as the first Biograph to be taken in Hollywood. The Hollywood Inn was at this time the only exclusive winter resort between the city and the ocean. We needed rooms where we could make up and dress, and Mr. Anderson, the genial young proprietor, welcomed us cordially.

Marion Leonard was playing the beautiful Spanish señorita in this movie and Frank Grandin the handsome young lover who afterwards became the governor of California. As we came out of the hotel in our make up and Spanish finery and quietly drove off into the foothills, guests were lolling on the broad front porch. With a start they came to. Whatever in the world was happening! "Did you see those people? What is it? What's going on? Let's get our motor and follow them and see," said they.

We had selected what we though a remote and secluded spot in the foothills, but soon in ones and twos and threes the guests appeared. For a time they seemed well-behaved spectators; they kept quiet and in the background. But Miss Leonard's dramatic scenes proved too much for them. They resented the love-making and began making derogatory comments about movie actors, and one "lady" becoming particularly incensed, shouted loudly, "Well, I wouldn't dress up like a fool like that woman and act like her, no, not for all the money in the world." That off her chest, she turned on her heel, and left us flat.

Paul de Longpré, the famous flower artist, lived only a few blocks from the Inn on Hollywood Boulevard. Many years ago he had left his native France and built a lovely château in the broad stretches of young Hollywood. In his gardens he had planted every variety of rose. A tangled profusion of them covered even the walls of his house. We offered fifty dollars a day for the use of the gardens. M. de Longpré went us one better. He offered to let us work if we'd buy a corner lot for three hundred dollars. But what could we do with a corner lot? We had no idea we would work six days and pay the three hundred dollars just in rental. But that we did. What we didn't do, was, take title to the corner lot. Had we done so we would have laid a foundation for fortune.

I recall M. de Longpré as the first person we met on location in California who seemed to appreciate that we were at least striving for something in an art line. To him we were not mere buffoons as we were to the ladies of the Hollywood Inn.

"Love Among the Roses" we aptly called the picture in which Marion Leonard played a great lady residing in the Kingdom of Never-never Land.

Monsieur de Longpré's lovely house and gardens—a

show place for tourists some twelve years ago—has long since been cut up into building lots on which have been erected rows of California bungalows. For when motion picture studios began to spring up like mushrooms in this quiet residential district, actors had to be domiciled and the boulevard was no longer desirable as a restful home locality. Also, the financial return on property thus manipulated was not to be lightly regarded. The town council voted a memorial to the kindly French artist. So Hollywood has a de Longpré Avenue.

The day we lunched at the Hollywood Inn marked an event for Hollywood. Few motion picture actors had desecrated the Inn's conservative grounds until that day. A few years later only motion picture actors lived there, and they live there now, though the old-maid régime is coming along rapidly. Aside from the movie intrusion, Mr. Anderson foresaw the changes that were to come. In due time he built the now famous Beverly Hills Hotel. But the movie actor, who has now achieved a social and financial standing that equals that of other professions, he still has with him.

Goodness gracious, how could we ever get all the scenic beauty on the screen! It was too distracting, what with Missions, desert, mountains, ocean, beaches, cliffs, and flowers. We wanted to send enough of it back in our pictures to ensure our coming again next winter.

We had a scenario that called for a wealthy gentleman's winter home. We hied ourselves out to Pasadena, to Orange Grove Avenue, Hillside Avenue, Busch's sunken gardens, Doheny's, and other famous show places. We found a place with gardens and pergolas, just the thing.

Asked permission to use the house and grounds, from very charming ladies wintering within, possibly a bit bored, for they seemed delighted with the idea.

It was not the custom in those days to explain the nature of the story for which one desired a place; and the ladies being so keen on seeing moving pictures being made, the matter ended right there. The scenario which had been selected for our pioneer work in Pasadena was called "Gold is Not All."

The day came to start work on the picture. We were all packed up in our motor car outside the Alexandria Hotel getting an early start, for the earlier we got to work, the fewer the days we would need to trespass on the borrowed property.

"Gold is Not All" was a story of contrasts. There were very wealthy people in it and very poor people. And the poor faction was so poor that mother, little mother, had to take in washing to help out, which washing she returned to the rich people's houses.

Like many other fallacies that have become identified with motion picture characterization, rich people are invariably represented as being unkind, selfish, penurious, and immoral—oh, always immoral. And the poor are loving, kind, true, surfeited with virtue. The poor mother idolized her children, worked and slaved for them; father always loved mother, never strayed from home. But the rich man, drat him, ah, he had sweethearts galore, he was dishonest on the stock market, he put marble dust in the sugar, his wife was something merely to be exploited, and his children were always "poor little rich boys and girls."

So we were primed for action and quite ready to make

our wealthy gentleman sojourning in his winter mansion an utter rake, a miserable specimen of the middle-aged debauchee who treated cruelly a long-suffering wife. But the little poor families were such models of all the virtues, they hadn't missed one; and their days were full of happiness.

The hostess of this charming home with some friends watched our performances. There was no limit to their hospitality. They brought out tables and a tea-service and they loaned us their "bestest" butler—there was a lawn party in the story. When the picture was finished, Mr. Griffith invited the owner and his family and their friends to the studio to see the picture.

The projection over, we noticed a strange lack of enthusiasm; and then Monsieur took Mr. Griffith aside and asked him if it would be absolutely necessary for him to release the picture.

"Really," said the gentleman, "we are a very happy family, my wife and I and the children, we like each other a lot. All my friends have been told about the picture and they'll watch for it—and I just don't like it, that's all. You know a person can have money and still be a respectable citizen in the community."

And that was that. But we learned something.

And here comes little Jack Pickford in his first leading part, a comedy directed by Frank Powell, and called "The Kid." It was full of impish pranks of the small boy who does not want his lonely daddy to bring him home a new mama, but he comes across in time and soon is all for her.

Two more pictures, "The Converts," and "The Way of the World," finished us at San Gabriel. Both were Christian preachments, having repentant Magdalenes as heroines, and were admirably suited for portrayal against the Mission's mellow walls.

Sleepy old San Gabriel, where dwelt, that first winter, but a handful of Mexicans and where no sound but the mocking bird was heard until the jangling trolley arrived and unloaded its cackling tourists!

Mission atmosphere got under the skin; so we determined on San Fernando for "Over Silent Paths," an American Desert story of a lone miner and his daughter who had come by prairie-schooner from their far-away Eastern home.

San Fernando Mission was twenty-two miles from Los Angeles, with inadequate train service, and the dirt road, after the first winter rains had swelled the "rivers" and washed away the bridges, was often impassable by motor.

The desertion and the desecration of the picturesque place was complete. For more than two hundred years the hot sun and winter rain had beat upon the Mission's adobe walls. It boasted no curio shop, no lunch room, not even a priest to guard it. A few Japs were living in the one habitable room—they mended bicycles. We were as free to move in as were the swallows so thickly perched on the chapel rafters. An occasional tourist with his kodak had been the only visitor until we came. Then all was changed.

It was in San Fernando that we first met up with the typical California rancher. This man, whose name I recall as "Boroff" had been one of the first settlers in the valley. On a "location hunt" we had spied Mr. Boroff's interesting-looking place with its flowers and its cows, and had decided to pay our respects and see if we could get the ranch for a picture, sometime. One of the "hands" brought Mr. Boroff to us. Rangy and rugged, oh, what health-in-the-cheeks he had! He swung us about the place and then suddenly we found ourselves in a huge barn drinking tall glasses of the most wonderful buttermilk.

"Do you know," said Mr. Boroff, downing his, "I drink a quart of whiskey every day to pass the time away, and a gallon of buttermilk so I'll live long."

Squatted one afternoon on the edge of the roadway in front of the Mission, I began idly scratching up the baked dirt with an old Mexican stiletto we were using in a picture. A few inches below the surface I noticed funny little round things that did not seem to be rocks. I picked up a few, broke off pieces of dry dirt, cleaned the small particles on my Mexican shawl, and found them to be old Indian beads, all colors, blue, red, and yellow. Through the leisure hours of that day I dug beads until I had an interesting little string of them. The Indians from whose decorated leather trappings the beads had fallen had been sleeping many years in the old cemetery back of the Mission.

Now there are grass and flower beds growing over my little burial place of the beads, for the Mission has been restored; but even were it not so, the movie actress of to-day would surely rather lounge contentedly in her limousine than squat on old Mother Earth, digging up Indian beads.

The third and last of the Missions we visited was romantic San Juan Capistrano, seventy miles south of Los Angeles, nestling in the foothills some three miles from the Pacific.

Our scenario man, Mr. Taylor, had prepared a Spanish story of the padre days, and this lovely rambling Mission with its adjacent olive ranches, live-oak groves, silvery aliso trees, and cliffs along the seashore, was to afford stacks of local color.

Our one automobile deposited its quota—Mr. Griffith and party—in San Juan Capistrano in the late afternoon. The evening train brought the rest of the actors.

There was one little Inn, the Mendelssohn—now fixed up and boasting all modern conveniences; then merely an airy wooden structure evidently built under the prevailing delusion that southern California has a tropical climate. There was a tiny office; the only parlor, the proprietor's personal one, which he was kind enough to let us use. He had a stove and it felt mighty good to get warmed up nights before turning in.

The bedrooms were upstairs. To reach them you had to go out in the yard, the back-yard, climb the rickety stairs to the porch, on to which each little bedroom by means of its own little door, opened. The bare-floored bedrooms were just large enough to hold a creaky double bed, wash-bowl and pitcher, and a chair.

We must see the Mission before dinner. The idea of dinner didn't thrill us much, and the thought of going to bed thrilled us less. But why expect the beauty of old things and modern comfort too? The thought of seeing old San Juan in the dim light of early evening should have sufficed.

Beautiful old ruin! The peace and the silence! We might have been in the Sahara.

Every member of the company was to work in this picture. There were no more than ten little bedrooms in the hotel. Actors slept everywhere, two and three in a bed; even the parlor had to be fixed up with cots. Miss Leonard and others of the women had been domiciled in a neighborly Spanish house—the only other available decent quarters.

Dell Henderson, who had put himself wise to the arrangement of sleeping partners, had copped little Jack Pickford as his bedfellow. Dell was one of our very largest actors and Jack being about as big as a peanut, Dell had figured that with the little fellow by his side he might be able to catch forty winks during the night.

Few of us managed to get unbroken winks. Between the creaking of one's own bed and the snores from other rooms down the line (the walls were like paper) and the footsteps on the shaking porch, of actors going from room to room looking for something better than what had been allotted them, it was a restful night! All through it, at intervals, Charlie Craig kept calling to his bedfellow, "Don't squash me—don't squash me." But the most disgruntled of all was Sennett. To every room he came calling "Hey, how many in this bed? Who's in there? Got three in my bed; I can't sleep three in a bed." But responses were few and faint, and from Dell Henderson's room came only silence. So after waiting in vain for help in his difficulty, and thoroughly disgusted, Mack returned to what must have been very chummy quarters.

There had been engaged for this picture a bunch of cowboys, rough-riders, headed by Bill Carroll, for we were to pull some thrillers in the way of horse stuff. The riders with their horses were leaving Los Angeles on the midnight train, due to reach Capistrano at 2 A.M.

It was all so weird and spooky that midnight had arrived before I had summoned sufficient courage to let myself go to sleep. No sooner had I dozed off than out of the black and the silence came a terrific roar, yells, and loud laughter, and pistol shots going zip, zip, zip.

These hot-headed Mexicans! Things happened here, and something dreadful was going to happen right now. I heard horses; and soon horses and riders galloped madly into the back-yard, right to the foot of our stairs, it seemed.

But it was only our cowboys who had arrived, feeling good, and full of the joy of life. Old Colonel Roosevelt knew all about this sort of thing, and would have appreciated the celebration. No thought had been given the boys' slumber places, and so after a look around they docilely crawled up into the barn and were soon asleep in the sweet-smelling hay.

"The Two Brothers," the picture we were to do, told the story of the good and bad brother. Good brother marries the pretty señorita in the Mission chapel.

An experienced and cultured gentleman was the French priest in charge of this Mission. He was most obliging and told us we could use whatever we liked of the wedding ceremonial symbols, which we did, but which we shouldn't have done on this particular day of days—Good Friday.

The wedding was some spread. There were Spanish ladies in gay satins and mantillas, and Spanish gentlemen in velvets and gold lace, and priest and acolytes carrying the sacred emblems. They paraded all over the Mission grounds. Then the camera was set up to get the chapel entrance. While all was going happily, without warning, from out the turquoise blue sky, right at the feet of the blushing bride and the happy groom, fell the stuffed figure of a man! Right in the foreground the figure landed, and, of course, it completely ruined our beautiful scene.

On Good Friday in these Spanish-Mexican towns of California a ceremonial called "burning Judas" used to take place (and may still, for all I know). Old carts and wheels and pieces of junk in the village are gathered in a heap outside the Mission grounds, and old suits of clothes are stuffed with straw, making effigies of Judas. The villagers set fire to this lot of rubbish and to the Judases as well, and the evil they have brought during the year is supposed to disappear in the smoke from their burning bodies. The handsomest Judas, however, is saved from the conflagration for a more ignominious finish. A healthy young bull is secured and to his formidable horns this Judas is strapped. Then the bull is turned loose, so annoyed by this monstrous thing on his horns that he madly cavorts until Judas's clothes are torn to shreds and his straw insides are spilled all over the place, and he is done for, completely.

Now while we had been rehearsing and taking the wedding scenes, the sacristan, a little old man to whom life meant tending the Mission and ringing the bells at the appointed hour, had been covertly taking us in, and when he saw our gay though holy processional start into the very sanctum of the Mission on Good Friday, his soul revolted. No, that he would not stand for!

Something even worse than riding the bull's horns could happen to Judas; and that was to be thrown at movie actors. So the sacristan picked the prize Judas, and at the climactic scene he dropped him on us, and then broadcasting a roar of Mexican oaths he went on his way, his soul relieved and his heart rejoicing.

But we felt differently. There was no telling now what these San Juan hot-heads might do to us. But the seeming

Mary Pickford as a picturesque Indian, before "curls" and "Mary" had become synonymous terms. (*See p. 168*)

The Hollywood Inn, the setting for "The Dutch Gold Mine," with Mack Sennett and Eddie Dillon. The players were thrilled at being received in such a hostelry, and the guests amazed at seeing picture actors.

(See p. 158)

From "Comrades," the first picture directed by Mack Sennett, with Mack Sennett and Dell Henderson. (See p. 204)

lack of reverence of our procession was explained to the little sacristan by the understanding priest.

The next day we did the abduction. We took ourselves miles from the Mission. We chose a treacherous-looking road along the ocean cliffs. In a ramshackle buggy the bride and groom were speeding on their honeymoon, but bad brother and his band of outlaws were hot on the trail to steal the bride. Our cowboys bringing up the rear were cavorting on their horses; the horses were rearing on their hind legs; and the director was yelling, "A dollar for a fall, boys, a dollar for a fall!" The boys fell, on all sides they fell; they swung off their horses, and they climbed back on, and they spilled themselves in the dust, their horses riding on without them. Some of the boys made ten and some twenty dollars that day, just for "falls." And not one was even scratched.

The next day was Easter Sunday, and our work being finished, in the gray dawn we folded our tents and silently slunk away.

But the curse of Judas was upon us. When the picture was projected, all was fine—scenic effects beautiful—and photography superb, until—we came to the wedding procession!

Judas, to our surprise, was nowhere to be seen; he had fallen out of focus evidently, but the effect of his anathema was all there. The scene was so streaked with "lightning" we could not use it. At San Gabriel we retook it later, but it never seemed the same to us.

Sierra Madre was another of our choice locations this first trip. Here were wonderful mountains with fascinating trails and canyons deep and long.   From Sierra Madre, Mount Wilson was climbed, by foot or donkey, for no magnificent motor road then led to its five-thousand-and-something-foot summit.

At the quarter-mile house we did "The Gold-seekers," a story of California in the days of '49, with Henry Walthall striking pay dirt in the west fork of the San Gabriel canyon.

Mary Pickford did one of her Indians here, "A Romance of the Western Hills."   David thought Mary had a good face for Indians on account of her high cheek bones, and usually cast her for the red-skinned maid or young squaw. A smear of brown grease paint over her fair face and a wig of coarse straight black hair made a picturesque little Indian girl of "our Mary."

Curls and Mary Pickford were not yet synonymous. She played, besides Indians, many character parts with her hair smacked straight back; and she "did" young wives with her hair in a "bun" on the top of her head to make her look tall and married.   When Mary wore curls, it meant an hour of labor at night.   The curls necessitated three distinct kinds of "curlers," the ones for the wave on top, others for the long curls, and little curlers for the shorter hair around the face.   I often thought Mary Pickford earned her slim salary those days for the time and effort she spent on her hair alone.

It was an unhappy Mary on that first trip to Los Angeles, Owen Moore having passed up his little sweetheart on account of the weekly ten dollars he thought Mr. Griffith should have added to his salary.   The day's work over, came her lonesome hour.   On the long rides home from location, cuddled up in her seat in the car, she dreamed of home and dear ones. And one day passing the eastbound Santa Fé Limited, out of a deep sad sigh the words escaped, "God bless all the trains going East and speed the one we go on"—the Irish in her speaking.

An urge to do "Ramona" in a motion picture possessed Mr. Griffith all the while we were in California, for the picturesque settings of Helen Hunt Jackson's deep-motived romance were so close at hand. Several conferences had been held on the subject in New York, before we left. But in order to make a screen adaptation of this story of the white man's injustice to the Indian, arrangements would have to be made with the publishers, Little, Brown & Company. They asked one hundred dollars for the motion picture rights and the Biograph Company came across like good sports and paid it, and "Ramona" went on record. It was conceded to be the most expensive picture put out by any manufacturer up to that time.

To Camulos, Ventura County, seventy miles from Los Angeles, we traveled to do this production of "Ramona." For Camulos was one of the five homes accredited to the real Ramona that Mrs. Jackson picked for her fictional one. She picked well.

What a wealth of atmosphere of beautiful old Spain, Camulos's far-famed adobe offered! Scenes of sheep-shearing; scenes in the little flower-covered outdoor chapel where Ramona's family and their faithful Indian servants worshiped; love scenes at Ramona's iron-barred window; scenes of heartache on the bleak mountain top but a few miles distant where Alessandro and Ramona bury their little baby, dead from the white man's persecutions; and finally the wedding scene of Ramona and Felipe amid the oranges and roses and grass pinks of the patio. Even bells that were cast in old Spain rang silently on the screen. The Biograph Company brought out a special folder with cuts and descriptive matter. The picture was Mr. Griffith's most artistic creation to date.

Nor did we neglect the oil fields, for oil had its romance. So at Olinda, that tremendous field, we "took" plungers innumerable and expensive oil spilling out of huge barrels into little lakes, all black and smooth and shiny. The picture, called "Unexpected Help," had Arthur Johnson and little Gladys Egan as star actors. One other oil picture we did, "A Rich Revenge," a comedy of the California oil fields, with Mary Pickford and Billy Quirk.

We had located a picturesque oil field. A crabbed-looking man in dirty blue jeans seemed the only person about. We asked him would there be any objection to our working, and he gruffly answered in the negative.

So we "set up," and got our scenes; and, work finished, looked about for our man, wishing to thank him. Feeling sorry for him, we went one better and tendered him a twenty-dollar gold piece. When he saw that money, he began to curse us so hard that we were glad when we hit the highway.

At the garage in the village we made inquiries and were enlightened. The man of the dirty blue jeans was none other than the millionaire owner of the oil well, an oil well that was gushing one fair fortune per day. And though he refused our money as though it were poison, three times a week that man walked to Santa Ana, ten miles distant, where he could buy a ten-cent pie for five cents.

Still more atmosphere we recorded in a picture called "As It Is In Life"—the famous old pigeon farm located near the dry bed of the San Gabriel River. Shortly after the time of our picture, the winter storms washed away this landmark and we were glad then that we had so struggled with the thousands of fluttering pigeons that just wouldn't be still and feed when we wanted them to, and insisted upon being good, quiet little pigeons when we wished them to loop the loop.

It seems we paid little attention to sea stories. Perhaps because we had our own Atlantic waiting for us back home, and we had done sea stories. We produced only one, "The Unchanging Sea," suggested by Charles Kingsley's poem, "The Three Fishers."

Charlie Ogle, who had worked in a few old Biographs but had been signed up with Edison before Mr. Griffith had a chance to get him, said to me one day out at the Lasky lot last winter—1924:

"What was that wonderful sea picture you played in? My, that *was* a picture, and you did beautiful work. I'll never forget it."

"You couldn't remember a sea picture I played in, Mr. Ogle. Heavens, that was so long ago you must mean some one else."

"No, I don't, and I remember it very well. What was the name?"

"Enoch Arden?"

"No."

"Fisher Folk?"

"No, now what *was* that picture?"

And at that moment we were interrupted in our game of guess as Leatrice Joy, whom we had been watching, came off the scene to revive from the heavy smoke of a café fire, before doing it over again.

"I've got it—'The Unchanging Sea.'"

"That's it, that's the one.   I'll never forget that picture."

"As I remember, it was considered quite a masterpiece."

The fishing village of Santa Monica was the locale of this story.   At this time there was but a handful of little shacks beyond the pier, places rented for almost nothing by poor, health-seeking Easteners.   No pretentious Ince studio as yet meandered along the cliffs some nine miles beyond. The road ran through wild country on to Jack Rabbit Lodge where a squatter had a shack that tourists visited occasionally and for twenty-five cents were shown an old Indian burial ground.

The only fellow movie actors we met this first winter in Los Angeles were two members of the Kalem Company, beautiful Alice Joyce and handsome Carlyle Blackwell, who often on fine mornings trotted their horses over Santa Monica's wet sands.

Occasionally, we met Nat Goodwin, who had cantered all the way from his home in Venice-by-the-Sea.

CHAPTER XXI

BACK HOME AGAIN

NOW we must pack up our troubles in our little black bag and go home. They must be lonesome for us at 11 East Fourteenth, for the studio has been dark and silent in our absence. Mr. Dougherty especially will be glad to see us. And others—the jobless actors. For things were coming along now so that Mr. Griffith didn't have to dig so hard for new talent.

Much talk there'll be about the pictures we did—how the public is receiving them—which ones are most popular —how worthwhile the trip was—how economical we were— and how hard we worked.

When once again we had donned our working harness, how stuffy and cramped the studio seemed! Four months in the open had ruined us; four months with only a white sheet suspended above our heads when we did "interiors" on our lot and the sun was too strong. We felt now like toadstools in a dark cellar, with neither sun nor fresh air.

There was so much to keep Mr. Griffith busy—cutting and titling of pictures, and conferences upstairs. But the blossoming pink and white apple orchards must be heeded, so we deserted a few days, hied ourselves to New Jersey's old stone houses and fruit trees and friendly hens, and did a picture "In the Season of Buds."

Dorothy West played a leading part in "A Child of the Ghetto," in which was featured more Eastern atmosphere—the old oaken bucket.

For a time we stayed indoors. We acquired a new actor, Joseph Graybill, and a few old ones returned, Vernon Clarges and Mrs. Grace Henderson, Jim Kirkwood and Gertrude Robinson. They now played leading parts. The public must not get fed up with the same old faces—Mr. Griffith always saw to that—so it was "go easy" on the California actors for a while.

The feeling of the old actors towards the new ones, this spring, was largely a jealous one. "Gee, Griff likes him all right, what are we going to do about it?" said Charlie West and Arthur Johnson when Joe Graybill was having his first rehearsals and the director was beaming with satisfaction and so happy that he was singing lusty arias from "Rigoletto."

"We'll fix him," they decided.

So this day Charlie and Arthur returned from lunch with a small brown bottle containing spiritous liquor, with which they would ply Joe Graybill surreptitiously in the men's dressing-room in the hope that they might incapacitate him. But Joe drank up, rehearsed, and Mr. Griffith's smile only grew broader. Better than ever was the rehearsal. So Charles went out for another little brown bottle and Joe disposed of it, and rehearsed—better still. Another bottle, another rehearsal—better than ever—until in a blaze of glory the scene was taken and Joe Graybill stood upon the topmost rung of the ladder, leaving Charles and Arthur gazing sadly upward.

There was another reason why Mr. Griffith welcomed new faces. He had a way of not letting an actor get all worked up about himself. When that seemed imminent, new talent would suddenly appear on the scene to play "leads" for two or three weeks so that the importance of the regular could simmer down a bit.

Now that they had developed an affection for their movie jobs, the actors didn't like this so well. They'd come down to the studio, sit around and watch, get nervous, and after drawing three or four weeks' salary without working (things had come along apace), they wouldn't know what to make of it. They'd carry on something awful. They'd moan: "When am I going to work? I don't like this loafing —I wonder if Griffith doesn't like me any more—I'd like to know if he wants me to quit and this is his way of getting me to make the overture." Finally, Eddie August, after suffering three weeks of idleness, on pay, got very brave and told Mr. Griffith he wished he'd fire him or else, for God's sake, use him. Mr. August was quite relieved to have Mr. Griffith's explanation that in his case he was merely trying out new people, and didn't want him to quit at all, would be very glad to have him stay.

When the Black-eyed Susans had reached full bloom, we went back to Greenwich, Connecticut, and did a picture called "What the Daisy Said," with Mary Pickford and Gertrude Robinson. We visited Commodore Benedict's place again, and again he brought out boxes of his best cigars. A good old sport he was.

To the Civil War again, in the same old New Jersey setting, with Dorothy West playing the heroine in "The House with the Closed Shutters." In her coward brother's clothes she takes his place on the battlefield, breaks through the lines, delivers a message, and is shot as she returns. And, forever after, inside the darkened rooms of the House with the Closed Shutters the brother pays through bitter years the price of his cowardice.

All our old stamping grounds we revisited this summer. At the Atlantic Highlands we did two pictures: one, "A Salutary Lesson," with Marion Leonard; and the other, "The Sorrows of the Unfaithful," with Mary Pickford.

At Paterson, New Jersey, we found a feudal castle. It belonged to one Mr. Lambert, a silk manufacturer. Here we did "The Call to Arms" where little Mary donned tights for the first and only time, playing a page, and looking picturesque on a medieval horse, but being a very unhappy Mary for a reason that none of us knew.

How she fussed about those tights—nearly shed tears. She sat on the lawn all wrapped up in the generous folds of her velvet cape, and wouldn't budge until she was called for her scene, and she talked so strangely. For Owen was there, and all the other actors were to see her in the tights, and Mary and Owen had a secret—a secret that made such a situation quite unbearable. She had confided it only to "Doc," but the rest of us had been wondering.

What a miserable, hot, muggy day it was. Tolerable only sitting on the grassy slopes of the Lambert estate, but how awful in the rooms of the little frame hotel over by the railroad tracks where we had made up and where some of the actors were still awaiting orders as to how they should dress.

Dell Henderson, who was assisting Mr. Griffith on this picture, was laboring back and forth from the castle to the hotel bringing orders to the waiting actors as they were needed. Sennett was one of the waiting ones, and he was all humped up in his pet grouch when Dell entered and said, "Here, Sennett, the boss says for you to don this armor."

"Armor, in this heat? Armor? I guess I won't wear armor." Then a short pause, "Are you going to wear armor?"

"Yes, I'm no teacher's pet," said Dell, as he gathered to himself the pieces of his suit of mail and began to climb into them. So the doubting Mack Sennett could do naught but imitate him, for no matter how balky his manner, one word from the boss and he became a good little boy again.

In August we were once more back in Cuddebackville. The O. and W.'s conductor was no longer skeptical of our visits. We brought so many actors sometimes that we not only filled the little Inn but had to find neighboring farmhouses in which to park the overflow.

We met all the old Cuddebacks again. We never realized what a tribe they were until we had to do a scene in a cemetery, and every grave we picked made trouble for us with some Cuddeback or other still living. How to get away with it we didn't know until we hit upon the idea of simultaneously enacting a fake but intensely melodramatic scene down by the General Store. That did the trick. All the villagers missed their lunch that day and were unaware of the desecration of their dead.

"Wally" Walthall gave his famous fried chicken luncheon at the minister's house. Talent was versatile. We'd worked through our lunch hour this day, so it was either go lunchless or beg the privilege of slaughtering some of the minister's wife's tempting spring chickens and cooking them in her kitchen. That's how "Wally" had the opportunity to prove his fried chicken the equal of any Ritz-Carlton's.

We met up with old Pete again. Although nearly ninety, he was worrying his faithful spouse into a deep and dark melancholia. Pete drove the big bus, rigged up for our use out of one of his old farm wagons. It was usually filled with "actresses"—wicked females from the city who wore gay clothes and put paint on their faces. What a good time old Pete did have once out on the highway! What a chatter, chatter, chatter he did maintain! Never had he dreamed of such intimacy with ladies out of a the-ayter!

But a wife was ever a wife. So no matter how old and decrepit Pete was, to Mrs. Pete he still had charm, so why wouldn't he be alluring to these city girls? Every night Mrs. Pete was Johnny-on-the-spot, when the bus unloaded its quota of fair femininity at the Inn, waiting to lead her errant swain right straight home.

Our friends the Goddefroys still held open house for us. Dear old Mr. Goddefroy told us of the disquieting notes that had crept into Cuddebackville's former tranquil life, due to our lavish expenditures the first summer—told Mr. Griffith he was "knocking the place to hell."

But they still loved us. In a smart little trap they'd jog over to location bringing buckets of fresh milk and boxes of apples and pears. Toward late afternoon of a warm summer day, when working close to their elaborate "cottage," the "Boss" would appear with bottles of Bass's Ale, and bottles of C-and-C Ginger Ale, both of which he'd pour over great chunks of ice into a great shining milk bucket—shandygaff! Was it good? For the simple moving picture age in which we were living we seemed to get a good deal out of life.

We enjoyed the other social diversions of the year before—canoeing, motoring, table-tipping. But one night, the night on which the Macpherson magicians broke up Mr.

Griffith's beautiful sleep, nearly saw the end of table-tipping.

Retiring early after a hard day David was awakened by noisy festivities downstairs, and getting good and mad about it he rapped a shoe on the floor. The group on occult demonstration bent, thinking how wonderfully their spooks were working, instead of quieting down became hilarious. The morning found them much less optimistic about spirit rapping.

We did an Irish story of the days when the harp rang through Tara's Hall—the famous "Wilful Peggy"—in which pretty Mary never looked prettier nor acted more wilfully. But the something that had happened to Mary since our first visits to Cuddebackville made her a different Mary now.

One day we were idling over by the Canal bank when, with the most wistful expression and in the most wistful tone, Mary spoke, "You know, Mrs. Griffith, I used to think this canal was the most beautiful place I'd ever seen, and now it just seems to me like a dirty, muddy stream."

What had happened to her love's young dream to so change the scenery for her?

Early that fall we went to Mount Beacon to do an Indian picture. The hotel on the mountain top had been closed, but we dug up the owner and he reopened parts of the place. At night we slid down the mountainside in the incline railway car to the village of Fishkill where we dined and slept at a regular city hotel.

We nearly froze on that mountain top. Playing Indians, wrapped up in warm Indian blankets, and thus draped picturesquely on the mountainside, saved us. Mrs. Smith, not yet Pickford, did an Indian squaw in this picture, which featured a picturesque character, one Dark Cloud, for years model to the artist Remington. Dark Cloud was sixty years old, but had the flexible, straight, slim figure of nineteen. How beautifully he interpreted the Harvest Festival dance!

There were other actor-Indians on this Mount Beacon picture, present-day celebrities who were thanking their stars they were being Indians with woolly blankets to pose in. There were Henry Walthall and Lily Cahill and Jeanie Macpherson and Jim Kirkwood and Donald Crisp, among others.

Donald Crisp had crept quietly into the Biograph fold as Donald Somebody Else. Occasionally, he authored poems in *The Smart Set*—reason for being Donald Somebody Else in the movies. Of late, Mr. Crisp has rather neglected poetry for the movies. He gave the screen his greatest acting performance as *Battling Burrows* in Mr. Griffith's artistic "Broken Blossoms."

The night that "Way Down East" opened in New York in 1920 (September 3) Donald was radiant among the audience saying his farewells, for on the morrow he was to sail for England to take charge of the Famous Players studio there, where he put on among other things "Beside the Bonnie Brier Bush."

Claire MacDowell and her husband, Charles Mailes, joined Biograph this season. Stephanie Longfellow returned to play in more pictures; Alfred Paget began to play small parts, as did Jeanie Macpherson; also beautiful Florence LaBadie, who afterwards became a fan favorite through Thanhouser's startlingly successful serial "The Million Dollar Mystery." As one of the four principals, along with James Cruze of "The Covered Wagon" fame, Sidney Bracy and Marguerite Snow, she attracted much attention.

A job as model to Howard Chandler Christie had preceded her venture into the movies. Her tragic death, the result of a motor accident, occurred in 1917.

Edwin August came, to look handsome in costume, playing his first part with Lucy Cotton (recently married to E. R. Thomas) in "The Fugitive," taken on Mount Beacon. Mabel Normand, who had peeked in on us the year before, returned after a winter spent with Vitagraph.

Mabel, as every one knows, had been responsible for the lovely magazine covers by James Montgomery Flagg, and had also been model to Charles Dana Gibson, before she came to pictures, which had happened through friendship for Alice Joyce, who had also been a model, but was now leading lady at the Kalem Company. It was at Kalem, playing extras, that Mabel Normand began her rather startling movie career. Dorothy Bernard made a screen début, as did the other Dorothy who afterward became the wife of Wallace Reid.

I recall Dorothy Davenport at the Delaware Water Gap where we took some pictures that fall. She was a modish little person; she wore brown pin-check ginghams and a huge brown taffeta bow on the end of a braid of luxurious brown hair that fluttered down her back. She looked as though she came direct from Miss Prim's boarding school for children of the élite—and so was distinctive for the movies.

Fair Lily Cahill of the tailored blue serge, plain straw "dude," and lady-like veil worked intermittently that summer; she was always immaculately bloused in "sun-kissed linen." Not long after the days of the Water Gap and Mount Beacon Indian pictures, Miss Cahill became a Broadway leading woman in support of that long-time matinée idol, Brandon Tynon, and somewhere along in this period she married him.

Henry Lehrman, alias Pathé, hung about. How he loved being a near-actor! How he adored getting fixed up for a picture! He was satisfied by now that his make-ups were works of art. From the dressing-room he would emerge patting his swollen chest, with the laconic remark, "Some make-up!"

Eddie Dillon returned, to smile his way through more studio days. He often engaged me in long converse. Eddie was quite flabbergasted when he learned my matrimonial status. He need not have been. For in Los Angeles on Mr. Griffith's busy evenings he often suggested my taking in a movie with Eddie. But Eddie never knew about that.

And there was Lloyd Carlton, who went all around the mulberry bush before he landed in the movies. He first heard of them in far-off Australia in 1908, when as stage manager for "Peter Pan" he met a Mr. West, who was "doing" Australia and the Far East with a "show" that consisted of ten- and fifteen-foot moving pictures, toting the films and projection machine and the whole works along with him. Back on home soil, Mr. Carlton bobbed up at Biograph where instead of Mr. Frohman's one hundred and fifty dollars weekly he cheerfully pocketed five dollars per day for doing character bits. Followed Thanhouser, Lubin, and Mr. Fox.

Mr. Carlton says he directed the first five-reel picture ever released—"Through Fire to Fortune"—written by Clay Greene and released March 2, 1914, by the General Film Company. Mr. Carlton also says his picture contained the first night scene. Through crude lighting manipulations Mr. Carlton secured it in the quarry at Betzwood where

Mary Pickford's first picture, "The Violin Maker of Cremona," June 7, 1909. David Miles as the cripple Felippo. (*See p. 100*)

Mary Pickford's second picture. Mary Pickford, Marion Leonard and Adele de Garde, in "The Lonely Villa." (*See p. 100*)

Mary Pickford and Mack Sennett in "An Arcadian Maid," Aug. 1, 1910.
(*See p. 78*)

Mary Pickford, Mack Sennett, Joe Graybill and Marion Sunshine, in "The Italian Barber," which established Joe Graybill. (*See p. 174*)

rocks were painted black and properties arranged to represent the interior of a mine.

And so from near and far, and from diverging avenues of endeavor, came the new recruits to Biograph; but in the late fall Mary and Owen, and the Smith family sailed for Cuba one fine day to produce some "Imp" pictures there. When safe aboard the steamer, Mary and Owen decided to brave mother's tears and anguish. They told her of the secret marriage.

CHAPTER XXII

IT COMES TO PASS

THERE were no social engagements during these Biograph years. Our dinner parties, which were concerned
with nourishment mostly, were with our co-workers. As
we never knew when we would be allowed to eat, it was
impossible to dine with friends. There was no time for
anything but work—a good, hard steady grind it was, and
we liked it.

The one, lazy, lenient affair of the week was breakfast
on Sunday morning. From ten to twelve it stretched, and
it was so restful to eat at home and not have to look at
a menu card or talk to a waiter, even though the conversation would be all about the movies.

"What are people interested in?" said he, one Sunday.

"Well, men like to make money, and women want to
be beautiful."

"That would make a good movie. Why don't you
write it?"

"Glad to, if you think it's any good."

So she wrote it, the part about the women wanting to
be beautiful, and called it "How She Triumphed," and in
it Blanche Sweet evolved from an ugly duckling with no
beaux to a very lovely bit of femininity with sighing swains
all around her. In the picture she did calisthenics according
to Walter Camp as one way of getting there.

After the leisurely Sunday morning hours had crept their way, to the studio David would hie himself to read scripts with Mr. Dougherty. And Sunday night would mean a movie show somewhere. And Monday morning it began all over again.

From "Wark," to "work," only the difference of a vowel, so what an appropriate middle name for David Griffith! What infinite patience he had. If we got stuck in the mud when going out to location—we were stuck, and we'd get out, so why worry? No cursing out of driver or car or weather; no, "What the——? Why the —— couldn't you have taken another road?" Instead would suddenly be heard baritone strains of "Samson and Delilah" or some old plantation negro song while we waited for horses or another car to pull us out.

And it did happen once when on location perhaps twenty miles out in the wilds, that the leading man suddenly discovered he had brought the wrong pair of trousers. Nothing to do but send back for the right ones. Mr. Griffith was not indifferent to the time that would be lost, but getting himself all worked up would not make the picture any better. He'd sing, perhaps an Irish come-all-you, or, were he out in the desert, get out the automobile robe and start a crap game.

Arthur Marvin never ceased to marvel at his chief's agility and capacity for hard work. Mr. Marvin had a sort of leisurely way of working.

Up and down a stubble field Mr. Griffith was tearing one day—getting a line on a barn, a tree and some old plows. Arthur was having a few drags on his pipe—the film boxes being full and everything in readiness to put up the tripod wherever the director should decide. David's long legs kept striding merrily all over the cut harvest field —most miserable place to walk—Arthur musing as he looked on. "There goes Griffith, he'll die working." In a few moments Mr. Griffith right-about faced and with not a symptom of being out of breath said, "Set her up here, Arthur."

That winter we lost our genial Arthur Marvin, but David Griffith is still hitting the stubble field. Well, he took good care of himself. He did a daily dozen, and he sparred with our ex-lightweight, Spike Robinson. The bell-boys at the Alexandria Hotel called him "the polar bear" because he bought a bucket of cracked ice every morning to make the Los Angeles morning bath more tonic-y.

One could not have better equipment for the trying experiences of movie work than patience, and a sense of humor. And the "polar bear" is well equipped with both.

But there were times when even a sense of humor failed to sustain one. Nothing was funny about the uncertain mornings when we'd gather at the 125th Street ferry for the 8:45 boat, having watched weather since daylight through our bedroom window, only to cross and recross the Hudson on the same boat, the cumulus clouds we delighted in for photographic softness having turned to rain clouds even as we watched from the ferry slip. Back to the studio then to begin another picture and to work late. And oh, how we'd grouch!

But when it rained while we were registered at some expensive place like the Kittatiny at the Delaware Water Gap, there was need for anxiety, with the actors' board bill mounting daily and nothing being accomplished.

Yes, we had worries. But we were getting encouragement too. The splendid reviews of our pictures in *The*

Dramatic Mirror helped a lot. The way our pictures were going over was a joy. With their first announcement on the screen, what a twitter in the audience! A great old title page Biograph pictures had. Nothing less than our National emblem, our good old American eagle, sponsored them. He certainly looked a fine bird on the screen, his wings benignly spread, godfathering the Biograph's little movie children.

Exhibitors were certainly getting keen about "Biographs"; the public was too. People were becoming anxious about the players as well, and commencing to ask all sorts of questions about them.

Stacks of mail were arriving daily imploring the names of players, but of this no hint was given the actor. How surprised I was that time my husband said to me, "You know we are getting as many as twenty-five letters a day about Mary Pickford?"

"Why, what do you mean, letters about her?"

"Every picture she plays in brings a bunch of mail asking her name and other things about her."

"You're not kidding?"

"Of course not."

"Did you tell her?"

"No. I don't want her asking for a raise in salary."

Biograph found it a difficult job sticking to their policy of secrecy. Letters came from fans asking about their favorites; the pretty girl with the curls—the girl with the sad eyes—the man with the lovely smile—the funny little man—and the policeman. What tears of joy Sennett would have wept had he known!

In bunches the postman soon began to leave the "who" letters at 11 East Fourteeenth Street. "Who played the tall,

thin man in 'The Tenderfoot'?" "Who played the little
girl in the Colonial dress and curls who danced the minuet
in the rose garden at midnight in 'Wilful Peggy'?" "Who
was the handsome Indian who did the corn dance on the
mountain top in 'The Indian Runner's Romance'?"

Other picture concerns than Biograph had not as yet
made the actor's name public. But they did give him his
mail when addressed with sufficient clarity. Arthur Mackley, the famous *Sheriff* of Essanay, was receiving, those
days, ten letters a day. They came addressed.

> The Sheriff
> Essanay Company
> Chicago

Some boy, the Sheriff, getting ten letters a day!

It remained for English exhibitors first to name the
Biograph players. For Biograph, long after all the other
picture companies had made the actor's name public, still
refused to come out into the open. Over in London the
fans were appeased with fictitious names for their favorites.
Beautiful names they were, so hero-ish and so villain-ish,
so reminiscent of the old-time, sentimental, maiden-lady
author. I recall but one and a half names of our players.
Dell Henderson was given the beautiful soubriquet of
"Arthur Donaldson" and Blanche Sweet became "Daphne
———" something or other.

But the yearning American youths and maidens continued to receive the cold, stereotyped reply, "Biograph
gives no names." The Biograph was not thinking as quickly
as some of its players.

Our friends from Cuddebackville, the Goddefroys, being
in New York one time this summer, Mr. Griffith thought

it would be rather nice to arrange an evening. They were interested in our California pictures, as they were planning a trip there. We fixed up the projection room and ran the better of the Western stuff. Afterward with our guests and a few of the leading people we repaired to Cavanagh's on West Twenty-third Street.

Busy chatter about the pictures, every one raving over Mary Pickford's work in "Ramona," when Mary, quietly, but with considerable assurance said, "Some day I am going to be a great actress and have my name in electric lights over a theatre."

I turned pale and felt weak. We all were shocked. Of course, she never meant the movies, that would have been plumb crazy. No, she meant the stage, and she was thinking of going back. The thought of losing Mary made me very unhappy. But just how had she figured to get her name in electric lights? What was on her mind, anyway?

This summer of 1910 Mr. Griffith signed his third Biograph contract. This contract called for a royalty of an eighth of a cent a foot on all film sold and seventy-five dollars per week, but the name "Lawrence" which had been signed on the dotted line the two preceding years, was this time scratched out and "David" written in.

"David" had gone into the silence and decided that the movies were now worthy of his hire, and couldn't dent his future too badly, no matter what that future might be. David W. Griffith and Mary Pickford were certainly growing bold.

CHAPTER XXIII

THE FIRST TWO-REELER

THOUGH the licensed picture companies—The General Film Group—kept a watchful eye on one another, each had pride in its own trademark and was satisfied with the little company of actors bringing it recognition.

But the independent companies, now beginning to loom on the horizon, were looking with envying eyes on the rich harvest the licensed companies were reaping, and they figured that all they'd need, to do as well, would be some of their well-trained actors, especially those of Mr. Griffith's quite famous little organization. Surely D. W. Griffith had less to do with Mary Pickford's success than Mary Pickford herself! She it was the public came to see; so they were out, red-hot for Mary, and offering publicity and more money. The little war was started.

Actors in the companies that comprised the General Film Company could not be bargained for except by the Independents. For instance, if an actor of the Biograph Company were discovered offering his services to Lubin or Edison or any of the General Film, that company promptly reported the matter to Biograph and the ambitious actor found himself not only turned down by Edison or Lubin or any other but his nice little Biograph job would be gone as well. That had happened to Harry Salter and Florence

Lawrence.   An actor in one of the General Film group
would have to resign his job before he could open negotia-
tions with any other company in that group.

We did grind out the work this fall and early winter.
The promise of California again was a big incentive.   We
might stay longer and have a new studio, a regular place.

While there was no more excitement pervading the
studio than there had been the year before, a more general
willingness was noticed among the leading people and more
tears and anguish on the part of the beseeching extras.
Jeanie Macpherson sat on the steps leading to the basement
of the studio, and cried, until Mr. Griffith felt remorseful
and took her.

But such conduct hadn't availed pink-cheeked lanky
"Beau," the year before, when he was the one property boy
left behind.   Then that unhappy youth's tearful parting shot,
"All I ask, Mr. Griffith, is that some day you take me to
California," kept intruding and spoiling the complete satis-
faction of our days.   Another year Mr. Griffith harkened
to his pleading.   For nearly ten years now "Beau" as
William Beaudine has been directing pictures in Los
Angeles.

And so, while some of the old guard would not be with
us, a goodly number would.

To the "Imp" had gone Mary and Owen; and while
Ma fussed terribly about it, there was nothing for her and
Lottie and Jack to do but follow suit.

David Miles and Anita Hendry, his wife, were already
with "Imp"; and they, with King Baggott and George
Loane Tucker, Joe Smiley, Tom Ince, Hayward Mack, and
Isabel Rae, made a fair number of capable people.   But

even so, Mary's "Imp" pictures fell far short of her Biograph pictures, and she wasn't very happy and she didn't stay so very long.

As a member of the "Imp" Company, the silence and mystery that had surrounded her when with Biograph instantly vanished. She now received whole pages of advertising, for that was how the "Imp" would put the pictures over. One of her first Independent pictures was "The Dream" of which a reviewer said: "The picture got over on account of Miss Pickford. Our feelings were somewhat sentimental when we saw 'Our Mary' as a wife arrayed in evening gown and dining with swells. In other words, we have always considered Mary a child. It never occurred to us she might grow up and be a woman some day."

Marion Leonard and Stanner E. V. Taylor had taken their departure. I believe it was Reliance-ward they went, as did Mr. Walthall, Mr. Kirkwood, and Arthur Johnson. Arthur had become not so dependable, and Mr. Griffith being unable to stand the worry of uncertain appearances, reluctantly parted with his most popular actor, and his first leading man. He never found any one to take his place exactly. For even so long ago, before he and Mr. Griffith parted, 'twas said of Arthur Johnson, "His face is better known than John Drew's."

Mary gone, Mr. Griffith located Blanche Sweet somewhere on the road and telegraphed an offer of forty dollars weekly to come with us to California, which Miss Sweet accepted. He was willing to take a chance on Blanche, being in need of a girl of her type. If she didn't work out right (he hardly expected her to set the world a-fire) the loss would be small, as he was getting her so cheaply.

Wilfred Lucas also received a telegram; but his tenderly

implored him to come for one hundred and fifty dollars—a staggering offer—the biggest to date. He also accepted.

Dell Henderson had been commissioned by Mr. Griffith to dispatch the Lucas-one-hundred-and-fifty-dollar telegram, and the high salary made him so sore that he promptly told it everywhere, causing jealous fits to break out all over the studio.

We had also in our California cast, Claire MacDowell, Stephanie Longfellow, Florence Barker, Florence LaBadie, Mabel Normand, Vivian Prescott, and Dorothy West for the more important parts; Grace Henderson, Kate Toncray, and Kate Bruce for the character parts; and little Gladys Egan for important child rôles. And of men—as memory serves me—there were Frank Powell, Edwin August, Dell Henderson, Charlie Craig, Mack Sennett, Joe Graybill, Charlie West, Donald Crisp, Guy Hedlund, Alfred Paget, Eddie and Jack Dillon, Spike Robinson, Frank Grandin, Tony O'Sullivan and "Big" Evans, and George Nichols.

And some wives: Mrs. Frank Powell, Mrs. Dell Henderson, Mrs. George Nichols, and Mrs. Billy Bitzer.

And one baby: Frank Baden Powell.

At Georgia and Girard Streets, Los Angeles, a ten-minute ride from the center of the city, on a two-and-a-quarter-acre plot adjoining some car barns, the carpenters were building our grand studio. An open air studio—no artificial lighting—we could get all the light effects we desired from the sun—and could begin to work as early as 8:30 and continue until late in the afternoon. We had not yet reached the stage where we felt that Mr. Electric Lamp could compete with the sun.

How joyful we were when we first beheld the new studio! The stage was of nice smooth boards and seemed almost big enough for two companies to work at the same time. The muslin light diffusers were operated on an overhead trolley system. There was even a telephone on the stage. The studio was then indeed the last word in modern equipment.

An elongated one-story building contained the office, projection room, rehearsal room, for nights and rainy days, and two large dressing-rooms for the men. In order to save wear and tear on the women's clothes, they were given the two dressing-rooms in the rear of the building which opened directly onto the stage.

To tell the world how secure our position—how prosperous financially—at the street entrance to our studio there now waited through the day one, and often two big, black seven-passenger touring cars—rented by the month, at six hundred dollars per. Now between sets in the studio we could dash out in the car and grab an exterior.

In our dressing-rooms we had make-up tables, mirrors, lockers, and running water. And oil stoves to keep us warm. For in the early mornings, before the sun had reached our room, it was a shivery place. Our cold cream and grease paints would be quite as stiff as our fingers.

So now, with the new studio, a larger company, and our knowledge of the surrounding country, there was nothing to it but that we must get right on the job and do better and bigger pictures.

With the one exception already noted we had neglected the sea the year before, and as yet we had attempted nothing important that had to do with "Ol' davil Sea," as Eugene O'Neill calls it. The sea was trickier than the mountains, and more expensive if one needed boats and things. But this year we would go to it right, with a massive production of Tennyson's "Enoch Arden"—a second production of the poem that had written history for us in our screen beginnings.

The first time we had taken most of it in the studio, with only one or two simple shots of the sea. Now we would do something g-r-a-n-d. "Enoch Arden" was such good movie stuff, and Mr. Griffith was wondering how he could get it all into one thousand feet of film.

An exhibitor in those days would accept eleven hundred feet of film, but that was the limit. The programs were arranged only for the thousand-foot picture; a thousand-foot Biograph being shown Mondays and Thursdays. How could two thousand feet be shown on Monday and none on Thursday? Even could the exhibitor have so arranged it, would the people sit through two thousand feet without a break?

Well, now, we could do this: we could take the picture in two reels, each of a thousand feet, show one reel Monday, the second Thursday, and take a chance on the people becoming sufficiently interested in the first reel to come back for the second—the only logical way of working out the problem. Mr. Griffith fully realized his responsibility. Again he would chance it.

Santa Monica would be the ideal place for this big production; so every day for a week—for a whole week was given to exteriors alone—we motored out to Santa Monica in the cold early morning.

The place had changed little in the year that had passed. The row of tiny shacks was now occupied by Japs and Norwegians who caught and dried fish and fought with each other at all other times.

One friendly Norwegian loaned his shack as a dressing-room for the women. We "shot" the same shack for Annie's bridal home. The men made up in a stranded horse car of bygone vintage that had been anchored in the sand. We sent out an S. O. S. for a sailing vessel of Enoch's day, and we heard of one, and had it towed up from San Pedro. What would we do next?

We did "Enoch Arden" in two reels. Wilfred Lucas played Enoch; Frank Grandin, Philip; and I played Annie Lee. Well, Jeanie Macpherson said I had "sea eyes," whatever that meant.

Mrs. Grace Henderson kept the Inn to which Enoch returns; Annie's and Enoch's babies grew up to be Florence LaBadie and Bobbie Harron (one of Bobbie's first parts), and Jeanie Macpherson powdered her hair and played nurse to the little baby that later came to Philip and Annie.

George Nichols departed via the Owl for San Francisco to get the costumes from Goldstein & Company. There was so little to be had in costumes in Los Angeles. Mr. Nichols had also journeyed to San Francisco for costumes for "Ramona" the year before.

The exhibitors said they would accept "Enoch Arden" in the two reels, show the first on Monday, and the second reel Thursday. And so it was first shown. And those who saw the first reel came back in all eagerness to see the second half. And that was that.

The picture was so great a success, however, that it was soon being shown as a unit in picture houses; also in high schools and clubs, accompanied by a lecturer. And so "Enoch Arden" wrote another chapter of screen history.

Sustained by its success Mr. Griffith listened to the call of the desert. With two thousand feet of celluloid to record a story, he felt he now could do something with prairie schooners, pioneers, and redskins, and so he answered the desert call with a big epic of pioneer romance, "The Last Drop of Water."

We set up camp in the San Fernando desert—two huge tents, one for mess, with a cook and assistants who served chow to the cowboys and extra men. Two rows of tables, planks set on wooden horses, ran the length of the tent— there must have been at least fifty cowboys and riders to be fed hearty meals three times a day. The other tent contained trunks and wardrobe baskets, and here the boys slept and made up.

The hotel in the village of San Fernando, three miles or so from the camp, accommodated the regular members of the company and all the extra women, to whom the director, as he dashed off for his camp in the morning, gave this parting advice, "Girls, stay together when you're not busy, for you're likely to hear some pretty rough stuff if you don't."

Prairie schooners to the number of eight made up our desert caravan, and there were the horses for the covered wagons, the United States soldiers, and the Indians; dogs, chickens, and a cow; for this restless element from a Mississippi town, making the trek across the land of the buffalo and the Indian to gather gold nuggets in the hills of California, brought with them as many familiar touches from their deserted homes as they reckoned would survive the trip.

Of course, conflicts with Indians, and the elements, resulted in a gradual elimination of the home touches and disintegration of the caravan, but there was a final triumphant arrival at their destination for the few survivors.

The picture was expensive, but quite worth it; we were at least headed the right way, in those crude days of our beginnings. We were dealing in things vital in our American life, and not one bit interested in close-ups of empty-headed little ingénues with adenoids, bedroom windows, manhandling of young girls, fast sets, perfumed bathrooms, or nude youths heaving their muscles. Sex, as portrayed in the commercial film of to-day, was noticeable by its absence. But if, to-day, the production of clean and artistic pictures does not induce the dear public to part with the necessary spondulics so that the producer can pay his rent, buy an occasional meal and a new lining for the old winter overcoat, then even Mr. Griffith must give the dear public what it wants. And for the past year or two it has apparently wanted picturizations daring as near as possible the most intimate intimacy of the bedroom.

The season closed with another "Covered Wagon" masterpiece called "Crossing the American Prairies in the Early Fifties." The picture was taken at Topango Canyon. There were hundreds of men and women and cowboys and a hundred horses from ranches near by, as well as eleven prairie schooners.

In the picture, guards had been posted at night, but being tired, they fell asleep, so the Indians pounced upon the emigrants, slaughtering some and taking some prisoners, to be burned at the stake. The few survivors who escaped left numbers of dead pioneers behind. The shifting desert sands would soon cover the bodies and remove all trace of the massacre. The dead bodies were represented by the living bodies of members of the company who had to be buried deep in the alkali waste; and the getting covered up was

Linda Griffith and Mr. Mackay in "Mission Bells," a Kinemacolor picture play taken at San Juan Capistrano.

(*See p. 162*)

A rain effect of early days at Kinemacolor's Los Angeles studio, known a year later as the Fine Arts Studio, where "The Birth of a Nation" and "Intolerance" were filmed. From "The House That Jack Built," with Jack Brammall and Linda Griffith.

going to be a dirty job for the living corpses. So those scenes had to be taken last.

Little grains of sand gently falling upon one from out the property boys' cornucopias, while unpleasant, could be silently endured; but when the property boys got the storm really started and the sand was being poured upon one thick and heavy, getting into hair and ears and eyes, no matter how protective the position one had assumed, there were heard smothered oaths from the dead people that no wild cowboy had ever excelled.

Dell Henderson, dying with little old Christie Miller, was all humped up and writhing in the desert sands. And while Dell was just about to be featured as the far-famed gambler of the West in a line of showy parts, and while he felt that Mr. Griffith had a friendly feeling for him, his ardor for his movie job was beginning to cool. And when, after being extricated from his earthy grave, he found the boss, he lost all restraint.

"Old man," said Dell to David, "this is too much, I quit pictures, I'm through." But the next day when all bathed and barbered up, he felt differently about it.

But Dell hadn't had it as rough as the atmospheric members of the company. Even the wives had been called upon for atmosphere, and were to make up and dress as men. They didn't like the old trousers and the greasy felt hats that were passed out to them, and they weren't keen on being recognized on the screen, in the unflattering costumes.

So Mr. Griffith compromised: "All right, I'll put you in the background and you can sit down." At that the women became more amiable and agreed to help out the perspective.   And in the last few hundred feet of the second reel, they joined the dead emigrants and were covered up in the whirlwind.

The final scenes were reserved for the days immediately preceding our departure for the East.   As soon as they were taken, the company would be dismissed to make the necessary preparations prior to leave-taking.   So to their pet establishment the women beat it to have their hair beautifully and expensively washed and lemon-rinsed, and were all in readiness for the California Limited, when a re-take was announced.   Static in the film!

To their burial places once more they were rushed, and again the boys stood by and again poured the cornucopias of sand over them, ruining completely the crop of nice clean heads.   Few got a chance at another fashionable shampoo. The majority had to be contented with just a home wash— or to take the sand along with them.

CHAPTER XXIV

EMBRYO STARS

WE fell to the lure of the Bret Harte story this winter. We advanced to the romances of the hardy Argonauts, and the "pretty ladies" of the mining towns. What a wealth of picturesque cinema material the lives of the rugged forty-niners afforded!

Dell Henderson was featured as the handsome gambler, *Jack Hamlin;* and Claire MacDowell as the intriguing lady of uncertain virtue; Stephanie Longfellow as the rare, morally excellent wife.

Blanche Sweet was still too much the young girl to interpret or look the part of Bret Harte's halo-ized Magdelenes. Mr. Griffith, as yet unwilling to grant that she had any soul or feeling in her work, was using her in "girl" parts. But he changed his opinion with "The Lonedale Operator." That was the picture in which he first recognized ability in Miss Sweet.

The outdoor life of the West had plumped up the fair Blanche, and Mr. Griffith felt at this stage in her development she typified, excellently well, buxom youth. Why wouldn't Blanche have plumped up when she arrived on location with a bag of cream puffs nearly every day and had her grandmother get up at odd hours of the night to fry her bacon sandwiches? She soon filled out every wrinkle of the home-made looking tweed suit she had worn on her arrival in Los Angeles.

Way, way up on the Santa Monica cliffs we built a log cabin for Blanche Sweet to dwell in, as the heroine of "The White Rose of the Wilds."

The location was so remote, the climb so stiff, that once having made it no one was going down until the day's work was over.

It was a heavenly day. Gazing off into the distances quite sufficed, until, whetted by clean, insistent breezes, little gnawings in the tummy brought one back to realities. It took more than dreamy seas and soft blue skies to deter a hungry actor from expressing himself around lunch time. And so, in querulous accents soon were wafted on the sage-scented air such questions as: "Gee, haven't they sent for the lunch yet? Gosh, I'm hungry. Hasn't the car gone? It'll take a couple of hours to get food way up here. Hope they bring us enough—this air—I'm starved."

Sooner or later lunch would be on the way. The car had to go for it as far as Venice. It was nearly three o'clock when the car returned and by that time every one was dog-gone hungry.

Mr. Griffith had tipped his two "leads" and Mr. Bitzer and myself to get off in a little group, for hot juicy steaks had been ordered for those select few—leading players must be well nourished—and it was just as well to be as quiet and unobtrusive about it as possible. For while it wasn't exactly fair, sandwiches and coffee was all the lunch the company usually afforded for the extra people.

Mack Sennett, who always had a most generous appetite, was wild-eyed by now, for he was just an "extra" in "The White Rose of the Wilds." And he was on to the maneuvers of the "steak" actors and so resentful of the partiality shown that he finally could contain himself no longer, and in bitter tones, subdued though audible, he spoke: "Steaks that way," with a nod of his head indicating Griffith and the leading people, "and sandwiches this way" —himself and the supers. And though Mack sat off on the side, and from his point of vantage continued to throw hungry glances, they brought him no steak that day.

This winter it was that Mr. Sennett invested in a "tux" and went over to the Alexandria Hotel night after night, where he decorated the lobby's leather benches in a determined effort to interest Messrs. Kessel and Bauman. (The Kay Bee Company.) His watchful waiting got him a job.

"The Battle of Elderberry Gulch" was a famous picture of those days. The star was a pioneer baby all of whose relatives had been killed by Indians. During the time the baby's folks were being murdered another party of pioneers, led by Dell Henderson, was dying of thirst near by. With just enough life left in them to do it, they rescued the baby from its dead relations, staggered on a few miles, and then they, too, sank exhausted in the sand and cacti.

Another cornucopia sand-storm blew up.

Kind-hearted Dell Henderson, now sunk to earth, had protectingly tucked the baby's head under his coat. But the tiny baby hand (in the story, and it was good business) had to be pictured waving above the prostrate figures of the defunct pioneers, to show she still lived. Otherwise, she might not have been saved by the second rescuing party, and saved she had to be for the later chapters of the story.

For though in the end of the story the baby became

the lily-white Blanche Sweet, it was, as matter of fact, a tiny, lightly colored, colored baby from a Colored Foundling Home, whom we often used for the photographic value of its black eyes, and Dell must see to it that the tiny pickaninny was in no way hurt, even though he had surreptitiously to wave the baby hand from under his rough outer garments.

Having succeeded so well at Santa Monica, we decided to work other beaches this year.   We became acquainted with them all—Redonda, Long Beach, Venice, and Playa del Rey.

The No. 2 company became especially familiar with the beaches, for they did numbers of bathing pictures.   Frank Powell was still directing the comedies, with Dell Henderson and Mack Sennett occasionally trying their hands at it.

It was in these bathing pictures that Mabel Normand began winning admirers both on the screen and off.   Even Mack Sennett began to take an interest in the beautiful and reckless Mabel, a slim figure in black tights doing dare-devil dives or lovely graceful ones.   Mabel was always ready for any venturesome aquatic stunt.   But her work was equally daring on land, for she thought nothing of riding the wildest bucking broncho bareback.   It took more than bucking bronchos to intimidate the dusky-eyed Mabel.

All of this Sennett was noting—clever kid was Mabel— and if he ever should be a director on his own——!

On the beach by the old Redonda Hotel, which the passing years had changed from a smart winter resort patronized by Easterners to a less stylish summer one patronized by Angelenos, one balmy winter day, some bathing scenes were being taken. This type of stuff was new to me and I was all eyes. Working only with the Griffith company, there were lots of things I didn't see.

But this day there were two companies working on the same location, and that was how I first saw Margaret Loveridge, of lovely Titian hair and fair of face, sporting the most modern black satin bathing suit, and high-heeled French slippers. Imagine, right in the seashore sand!

I was interested in this Loveridge girl, for she was pretty, and had a rather professional air about her.

Sometimes when rehearsing we'd suddenly find ourselves in need of a little two- or three-year-older, which need would be supplied by Mr. Griffith or Mr. Powell or Dell Henderson calling right out at rehearsal: "Who's got a kid?" Margaret Loveridge on one such occasion had replied affirmatively. And so we came to use her small son occasionally; and when Margaret was working and we needed the child, and Margaret couldn't bring it or take care of it, she'd press her little sister into service.

For Miss Loveridge had also a little sister. And it was some such situation that led little sister to the movies and to Redonda at this time.

Little sister was a mite: most pathetic and half-starved she looked in her wispy clothes, with stockings sort of falling down over her shoe-tops. No one paid a particle of attention to the child. But Mr. Griffith popped up from somewhere and spied her, and gave her a smile. The frail, appealing look of her struck him. So he said, "How'd *you* like to work in a picture?"

"Oh, you're just fooling—you mean *me* to work in a picture?"

"Yes, and I'll give you five dollars."

No stage bashfulness in the hanging head, the limp arms, and the funny hop skip of the feet.

"Oh, you couldn't give me five dollars."

"Oh, yes I can."

"You sure you're not fooling?"

"No, you come around some time, and you'll see, I'll put you in a scene.   What's your name?"

"Mae Marsh."

"I'll remember, and I'll put you in a movie some day."

Right about now Dell Henderson was directing a picture in which Fred Mace was playing the lead and Margaret Loveridge had a part.   It was understood about the studio that Mr. Mace was quite taken with the charms of the fair Margaret.   Now Margaret couldn't get out on location, and she wanted to send a message to Fred Mace, so she sent little sister, and little sister looked so terrible to Mr. Mace that he said to her, "Don't let Griffith see you or your sister will lose her job."

When Mace saw Margaret again he said, "Don't have your sister come around the studio looking like that."

And Margaret answered, "Well, I will, for Mr. Griffith is going to use some children at San Gabriel and she is going to be one of the children."

"All right," answered Mace, "take your chance."

And at San Gabriel Mae did a little more of the funny hop skip, and she talked up rather pert to the director, "You think you're the King" sort of thing, and he liked it, and he said to Dell, "The kid can act, she's great, don't you think so?"

Dell answered "yes," but he didn't think so.   No one thought so but Mr. Griffith.

A few weeks later when little Mae Marsh came to the

studio carrying a book and the boys made jokes about it, Dell said to himself, "When she puts that down, I'm a-going to see." The book was Tennyson's poems. The boys knew when a new actress came with such literature that Mr. Griffith was already seeing her bringing home the cows, or portraying some other old-fashioned heroine of the old-fashioned poets.

As intended, our stay in California this second year was much longer than the first. The three months lengthened to five, and it was May when the company returned East.

It did seem a pity to close up the new studio, for it was the last word in organization. Why, we'd even a separate department for finances. The money end of things had grown to such proportions that David could no longer handle it as he had the first year. And Mr. Dougherty was along too, in charge of the front office.

With Mabel Normand and Blanche Sweet well started on their careers, the second winter's work in California ended. Another milestone had been passed, the birth of the two-reeler, which having been tried was not found wanting.

What otherwise came out of the winter's work as most important was Biograph's acquisition of the little hop-skip girl, Mae Marsh. She played no parts this season, made very few appearances even as an insignificant extra girl, and when the company returned to New York they left little Mae behind them.

CHAPTER XXV

MARKING TIME

THE serious students of the motion picture, for they had arrived, were at this time writing many and various articles in the trade papers. Epes Winthrop Sargent was a-saying this:

The Moving Picture World more than advocates the ten cent theatre. It looks forward to the time when the dollar photoplay theatre will be an established institution following the advance in quality of the films. But there will always be five cent theatres in localities that will not support the ten cent houses and ten cent houses for those who cannot afford fifty cents or a dollar. It is the entertainment for the whole family.

And W. Stephen Bush, the reviewer, this, of a Biograph:

"The Battle" is a perfect picture in a splendid frame. I cannot close without a well-deserved word of praise regarding the women's dresses and coiffures of the wartime period. It is in the elaboration of such details that the master hand often betrays itself as it does here to the last chignon on the young girls' heads.

And an unsigned article is headlined:

Will Moving Pictures Save Madison Square Garden?

And the late Louis Reeves Harrison in his "Studio Saunterings" in *The Moving Picture World:*

I did not meet the mighty Griffith until after I had had an opportunity to study some examples of his marvelous work—he is the greatest of them all when he tries—but I found him to be keenly alive to the future possibilities of the new art to which he has so materially contributed. . . . His productions show lofty inspirations mixed with a desire to help the world along, a trend of thought that is poetic, idealistic with a purifying and revivifying influence upon the audience that can best be excited through tragedy.

The inquiry department of magazines published replies of this sort almost every week:

Since the lady is in the Biograph, we premise her name is Jane Doe. 'Tis the best we can do.

Or this:

No, John Bunny is not dead, report to the contrary notwithstanding. Miss Turner, Miss Lawrence, Miss Pickford, Miss Gauntier, and Miss Joyce are all alive, and there have been no funerals for Messrs. Costello, Delaney, Johnson, Moore, or others.

Or this:

Questions about tall, thin girls two years old are barred. Keep up to date.

Or this:

All Biograph players are either John or Jane Doe.

So while Biograph players were still nameless, Vitagraph, Lubin, Kalem, Edison, Essanay, Melies, and Selig not only gave out players' names but offered exhibitors trade photos at twenty cents each, and stereoptican slides of all players. Ambitious actors were getting out postcards with their photos to send the fans.

The flow of Biograph players into the ranks of the Independents left the Biograph Company temporarily weakened. So much so that when "His Daughter" was released in the spring of 1911 a critic said:

The picture has something of the spirit and character of the *old* Biograph stock company's work.

And another speaking for an open market said:

The best argument that I can offer for an open market is the well-known fact that when Biograph was supreme, a mere sign of "Biograph to-day" would draw the crowd. Yes, folks would rather pay a ten cent admission and be satisfied with only two reels as long as there was a Biograph than to visit the neighbor house with three reels and four vaudeville acts and no Biograph. Everybody knows what a magnet was the word "Biograph."

But other good actors were coming to the front and the loss of the old ones made but a brief and shallow dent in the prestige of Biograph. On a June day in 1912 arrived little Gertrude Bambrick. She came on pretty sister Elsie's invitation—just to look. Sister Elsie liked the movies, liked it at Biograph, but to get Gertrude down to the place had required considerable coaxing. Gertrude didn't like the place when she finally got there. "How terrible," said she; "why, they haven't even chairs, what an awful place!" She was almost ready to beat it before she had had a good look around.

A tall, angular man had noticed the pretty little girl, and he kept passing and repassing before her, giving her a searching look each time. Then, one time, when directly in front of her he made an abrupt stop and a significant beckoning of his right forefinger plainly said, "Youngster, I would speak with thee."

But Gertrude paid no attention to the beckoning finger. She only thought what a funny thing for any one to do. If the man wanted to speak to her, why didn't he speak? Sister Elsie gave her a poke and whispered to her secretly that it was the "great Griffith" who was beckoning, and when he beckoned the thing to do was to follow. So, somewhat in a daze, Gertrude started off and as she did so the actors and others in the studio cleared a way for her much as they might for a queen.

Mr. Griffith led the way into the ladies' dressing-room, which, when the actresses were out on the stage, was the only place of privacy in the studio. There his eagle eye scrutinized the girl some more. Gertrude now figured, being in the studio and having no business there, she was in for a call-down, and quick on the defensive she let it be known she was only visiting her sister—she didn't want to work in the pictures—she had a good job as a dancer in vaudeville with Gertrude Hoffman—dancing was what she loved most of all, and, well——

"Well, who are *you?*" asked Gertrude.

"I'm the director down here, I'm Mr. Griffith."

As far as Gertrude was concerned, Mr. Griffith was entirely without honor even in a picture studio.

"So you dance," said he, "and you don't want to work in pictures. Well, come down to-morrow anyhow, I want to make a test of you. And I am going over to-night to see your show."

"Well, all right," said Gertrude with tolerance, "but I must get on home now. I have to have dinner with my family." (If one so young could be bored, Gertrude Bambrick was just that thing.)

"I'll send you home in my car," said Mr. Griffith, which frightened little Gertrude almost to pieces and which would have frightened her more had she known that the car was a gorgeous white Packard lined with red leather. But in she hopped, nevertheless, and when she arrived home, and her mother opened the door, and saw a huge touring car of colors white and red, in the days when any kind of a touring car was a conspicuous vehicle, mother said, "Now don't you ever do that again—come home here in a car like that for all the neighbors to talk about." Gertrude promised she wouldn't.

That evening she went to her show like a good little girl and did her bit, and Mr. Griffith and Eddie Dillon sat out front. To show how much he liked her work, D. W. Griffith's big white touring car next morning, entirely unexpected, drove up again to the Bambrick home. Gertrude had to forego her morning sleep that day—the neighbors must not see that rakish motor car outside the house again any longer than was necessary. "What kind of girls will the neighbors think I have, anyhow?" said Mrs. Bambrick, very much annoyed at the insistent person who had sent the car.

To such extremes Mr. Griffith went to land a new personality—particularly if that personality was so wholly indifferent to him and his movies as Miss Gertie was. But Gertie was pretty and graceful, and pictures were just arriving at the place where it was thought dancing could be photographed fairly well and cabaret scenes might be introduced to liven things up, now that picture production was advancing toward the spectacle.

The next day little Gertrude had her "test" and sat around, and looked on, and felt lonesome, until she suddenly spied an old friend who had been with her in Gertrude Hoffman's dancing chorus. Gertrude called out, "Oh, hello, Sarah." But Sarah Sweet, since become Blanche Sweet, only looked blankly at the new girl. Oh, the fear that

gripped at the possibility of a new rival! Mr. Griffith was
"getting it," and he wasn't going to stand for it, so em-
phatically he spoke, "Blanche, you know Gertie Bambrick,"
at which Blanche capitulated.

"Little Mary" returned to Biograph. From "Imp," in
the fall of 1911 she had gone over to the Majestic, where
she and Owen put in a brief season. Then back to Biograph
she came, but without Owen. He went to Victor with
Florence Lawrence.

Mary Pickford was now so firmly entrenched that she
had no fear of bringing other little girls to the studio. And
so, on her invitation, one day came a-visiting two sisters,
one, decidedly demure; the other, decidedly not. Things
were quiet in the theatre and Mary saw no reason why,
when they could find a ready use for the money, her little
friends shouldn't make five dollars now and then as well
as the other extra people.

Mr. Griffith rather liked the kids that Mary had brought
—they were little and slinky. He liked the elder the better
of the two, she was quiet and reserved. Dorothy was too
forward. She even dared call the big director "a hook-
nosed kike," disregarding completely his pure Welsh descent.

The little Gish sisters looked none too prosperous in
mama's home made dresses.

I'll say for the stage mamas of the little Biograph girls
that they did their bit. Mrs. Smith would sometimes make
her child a new dress overnight, and Mary would walk in
on a bright morning sporting a new pink frock of Hearn's
best gingham, only to make Gertrude Robinson feel so
orphaned, her mama seemingly the only one who had no
acquaintance with a needle.

Lillian and Dorothy Gish just melted right into the

studio atmosphere without causing a ripple. For quite a long time they merely extra-ed in and out of the pictures. Especially Dorothy—Mr. Griffith paid her no attention whatever, and she cried because he wouldn't, but **he** wouldn't, so she just kept on crying and trailed along.

But she let out an awful howl when Gertie Bambrick was put on a guaranty and she wasn't. Their introduction to Biograph had happened the very same day. Lillian didn't mind so much, as she was still full of stage ambitions. When the company left for California, Lillian went back to the stage as a fairy in "The Good Little Devil" with Mary Pickford. Dorothy paid her own fare to the coast. That was how popular she was just then.

It was going to be a "big time" for Gertie Bambrick and Dorothy Gish in Los Angeles, away from home and mothers. They ducked to the Angelus Hotel to be by themselves, and not to be bothered by elders and fuss-budgets. They had an idol they would emulate, and wanted to be alone where they could practice. The idol was Mabel Normand. Could they be like Mabel Normand, well, then they would be satisfied with life. So bright, so merry, so pretty; oh, could they just become like Mabel! Perhaps cigarettes would help. They bought a box. And at a grocery store, they bought—shush—a bottle of gin. Almost they would have swallowed poison if it would have helped them to realize their youthful ambition. But their light had led them only as far as gin, and this they swallowed as a before-dinner cocktail, a whole teaspoonful which they drank right out of the teaspoon.

Yes, Mabel Normand was the most wonderful girl in the world, the most beautiful, and the best sport. Others have thought of Mabel Normand as these two youngsters

A corner of Biograph's stylish Bronx studio. A scene from "The Fair Rebel," with Clara T. Bracey, Linda Griffith, Charles Perley, Dorothy Gish and Charles West. (*See p. 225*)

The beginning of the Griffith régime at 4500 Sunset Boulevard. A tense moment in comedy. From left to right: D. W. Griffith, Teddy Lampson, Mae Marsh, Donald Crisp, W. E. Lawrence and Dorothy Gish.
(See p. 248)

did. Daring, reckless, and generous-hearted to a fault, she was like a frisky young colt that would brook no bridle. The quiet and seemingly demure little thing is the one who generally gets away with things.

The gay life of Dorothy and Gertrude was short-lived. Their first night of revelry on Los Angeles' Gay White Way was their last. Up in their room, the night of arrival, they had planned their evening: dinner in the grill, the movies afterward, the grill again as a finish. They put up their hair, they slipped their skirts to the hip, the jacket just covering the lowered waistline, and the lengthened skirt the legs. So they sallied forth.

Their program was well-nigh fulfilled; they finished with two-thirds of it. As they were leaving Clune's big movie palace they were apprehended by two men, David Griffith and Dell Henderson, who, having been out scouting for the youngsters all evening, were just beginning to get seriously worried over their disappearance.

Mr. Griffith had made Mr. and Mrs. Henderson responsible for the girls, and at his suggestion they had already found an apartment for them, not only in the same house with themselves but on the same floor, and—adjoining. All the fun was gone out of life. This arrangement would be worse than boarding school.

But it got worse still. Sister Lillian, at Mary Pickford's suggestion, decided she'd return to the movies, and so she and mother came on to Los Angeles. That meant Dorothy and Gertrude would be transferred to Mother Gish's care, where their bubbling spirits and love of noisy innocent fun would be frowned upon by the non-approving eyes of the more sober elder sister.

Things became more complicated when Marshall Neilan

began paying ardent attentions to little Gertrude. Marshall had fallen in love with Gertrude from seeing her on the screen, and he told Allan Dwan with whom he had worked at the American Film Company in Santa Barbara that he was going to marry the cute little kid.

In the fall of 1912 the funny little hop-skip girl had arrived on the scene in New York. When he got back to the City, Mr. Griffith had found need for her, and he fussed; and finally Mr. Hammer told him to send for her. Two tickets were accordingly rushed west to Los Angeles, one for Mae and one for Mae's mama. In due time two members of the Marsh family arrived. The day they reached the East the company was working outside at some place with a meaningful name like "Millville," where we took small country-town stuff. The two Marshes were so excited when they got off the train in New York and dashed to the studio at 11 East Fourteenth Street and found the company working outdoors that they departed immediately for "Millville." They must get right on location. So to "location" they hied. And when they had fluttered on to the scene, and Mr. Griffith looked up and saw his Mae, and not his Mae's mama, but the fair Margaret, Mae's sister, he was pretty mad about it.

Margaret Loveridge, as soon as sister Mae's star began to rise in the movie heavens, changed her name to "Marguerite Marsh"; but to her intimates she became "Lovey Marsh."

Little Mae Marsh back on the job, did a lot of extra work before she got a part. Mr. Griffith worked hard with her, especially when a scene called for a sudden transition from tranquillity to terrible alarm. But a bright idea came to him. He had noticed in battle scenes that young Mae became terribly frightened; so when he didn't have war's aid to get the needed expression of fright, without her knowledge he would have a double-barreled shotgun popped off a few feet from her head, and the resultant exhibition of fear would quite satisfy the exacting director.

Mae Marsh's first hit was in "Sands O' Dee," a part that Mary Pickford had been scheduled to play, and there was quite a to-do over the change in cast. But it was the epochal "Man's Genesis" that brought her well to the front, as it did also Bobby Harron. In the parts of *Lilly White* and *Weakhands* their great possibilities were discerned, with no shadow of doubt.

"Man's Genesis" was produced under the title "Primitive Man," and Mr. Griffith and Mr. Dougherty had an awful time because Doc said he couldn't see the title and he couldn't see the story as a serious one—as a comedy, yes! But Mr. Griffith was determined it should be a serious story; and he did it as such, although he changed the animal skin clothing of the actors to clothes made of grasses. For if the picture were to show the accidental discovery of man's first weapon, then the animal skins would have had to be torn off the animal's body by hand, and that was a bit impossible. So Mae and Bobby dressed in grasses knotted into a sort of fabric.

"Man's Genesis" wrote another chapter in picture history. It *was* taken seriously by the public, as was meant, and every picture company started right off on a movie having some version of the beginning of man. For Mr. Griffith it was the biggest thing he had yet done, and one of the most daring steps so far made in picture production.

Again, against great opposition David had put it over, not only on his studio associates, but on the entire motion picture world. Besides "Man's Genesis," our most talked of picture of the winter—our biggest spectacle—was "The Massacre."

It was taken at San Fernando. There were engaged for it several hundred cavalry men and twice as many Indians. A city of tents, as well as the two large ones, similar to the ones of the year before, was built outside the borders of the town.

There was so much preparation, due to the magnitude of the production, that the secrecy usually attending a Biograph picture did not hold in this case, and the village of San Fernando, two miles away from the place of the picture, declared a holiday.

The townspeople having found out just when the raid on the Indian village and the slaughter of the men and women of the tribe was to take place, closed up shop and school, and swarmed out to within a safe distance of the riding and shooting incidental to Custer's Last Fight, and spent the day in the enjoyment of new thrills.

There was a two weeks' fight over a sub-title in "The Massacre"—the scrappers Mr. Griffith and Mr. Dougherty.

David never used a script, and a sub-title never was written until he was convinced that one was necessary to elucidate a situation. A picture finished, at its first running we would watch for places where the meaning seemed not sufficiently clear; where we doubted if the audience would "get" it. And in such a place in the film, a title would be inserted. So "The Massacre" finished, and being projected, this scene was reached:

Horses with riders dashing madly down the foreground, the enemy in pursuit, then the riders dismounting and using the horses as a barricade, shooting over them.

Here arose the disagreement about the sub-title. Mr. Griffith wanted to insert a caption "Dismounting for Defense." Mr. Dougherty said, "The audience will know that is what they are doing." But Mr. Griffith was not so sure about it, so he said: "Now I think, I'd just like to have the title; they may not know what I am trying to show."

"Yes, they will," said Doc.

Even Mr. Kennedy was swept into the debate. As the argument continued his morning greeting became, "Well, are you still at it, you Kilkenny cats?"

The title went in. How it would improve some pictures in these days to have two weeks of conversation over a sub-title. How a good old row with the whole force would perk things up for some directors, for too many of them, poor things, have had their pictures yes-ed to death by the fulsome praise of their assistants; the "yes-sirs" who, grouped in friendly intimacy about their director, have only one answer when he says: "Do you like that scene?"

"Oh, yes, sir, the scene is wonderful."

"Do you like that title?"

"Oh, yes, sir, the title is great."

But that is how the "yes-sirs" hold their jobs!

Before the year 1912 ended, Lionel Barrymore had been acquired. His plunge movie-ward was inauspicious.

"Who's the new man?"

"That's John Barrymore's brother."

"Never heard of him—is he an actor?"

"No, he's an artist, just back from Paris, been studying painting," answered the wise guys.

On the return trip east this winter, a stop-over was made at Albuquerque to secure legitimate backgrounds for some Hopi Indian pictures. One, especially atmospheric, was "A Pueblo Legend" with Mary Pickford.

CHAPTER XXVI

THE OLD DAYS END

IT was being hinted in the spring of 1913 that Biograph was having a change of heart about the secrecy regarding their players, and that they might end it. Contrary to the policy of other companies, their scheme was not to give the popular players the first publicity, but the directors and camera men. D. W. Griffith would thus head the honor list—his name to become identified with a certain class of strong and highly artistic drama; Dell Henderson next—farce comedies; Tony O'Sullivan—melodrama; Billy Bitzer —photography; lastly—the actors.

The Biograph had always held to the policy that they were an "institution," and as such, the value of their pictures did not depend on an individual. Sufficient that it was a "Biograph." Apparently, they now felt they had reached a place so firmly fixed in public esteem through the fine quality of their pictures, that giving credit to individuals could not in any way react on them.

So D. W. Griffith became the first Biograph star. Biograph's policy he afterwards took to himself. He is still the "star" of his productions. His actors continue as "leading people" as long as they stay with him. And when they go on to bigger money and names in bigger type with other companies and under other directors, some succeed and some do not. Mary Pickford was one who did.

In the picture world, especially abroad, big things were now happening. "Quo Vadis," a great spectacle, splendidly acted, had been produced in Italy by the Società Italiana Cines, in three acts of four reels. It came to America and had a run in a Broadway theatre.

From France, this same time, April, 1913, the steamer *La Touraine* arrived in America bringing "Les Misérables" in four sections and twelve reels.

"The Miracle," which Morris Gest presented in the year of 1924 in the Century Theatre, New York, as a pantomime, had been filmed by Joseph Mencher and was shown at the Park Theatre, New York, in February, 1913. It was a "filmed pantomime" (not a moving picture drama), based on the Wordless Mystery Play which, under the direction of Max Reinhardt, had had a wonderful run at the Olympic, London.

A reviewer said of it:

> What was seen and heard last night only went to emphasize that the moving picture under certain conditions, conditions like those that prevailed last night, may be capable of providing entertainment to be taken seriously by audiences which have never seen the inside of an electric theatre.

Eugene Sue's "Wandering Jew" came over, the work of the Roma Film Company.

In our own country, Helen Gardner in her own productions was appearing as *Cleopatra* and like characters.

The Vitagraph started on a trip around the world with Clara Kimball Young to do a picture in each country visited, but that rather fell by the wayside; Miss Young, however, had somewhat contented herself with having charming "still" photos taken in costume in each country on their route; when the company reached Paris, Vitagraph cabled for the actors to come home.

Kalem had already made some beautiful pictures in Ireland, and in Egypt had made "From the Manger to the Cross," under Sidney Olcott.

Vitagraph answered an inquiry as to when they made "Macbeth" by saying they "made it so long ago they wanted to forget it in these days (1913) of high art production."

Keystone Comedies were coming along, directed by Mack Sennett, featuring the two famous detectives, Mack Sennett and Fred Mace. In these comedies Mabel Normand began to daredevil. Henry Lehrman joined Sennett.

Hal Reid, Wally Reid's father, was directing Reliance pictures.

"Traffic in Souls," written by Walter McNamara and directed by George Loane Tucker, opened at Weber's Theatre, Twenty-ninth Street and Broadway, at twenty-five cents the seat. People clamored for admission, with thousands turned away.

So Biograph, concluding to get into the march of things, ordered posters for twelve of their players whose names they would make public.

"David Belasco Griffith" became Mr. Griffith's nom-de-moving-pictures. It was a time of tremendous ambitions to him. In California, during that winter, was filmed his "masterpiece"—"Mother Love"—seven hundred feet over one reel. Mr. Griffith refused to have it the conventional length, refused to finish it in a stated time, refused to consider expense, introducing a lavish cabaret scene, costing eighteen hundred dollars exclusive of salaries. Miss Bambrick arranged the dances and coached the dancers.

Mr. Griffith said of it, "If it serves no other use, it will teach café managers in the interior how to run a café."

There was also "Oil and Water" in which Blanche Sweet surprised both exhibitors and fans by her splendid work in an unfamiliar rôle. It was strange that the one woman in whom Mr. Griffith had seen the least promise came to play the most important rôles in his Biograph pictures. Strange also that Mary Pickford, who had played in so many more pictures than any of his stars, and was by far the most popular of them all, never played in a big Griffith picture.

Before the end of the season, much curiosity was abroad as to what David Griffith was up to. Way out to the wilds of Chatsworth he was beating it day by day—this remote spot having been chosen to represent the Plains of Bethulia. For the story told in a book of the Apocrypha of Judith and Holofernes was the big thing Mr. Griffith was doing, and being so secretive about it, he had aroused everybody's curiosity.

Blanche Sweet played the lead in this picture—"Judith of Bethulia"—Mr. Griffith's most pretentious movie so far, and his "Old Biograph" swan song. Henry Walthall and the late Alfred Paget were the male leads.

How hard and how patiently the director worked with the temperamental Miss Sweet. For hours one day he had been trying to get some feeling, some warmth out of her, until the utter lack of response got his goat. So with bended knee he went after the fair lady and he gently but firmly kicked her off the stage—just politely kneed her off. Then, as was his wont, he burst forth in song, apparently oblivious of the situation.

It was now Blanche's turn to worry. She backed up

on to the stage and over to her discouraged director. He escaped her—stretching his arms and singing louder than ever he took large strides away from her. Finally, the penitent reached him, and on her bended knees begged: "Please, Mr. Griffith, please take me back." When he thought she had begged hard enough he took her back, and he got results for the rest of that day.

"Judith," owing to expensive sets, cost thirty-two thousand dollars, but that was not advertised as a point of interest in the picture. Much excitement prevailed over "Judith," D. W. Griffith's first four-reeler. It was shown to financiers. Wall Street was to be brought into intimate conversation.

The old days and the old ways of 11 East Fourteenth Street, how brief they had been! Those vital Biograph days under the Griffith régime, how soon to pass! For when, late in the winter of 1912, the company left for the West coast studio, they said good-bye to the nursery, and to the intimate days and the pleasant hours of their movie youth.

The big new studio up in the Bronx was now finished, with two huge stages—one artificially lighted, and one a daylight studio. There was every modern convenience but an elevator. Of course, one director couldn't utilize so much studio; so while Mr. Griffith was still in California and without saying anything to him about it, the Biograph made a combine with Klaw & Erlanger by which all the K. & E. plays were to be turned over for Biograph production in three-, four-, and five-reel pictures.

Mr. Griffith didn't fancy the idea; he felt also that Biograph might have consulted him before closing the deal.

There was nothing to interest David in supervising other directors' movies or in giving them the "once over" in the projection room. After watching the other fellow's picture for a while, even though he'd be considering it very good work, he'd yawn and declare, "Well, it's a hell of a way to earn a living." But that slant never occurred to him when watching his own pictures.

But a growing restlessness was noticeable; threats to leave were in the air; rumors floated all about.

However, he lingered through the summer, a busy one, as in those introductory months the new studio had to be got thoroughly into a moving and functioning affair.

Among the many to whom it gave opportunities was Marshall Neilan. For his years young Mr. Neilan hadn't missed much. At the age of fourteen he had run away from Los Angeles, his home, to Buffalo. There he washed cars for a living—which he probably didn't mind much, for it enabled him to satisfy somewhat his fascination for mechanics. Then, back in Los Angeles once more, he got a job as chauffeur for a kindly person, a Colonel Peyton, who also sent him to the Harvard school in Los Angeles.

From chauffing to the movies was then but a natural step. For Marshall, a nice-looking Irish boy with Irish affability, soon had a "stand" at the Van Nuys hotel, which was a wonderful way to meet the movie people. Alice Joyce it was who enveigled him. She kept asking him, "Why don't you come on in?" It was just like an invitation to go swimming. So he took the plunge via Kalem, but not until after he had become manager of the Simplex Automobile Company in Los Angeles.

When the Biograph Company returned East after that winter in which young Neilan had met his heart's desire, he wrote to New York to ask Mr. Griffith for a job. Mr. Griffith asked Miss Bambrick if it was her wish to have Marshall come on, but Gertrude wasn't so anxious. David had him come just the same.

The K. and E. pictures, especially "Men and Women" and "Classmates," gave Marshall Neilan his big chance. He soon fell into the producing ranks, where recognition came quickly.

And he married his Gertrude. Marshall Neilan, Jr., is now nine years old. But they didn't live happily forever after. Many years ago they parted. Just recently Mr. Neilan married Blanche Sweet.

By fall, with four and five companies working, there were so many actors that it wasn't interesting at all any more. There was Millicent Evans and Georgie O'Ramey, Louise Vale, Travers Vale, Louise Orth, Jack Mulhal, Thomas Jefferson, Lionel Barrymore, Franklin Ritchie, Lily Cahill, Donald Crisp, Dorothy Bernard, Edwin August, Alan Hale, William Jefferson—oh, slews and slews of new ones, besides the old guard minus Mary Pickford.

From Chatsworth's lonely stretches and prehistoric atmosphere to the spic-and-span-ness, and atmosphere-less Bronx studio came "Judith of Bethulia" to receive its finishing touches. "Judith" was about the last of Blanche Sweet in anything as pretentious directed by Mr. Griffith.

Mae Marsh was coming along and so was Lillian Gish. Lillian was beginning to step some, and it was interesting to watch the rather friendly rivalry between the three, Blanche, and Mae, and Lillian.

Dorothy Gish was still a person of insignificance, but she was a good sport about it; a likable kid, a bit too perky to interest the big director, so her talents blushed unnoticed by Mr. Griffith. In "The Unseen Enemy" the sisters made their first joint appearance.

Lillian regarded Dorothy with all the superior airs and graces of her rank. At a rehearsal of "The Wife," of Belasco and De Mille fame, in which picture I played the lead, and Dorothy the ingénue, Lillian was one day an interested spectator. She was watching intently, for Dorothy had had so few opportunities, and now was doing so well, Lillian was unable to contain her surprise, and as she left the scene she said: "Why, Dorothy is good; she's almost as good as I am."

Many more than myself thought Dorothy was better— for she was that rare thing, a comedienne, and comediennes in the movies have been scarcer than hen's teeth. She proved what she could do when she got her first real chance as the bob-haired midinette in "Hearts of the World."

Four or five companies working on the big stage these days made things hum like a three-ring circus. From the dressing-rooms a balcony opened that looked down on the studio floor, and here Blanche Sweet could often be seen, her feet poked through the iron rails of the balcony, her elbows resting on the railing, her chin cupped in the hollow of her hands, her eyes bulging as she watched every move the director made. For Blanche was worried. Would Lillian or Mae be chosen to play in the next big picture?

Mr. Griffith kept all the girls worried. All but Mary Pickford. She was the only one who dared demand. With Mother, Mary came up to the new studio to see what she could put over in the way of a job. She'd now a legitimate reason for making herself costly. In January, 1913, Miss Pickford made a second appearance on the dramatic stage

under David Belasco's wing.   On her opening, the papers
said that the success of Miss Pickford as the little blind
princess was so marked that it practically precluded her
return to the screen.

Adolph Zukor had followed up his first Famous Players
picture, the four-reel "Queen Elizabeth" with James K.
Hackett in "The Prisoner of Zenda" and Mrs. Fiske in
"Leah Kleschna."   Astute business man that he was, as
soon as "The Good Little Devil" closed, he secured the play
for the screen with the dramatic company intact and Mary
as a Famous Player.

No, her dramatic success would not preclude her return
to the screen.   It would merely fortify her with great assurance in making her next picture contract.   I am told it
happened thus:

Mother and Mary bearded the lion in his den.

"Well, what are you asking now?" queried Mr. Griffith.

"Five hundred a week," answered Mrs. Smith.

"Can't see it.   Mary's not worth it to me."

"Well, we've been offered five hundred dollars a week
and we're going to accept the contract, and you'll be sorry
some day."

They could go ahead and accept the contract as far as
Mr. Griffith was concerned.   Indulging in his old habit of
walking away while talking, he brought the interview to
an end, calling back to the insistent mother, "Three hundred
dollars is all I'll give her.   Remember, I made her."

And so the Famous Players secured Mary Pickford for
a series of features, the first of which was "In the Bishop's
Carriage."

But whether Mr. Griffith has ever been sorry, nobody
knows but himself.

Kate Bruce, the saintly "Brucie" to so many, pillowed in her lap or on her shoulder by turns, all the feminine heads of sufficient importance, and at times, with her arm about me, it was even "Oh, dear Mrs. Griffith." But Miss Bruce was thoughtful, indeed, for her little room often made night lodging, when we had an early morning call, for the girl whose home was distant. Dorothy West, who lived in Staten Island, often accepted Miss Bruce's hospitality.

For Lillian Gish, "Brucie" had an especially tender heart. Miss Gish, at this time, affected simple, straight, dark blue and black dresses. She had long ago reached the book-carrying stage, being one of Mr. Griffith's most ambitious girls. Many times she'd arrive at the studio an hour or more ahead of time and have Billy Bitzer make tests of her with different make-ups.

With a tight little hat on her head, and a red rose on the side of it from which flowed veils and veils, and a soulful expression in her eyes, Miss Gish was even then, so long ago, affecting the Madonna.

But reclining in the arms of "Brucie," purring "Brucie, do you still love me?"—that was the perfect picture of the fair Lillian those days. And Brucie's reply came in honeyed words, "Oh, you sweet, little innocent golden-haired darling." Then turning to the girl sitting next her on the other side, she'd say, "You know this girl needs to be protected from the world, she's so innocent and so young." She had a strong maternal complex, had the maidenly Kate Bruce.

In need of a gown for a picture at this time (the Biograph was just beginning to spend a little money on clothes

Blanche Sweet and Kate Bruce in "Judith of Bethulia," the first four-reel picture directed by D. W. Griffith. (*See p. 224*)

Lillian Russell and Gaston Bell, in a scene illustrative of her beauty lectures, taken in Kinemacolor. These lectures were a headline act in vaudeville. (*See p. 247*)

Sarah Bernhardt, the first "Famous Player," as Jeanne Doré, and little Jacques. (*See p. 105*)

for the women), Miss Gish spied Louise Orth one day wearing just the very thing her little heart craved.

"Oh, what a lovely gown you have on. Where did you buy that?"

Madame Frances then had a tiny shop on Seventh Avenue, near the Palace Theatre: Polly Heyman had Bon Marché gloves on one side and Frances had gowns on the other. Frances had just made some thousands of dollars' worth of gowns for Valeska Surratt's show, "The Red Rose," which were so beautiful they won Mme. Frances prestige and recognition from Al Woods. Miss Orth had been a member of the Eltinge show for which Mme. Frances had made the dresses, which is the long story of how Lillian Gish got her first Frances gown.

The K. & E. pictures were going to be "dressed up," and we were being allowed about seventy-five dollars for gowns. Miss Gish's selection at Mme. Frances's was price-tagged eighty-five dollars; so back to the studio flew Miss Gish. With as much pep as she had, which wasn't so much, she slunk up to her director and coaxingly said:

"Mr. Griffith, I must have that dress, it's just beautiful; it's just what I must have for the part, and it costs eighty-five dollars."

"Who in the world ever heard of eighty-five dollars for a dress?"

"I don't care—now—I've *got* to have it."

"Don't bother me—it's too expensive—we cannot afford it."

Then growing bolder, as she followed him about she reached for his coat-tail, and twisting it and shaking it she implored:

"Oh, please, Mr. Griffith, buy me that dress."

"Will you get away?"

"Well, I won't play in the picture if you don't get me that dress—I've *got* to have it."

"All right, for heaven's sake, get the dress—but don't bother me."

Lillian got the dress.

Occasionally, Miss Gish took advantage of a beauty sleep. On such occasions she seldom arrived before eleven in the morning. And when she went to a party she played the rôle of the sphinx, and all evening long never spoke. But little Mae Marsh made up for her; she chattered incessantly.

Lillian's dope was to come and go without being noticed. She appeared one time at a midnight performance of "Shuffle Along" done up in black veils to the tip of her nose and a fur collar covering her mouth, with only little spots of cheek showing. Dorothy, on the other hand, acting like a real human being, was calling out to her friends, "Hello there, hello, hello," but Lillian, passing an old acquaintance, merely said, "Forgive me for not stopping and speaking; I don't want any one to know I am here." But as everybody was awfully busy having a good time and no one seemed to be particularly disturbed by Miss Gish's hiding away, she finally took her hat off and revealed herself.

But she came out of her seclusion that time she preached in answer to the Rev. John Roach Straton at his church on Fifty-seventh Street. Some one was needed to answer the Rev. Mr. Straton's knocks on the theatre and its people. Lillian came forward, and she so impressed her brother-in-law, James Rennie, Dorothy's husband, that he arrived late at a Sunday rehearsal of a George Cohan show. In perfect Sunday morning outfit, striped pants and gloves and cane he burst upon the rehearsal and quite breathlessly spluttered, "Please forgive me for being late, but I have just heard my sister-in-law preach a sermon, and never in my life have I heard anything so inspiring in a church. Don't go very often. More in Lillian than one suspects."

Mr. Cohan gave himself time to digest Mr. Rennie's outburst, and then went on with the rehearsal.

Inevitable the parting of the ways. Though the last word as to modern equipment, the new studio merely chilled. That atmosphere of an old manse that had prevailed at 11 East Fourteenth Street, did not abide in the concrete and perfect plumbing and office-like dressing rooms at East 175th Street. The last word in motion picture studios brought Biograph no luck. For as a producing unit, after a few short years they breathed their last, and quietly passed out of the picture. When the doors at the old studio closed on our early struggles, when Biograph left its original nursery of genius, was the proper time for Mr. Griffith to have left the company. In the fall, less than a year later, he did.

CHAPTER XXVII

SOMEWHAT DIGRESSIVE

FROM the old Biograph Stock Company they graduated, scenario writers as well as actors; and here and there they went, filling bigger jobs in other companies, as actors, directors, and scenario editors.

And as manager and head director of the Kinemacolor Company went David Miles. Directly upon leaving Biograph, Mr. Miles had spent a short time at the "Imp" with Mary Pickford and her family, King Baggott, George Loane Tucker, Gaston Bell, Isabel Rea, and Tom Ince. Leaving "Imp," he had gone over to Reliance. While at Reliance, and in need of a handsome young juvenile, there came to mind his friend Gaston Bell.

Mr. Bell already was signed up for a ten weeks' stock season in Washington, D. C.; with "Caught in the Rain" by William Collier and Grant Stewart, as the opening bill; Julia Dean, the leading lady; Mr. Bell's part that of the dapper Englishman, the Grant Stewart part. Mr. Miles suggested that Gaston play the needed juvenile in the Reliance Company's movie while rehearsing the opening bill of his Washington stock season in New York, and promised a good movie job when the Washington season ended. Said he'd rush him through at odd hours, so as not to interfere with rehearsals, and finish with him in time for the opening.

Well, everything went along fine, and for the last scene

Gaston reported beautifully arrayed in a new spring suit purchased especially for his stock opening.

Suavely spoke the director, "Now, Gaston, we have saved this scene for the finish—we must take you out somewhere and run you over."

"Take-me-out-and-run-me-over?—in my beautiful new suit? Oh, no, you can't."

But no one heeded Gaston's distress.

Everybody piled in the automobile—after a couple of turns it landed on a quiet street. "All out." The car emptied—camera was soon set up and Mr. Bell shown the place where he was to be run over.

These were amateur days in fake auto killings and injuries, but they did the "running over" to the director's satisfaction and Gaston's, as he escaped with no damage to his clothes or himself.

But Gaston had reckoned without a thought of static. How many hours of anguish "static" caused us—static, those jiggly white lines that sometimes danced and sometimes rained all over the film. Early next morning his 'phone rang—Mr. Miles on the wire. "Awfully sorry, Gaston, but we'll have to take you out and run you over again because there was static." So they did it again, and again was Gaston dismissed as finished. It came close on to train time: another 'phone—ye gods, static again! He'd be bumped from juvenility to old age in this one running-over scene, first thing he knew, and hobble onto the stage with cane and crutch, which would never do for his precious little Englishman in "Caught in the Rain."

Well, they ran him over again. This was Saturday. The following Sunday the company was to leave for Washington. Thinking to cinch things, Mr. Miles offered, should anything be wrong with the scene this last time, to pay Mr. Bell's fare to Washington and his expenses if he would stay in New York over Sunday. "Wildly extravagant, these picture people," thought Mr. Bell, as he departed for Washington with the company.

But no sooner was he nicely settled in his hotel, "static" and "being run over" quite forgotten, and all set for his opening—when a long distance came. Mr. Miles on the wire: "Awfully sorry, Gaston, but there was more static and we will have to take you out and run you over again." And before Gaston had time to recover from the shock, the movie director and his camera man were right there in Washington!

"Good night," said Gaston, despairingly, to himself. But to Mr. Miles he said, "Now I'll tell you what you have to do, you must have another actor handy to go on for me to-night, for I cannot take any more chances."

Well, they took the scene another time, ruining neither Mr. Bell nor his grand new suit, and as this time the scene was static-less, the day was saved for Gaston. But "never again" vowed he. And "never again" vowed the director.

David Miles kept good his promise and when Gaston's season in Washington closed, he joined Reliance. There he and George Loane Tucker soon became known as the "Hall Room Boys." For in an old brownstone they shared a third floor back—also a dress suit. And if both boys happened to be going out into society the same night, whoever arrived home first and got himself washed up and brushed up first, had the option on that one tuxedo.

The hall-room days of George Loane Tucker were brief. "Traffic in Souls," the white-slave picture that he produced for Universal, put him over. An unhappy loss to the motion picture world was Mr. Tucker's early death; for that truly great picture, "The Miracle Man," his tribute to the world's motion picture library *de luxe,* promised a career of great brilliance.

Mr. Tucker had come rightfully by his great talent, for his mother, Ethel Tucker, was an actress of note and a clever stage director also. As leading woman in stock repertoire at Lathrop's Grand Dime Theatre of Boston, she had a tremendous popularity in her time. And long years afterward, she too went into "the pictures" in Hollywood, for a very brief period.

Mr. Tucker's "Miracle Man" brought stardom to its three leading players, Lon Chaney, Betty Compson, and Tommy Meighan.

Tommy Meighan's leap to fame was surprising to both friends and family. For Tommy had been considered, not exactly the black sheep of the family, but rather the ne'er-do-well. During the run of "Get-Rich-Quick Wallingford," both being members of the cast, Frances Ring, sister to the lustrous Blanche of "Rings on My Fingers" and "In the Good Old Summertime" fame, had married Mr. Meighan, Tommy becoming through this matrimonial alliance the least important member of the Ring family of three clever sisters, Blanche, Frances, and Julie. An obscure little Irishman, Tommy trailed along, with a voice that might not have taken him so very far on the dramatic stage.

Like weaving in and out the paper strips of our kindergarten mats is the story of the Ring sisters and Tommy. For Los Angeles beckoned, with Blanche headlined at the Orpheum, Frances in stock, and Tommy playing somewhere or other.

Blanche and her husband, Charles Winninger, a member

of her company, were invited by Louise Orth for a week-end out Las Palmas way. The week-end proved very significant in results; for through their hostess, who was leading woman at the Elko Studios, a meeting between Mr. Winninger and Mr. Lehrman was arranged the next week which led directly to Charlie's signing on the dotted line at the fabulous salary of two hundred and fifty dollars a week—to do comedies. But Charlie's pale blue eyes did not register well enough on the screen, and the comedy note in his characterizations thus being lost, the good job just naturally petered out.

Then Miss Ring, who had now taken over one of Los Angeles's show places, on the Fourth of July gave a party —a red, white, and blue party at which were gathered more notables than had as yet ever been brought together at a social function in Los Angeles. It was Broadway transplanted. There were David Belasco, Laura Hope Crews, Charlie Chaplin, Edna Purviance, Julian Eltinge, Geraldine Farrar, Jesse Lasky, Mr. Goldwyn, Wallace and Mrs. Reid, Mr. Morris Gest, then representative for Geraldine Farrar and Raymond Hitchcock, who viewing from the back piazza the distant lights of Los Angeles was supposed to have said something when he remarked, "This reminds one of a diamond bar pin."

It was an illustrious and patriotic party. Before the festivities were over, Mr. Gest unwound the maline scarf from Miss Orth's neck while Charlie Chaplin sang the Spring Song, and Mr. Gest danced on the lawn waving the scarf and crushing the slimy snails that in droves were slowly creeping up to the house.

The party was illustrious in that it was here voted that Tommy Meighan would photograph well in pictures, and

Mr. Lasky invited him to the studio and offered him, perhaps, fifty dollars a week, and he made a hit in his first picture with Geraldine Farrar and was then given a substantial raise. At which Blanche, the astounded sister-in-law said, "And to think that at times I've had to support that Irishman." There had been enough job uncertainty to discourage her, so that she had wondered sometimes whether she would have him on her hands for the rest of her life. Even after Mr. Tommy Meighan's advent into pictures, sister Blanche rather expected, every now and then, than he would be "canned."

And so Tommy evolved from a liability into an asset, and became the idol of innumerable feminine hearts. It was a colorful paper mat the Ring family wove.

While out at the Elko studio Charlie Winninger, with all his brilliant and sustaining background, had so disastrously flopped, at Mack Sennett's studio another Charlie was very busy thinking out stunts that would make people laugh. For the more people laughed, the more dollars could Charlie Chaplin add to the savings for the rainy day, against which, if he ever got the chance, he would make himself fool-proof.

For, so I have been told, Charlie Chaplin had known rainy days even when a youngster. He was only seven when, in a music-hall sketch, he made his first theatrical appearance. Later, he toured for some time through the United Kingdom as one of the "Eight Lancashire Lads." There was an engagement with "Sherlock Holmes," and then the association with Fred Karno in "The Mumming Birds." To America with Mr. Karno he came, appearing as *Charlot* in the now famous "A Night in an English

Music-hall." When he debarked he was far from being the richest man on the boat.

The movies claimed him. He was discovered by Mack Sennett in this way. Mr. Sennett at this time was busy on the lot out in Los Angeles. He heard of a funny man in an act called "A Night in an English Music-hall" playing at Hammerstein's Victoria Theatre, which used to stand at Broadway and Forty-second Street, now replaced by the Rialto Motion Picture House. Mr. Adam Kessel and Mr. Bauman, the firm for whom Mack Sennett had nightly warmed the Alexandria's leather benches in the hope of landing a job, and for whom he was now producing comedies, were both in California, and so in September, 1913, a wire was sent to Charles Kessel, brother of Adam, to go over to Hammerstein's and get a report on the comedian about whom Mr. Sennett was so anxious.

Mr. Charles Kessel, the secretary of the company, heartily approved of the comedian, who was none other than Charlie Chaplin. He thought so well of him that he sent a letter asking Chaplin to come in and see him. This Mr. Chaplin did. Mr. Kessel asked him how'd he like to go into moving pictures. Mr. Chaplin answered that he had never given them any thought.

Said Mr. Kessel: "I've seen you act and like you, but you needn't make any assertions now, nor any answers, but go out and make inquiries as to Kessel and Bauman and if you think well enough of them, well then we'll talk."

Mr. Chaplin found out that the firm was O. K. So Mr. Kessel said: "I'll give you a contract for a year and gamble with you—I'll give you the same salary that you're getting on the stage."

"One hundred and fifty dollars," said Mr. Chaplin

quickly. He really was getting sixty dollars. "All right," said Mr. Kessel so quickly that Charles as quickly swallowed his Adam's apple, and regretted he hadn't said more.

"But I don't think I care to change from the stage to the pictures."

"Well, our contracts are for fifty-two weeks, no Sunday work, no intermissions between pictures; in vaudeville you get thirty-two weeks and you pay your own traveling expenses."

Mr. Chaplin said he'd make up his mind and let Mr. Kessel know.

So in about six weeks a letter came from Mr. Chaplin from Omaha saying he was ready to start. The contract was mailed December 19, 1913, and signed January 2, 1914.

"Mabel's Predicament," a one-reeler, was Charlie Chaplin's first picture. "Dough and Dynamite" the first two-reeler. Mr. Chaplin's success was instantaneous. It also must have been tremendous, for the Keystone Company (Kessel and Bauman) within five months dared to do a comedy five reels in length. When the five-reel comedy was announced, there were many who thought that now surely the picture people were going cuckoo. No one believed an audience would stand for a *five-reel comedy*.

They did. The picture was "Tillie's Punctured Romance," adapted from the Marie Dressler play, "Tillie's Nightmare." Marie Dressler was engaged for the picture and for fourteen weeks she received the unbelievable salary of one thousand dollars weekly and fifty per cent of the picture, which, released in June, 1914, was one of the sensations of the picture world.

All sorts of offers now began coming to Mr. Chaplin. Carl Laemmle was one who was keen to get Charlie under contract; he kept himself informed of Mr. Chaplin's activities even to the social side of his life so that he would know when and where best to set the bait.

Out at Sunset Inn, a place by the ocean where movie people then made merry, Charlie Chaplin was to be one of a party. Mr. Laemmle being wised up to it, gave a party of his own the same night, a most expensive and grand party. Well, he would have Charlie's ear for a moment anyhow, and one never could tell.

The party in full swing, Mr. Laemmle invited Mr. Chaplin over to his table, and after a few social preliminaries said, "Let's talk business; I want you to come and work for me." But Mr. Chaplin, always a clever business man, answered, "I'm enjoying myself—I don't want to talk business to-night, I'm on a party."

Mr. Laemmle was all set to secure the services of the rising young comedian, so he would not be daunted. Charles could talk "party," but *he* would talk "business"; Mr. Laemmle offered a little better salary; promised to advertise Chaplin big, and make him a tremendous star.

But Mr. Chaplin was too clever for Mr. Laemmle. With a most sweet smile he turned to one of Mr. Laemmle's guests, Louise Orth of the corn yellow hair, and said, "Gee, that's great music; I like blonds, and I am going to dance with a blond, may I?"

It *was* great music, about the first syncopated music with a saxophone heard in that neck of the woods. There was a great horn into which the dancers, if they desired an encore, threw a silver dollar. There needed to be five particularly anxious dancers to get the expensive orchestra to repeat an orchestration. The dollars clicked down the horn into a sort of tin bucket on the floor below, and the loud jangle of the silver money could be easily heard by the dancers who would listen attentively for jangle number five, and then "On with the dance."

As the music finished for the first dance this night, the dancers stopped and with much excitement waited for the click of the silver dollars. Charlie Chaplin was out for a big time; also he wanted to worry Mr. Laemmle, and, one thing sure, he was not going to talk business this night. So he was the first to say, "This dance is worth an encore," and he threw a silver dollar into the horn.

It was perhaps the first time Mr. Chaplin had been known to spend money in public either for food or music, for every one was so tickled and flattered to have him as a guest that he never was given a chance to spend money. So Charlie's Chaplin's silver dollar nearly caused a riot on that dance floor. The guests hooted and screamed and those who knew him well enough and had been given stray bits of confidence, called out, "You cannot plant your first dollar now because you've spent it." And Mr. Chaplin answered, "Oh, don't you worry, I planted my first dollar some time ago."

Mr. Chaplin could never squander money; memories of lean days inhibited him from doing that. But he must hold off Mr. Laemmle; and he was enjoying the dance.

Two other dollars had joined Charlie Chaplin's first one, and clicked their way down the yawning chasm of the brass horn, and then a pause, but just for a second. Grabbing his blond partner, Mr. Chaplin threw the two needed dollars into the horn's hungry maw, and the moaning saxaphone started off again while Mr. Laemmle looked sadly on. He never did secure the screen's greatest funny man.

In six months Charlie Chaplin's rise to fame and fortune was phenomenal. Not only had a kind Providence richly endowed him, but he worked very hard, as genius usually does. Even back in those days, Mr. Chaplin often began his day making excursions with the milkman. From the cold gray morning hours of three and four until seven, the two would ramble through the poor districts, and while the milkman would be depositing his bottle of milk, Mr. Chaplin would hobnob with drunks and derelicts, and in the later hours, talk with the little children of the slums, drawing out a story here, getting a new character there, and making the tragic humorous when finally the story was given life on the screen. The story of "The Kid" as Mr. Chaplin and Jackie Coogan told it, was nearer the truth than any audience ever guessed.

The ups and downs of the movie world!

Mack Sennett all dressed up and grouching on a leather settee in the hotel lobby, waiting for his prey! He would not be handed dry, old sandwiches all his days. He was out for steak, red and juicy. He got there and has stayed put.

Henry Lehrman patting his inflated chest! He got there, but stayed put the littlest while.

Charlie Chaplin, who topped them all, working while others slept, out on excursions with the milkman!

Tommy Meighan of the genial smile and Irish red-bloodedness. He got a chance, and the ladies liked him. Nice personality, and good actor, even so.

Not alone in the movies is it easier to get there than to stay there. Chance sometimes enters into the first, but to stay there means ears attuned, feet on the ground, and heaps and heaps of hard work.

CHAPTER XXVIII

"THE BIRTH OF A NATION"

L ATE in the summer of 1912 the Kinemacolor Company
of America, a subsidiary of the English company,
started the production of movies in color at a studio in
Whitestone, Long Island. The year of Kinemacolor's
endeavor also marks Mr Griffith's last year with Biograph,
for he went to the Mutual with Harry Aitken while I became leading woman with the Kinemacolor.

Messrs. Urban and Smith had rather startled the world
with their color pictures of the Coronation of George the
Fifth of England, and the Durbar Imperial at Delhi; and
even though their pictures were a bit fringy, they were
becoming ambitious for honors in color movies along
dramatic lines.

Great things were achieved in America in the movies,
and great things might have been achieved in America in
Kinemacolor, but it was destined otherwise. Kinemacolor
was fated to be but a brief though fruitful interlude in
color-photography in the movies, which, for some seemingly
mysterious reason, is so long in arriving.

Sunshine being imperative for Kinemacolor, southern
California's staple brand could not be denied, and soon the
company left its studio in Whitestone and repaired to the
modest little town of Hollywood where it took over the
Revier Laboratories at 4500 Sunset Boulevard.

That the place had been used as a studio was not discernible from the front. It was a pretty corner on which, some distance apart, stood two simple cottages, Middle Western in character. They represented office and laboratory. Dressing-rooms and stages of a crudeness comparable to the orginal Biograph studio were at the back.

No fence gave privacy from passers-by, but a high board fence, decorated with pictures of foxes and the words "Fox Pictures," protected the lot in the rear. It was not the William Fox of to-day who thus sought to advertise his trademark and his wares. Another Mr. Fox it was of whom we seem to hear nothing these days.

Here Kinemacolor moved in, with David Miles at its head, Jack Le Saint director of the No. 2 company, and our old friend Frank Woods making his movie-directing début as teacher to the actors of the No. 3 company. For Mr. Woods having tasted movie blood through his little Biograph scenarios and his position as chief reviewer of the movies, had grown anxious to plunge more deeply into the swiftly moving waters of reel life. So Mr. Miles opened the way for him. And although Kinemacolor opened up financially to a salary of only seventy-five dollars a week, the Woodses made the most of it, for from that humble beginning in less than ten years they have come to own a town near Barstow, California. They have named it "Lenwood." Charles H. Fleming, who was assistant to David Miles, afterwards became a director and tastefully executed a number of pictures.

When the Kinemacolor Company was gathering in what youth and looks and talent it could afford, Mr. Miles, remembering a little deed of kindness, recalled Gaston Bell and took him to Hollywood, and when the much-loved and generous-souled Lillian Russell came out to do some pictures in Kinemacolor, Mr. Bell was rewarded by being made her leading man. Mahlon Hamilton loaned his good looks to the same films. The Russell pictures were used to illustrate "Beauty Talks" in an act in which Miss Russell was headlined on big vaudeville time throughout the United States.

Mahlon Hamilton and Gaston were the company's two best "lookers." As to "acting," Mahlon made not a single pretense. He and the company quite agreed as to his dramatic ability. To be so perfectly Charles Dana-ish, and histronic also, was not expected of one man in those days. We had not reached the Valentino or Neil Hamilton age. Mr. Mahlon Hamilton, of late, not quite so Gibsonesque, has become a surprisingly good actor. So do the years take their toll and yield their little compensations.

The wonderful possibilities of Kinemacolor had not even been scratched when the American subsidiary was formed, for the foreign photographers—English, French, and German—who had "taken" the Coronation and also some picture plays that were produced in southern France, insisted that the close-up was impossible in color. But Mr. Miles, having had Biograph schooling, insisted contrariwise, and after a long and hard scrap with his photographers, he succeeded in inducing them to do as he said. The result proved his contention. The Kinemacolor close-ups were things of great beauty.

During its short life, Kinemacolor made some impression; for Dan Frohman after seeing some of the pictures said that "The Scarlet Letter" was the most artistic movie he had seen up to that time. Many distinguished visitors stopped at its Hollywood studio to see the new color pictures.

Madame Tetrazzini, the opera singer, among many others, was tremendously enthusiastic.

It has been stated in error that the Kinemacolor pictures were never released. They were very much released, being shown at the New York Theatre Roof, besides many other theatres in New York, and contracts for their service all through the country were made by the Kinemacolor Company. Things started off with such a bang, we never did get over the shock of the sudden closing.

It was one exciting year with Kinemacolor, but it ended suddenly and tragically with the death of the president, Mr. Brock. While preening our wings for a flight to southern France, a telegram arrived from the New York office announcing the finish of picture production in Kinemacolor.

The sudden disruption of the Kinemacolor Company sent a flock of actors and a few directors scouting for new jobs. Frank Woods took up with Universal, only to suffer a six weeks' nightmare. Being unable to turn out the class of stuff wanted, and anticipating what was coming, he resigned, dug up the return half of his Kinemacolor round-trip ticket, and was not long in New York before he got busy as a free-lance; and not so long after that a telephone from D. W. Griffith asked him to become his scenario writer. With great joy he accepted, filling the position with Mr. Dougherty, who was now back at Biograph after a short spasm with Kinemacolor.

Right away Mr. Woods and Mr. Griffith got busy on "Judith of Bethulia," for having produced such a classic, Mr. Griffith wanted some special titling for it. He turned it over to Frank Woods, who phrased the captions in the style of language of the day—the first time that was done. However, it proved too much of a strain for the exhibitors, for they afterward fixed the titles up to suit themselves in good old New Yorkese.

Mr. Griffith's connection with the Mutual Film organization and his association with H. E. Aitken resulted in the production of such eventful and popular pictures as "The Tell-tale Heart," "Home, Sweet Home," "The Escape," "The Avenging Conscience," and "The Battle of the Sexes." The Clara Morris home out on Riverdale Road served as a studio until the 29 Union Square Place was acquired.

Billy Bitzer, D. W.'s photographer, went with him in his new affiliation, as also did Frank Woods and Christy Cabanne. As Mr. Griffith's work with the Mutual became organized, one by one he took over his old actors, but he left them working with Biograph until he could put them directly into a picture. So they trailed along; Henry Walthall, Blanche Sweet, James Kirkwood, Mae Marsh, Lillian and Dorothy Gish, Eddie Dillon, and many others.

After a short time at the Mutual studio, Mr. Griffith and his company went to California. At the old Kinemacolor lot they encamped, the Mutual having taken over that studio. The carpenters got busy right away, and soon little one-story wooden buildings crowded to the sidewalk's edge, and the place began to look like a factory. The sprinkling can that had given sustenance to red geraniums and calla lilies was needed no more.

Now before the Kinemacolor Company had started work at Whitestone they had held a contract with George H. Brennan and Tom Dixon for the production in color of Tom Dixon's "The Clansman." The idea was that the dramatic company touring through the Southern States in

"The Clansman" would play their same parts before the camera. In these Southern towns all the Southern atmosphere would be free for the asking. Houses, streets, even cotton plantations would not be too remote to use in the picture. And there was a marvelous scheme for interiors. That was to drag the "drops" and "props" and the pretty parlor furniture out into the open, where with the assistance of some sort of floor and God's sunshine, there would be nothing to hinder work on the picture version of the play.

But the marvelous scheme didn't work as well as was expected; and eventually the managers decided that trying to take a movie on a fly-by-night tour of a theatrical company was not possible, so the company laid off to take it properly. They halted for six weeks and notwithstanding the sum of twenty-five thousand dollars was spent, it was a poor picture and was never even put together. Although Tom Dixon's sensational story of the South turned out such a botch, it was to lead to a very big thing in the near future.

Frank Woods, after several others had tried, had written the continuity of this version of "The Clansman," and had received all of two hundred dollars for the job. That the picturizing of his scenario had proved such a flivver did not lessen his faith in "The Clansman's" possibilities.

Mr. Griffith was doing some tall thinking. His day of one- and two-reelers having passed, and the multiple-reel Mutual features having met with such success, he felt it was about time he started something new. So, one day, he said to Frank Woods: "I want to make a big picture. What'll I make?" With his Kinemacolor experience still fresh in mind Mr. Woods suggested "The Clansman."

With the Dixon story and the play Mr. Griffith was quite familiar as he had heard from his friend Austin Webb, who had played the part of the mulatto *Silas Lynch,* about all the exciting times attending the performance of the play—the riots and all—and more he had heard from Claire Mac-Dowell, who was also in the show, and more still from Mr. Dixon himself.

So David Griffith said to Frank Woods: "I think there's something to that. Now you call Mr. Dixon up, make an appointment to see him, and you talk it over, but say nothing about my being the same actor who worked for him once."

So the meeting was arranged; the hour of the appointment approached; and as Mr. Woods was leaving on his important mission Mr. Griffith gave final parting instructions, "Now remember, don't mention I'm the actor that once worked for him, for he would not have confidence in me."

So while Tom Dixon nibbled his lunch of crackers, nuts, and milk, Mr. Woods, without revealing his little secret, unfolded the mighty plan, "We are going to sell Wall Street and get the biggest man in the business."

"Who?"

"D. W. Griffith."

"Oh, yes, I've heard a lot about him—he used to work for me."

Mr. Dixon was greatly interested and evinced no hesitation whatever in entrusting his sensational story of the South to his one-time seventy-five dollars a week actor. He'd already taken one sporting chance on it, why not another? Yes, Mr. Griffith could have his "Clansman" for his big picture.

H. E. Aitken, who had formed the Mutual Film Company, had had on his Executive Committee Felix Kahn, brother of Otto Kahn, and Crawford Livingston. They had built the Rialto and Rivoli Theatres. The Herculean task of financing the "big picture," Mr. Aitken presented to Mr. Kahn, and he genially had agreed to provide the necessary cash—the monetary end was all beautifully settled—when the World War entered the arena and Mr. Kahn felt he could not go on. So Mr. Aitken had to finance the picture himself. He financed it to the extent of sixty thousand dollars, which was what "The Birth of A Nation" cost to produce. With legal fees and exploitation, it came to all of one hundred and ten thousand dollars. Mr. Felix Kahn and Mr. Crawford Livingston afterwards offered to help out with fifteen thousand dollars but there were fifteen directors on the executive committee of the Mutual Film, and they over-ruled the fifteen thousand dollars tender, leaving Mr. Aitken as sole financier.

Mr. Dixon received two thousand five hundred dollars cash and twenty-five per cent of the profits. He wanted more cash—wasn't so interested in the profits just then. But afterwards he had no regrets. For it happened sometimes in later days, when the picture had started out to gather in its millions, that Mr. Dixon casually opening a drawer in his desk, would be greeted by a whopping big check—his interest in "The Birth of A Nation," and one of these times, happening unexpectedly on one such check, he said, "I'm ashamed to take it"—a sentiment that should have done his soul good.

Well, Mr. Dixon is one who should have got rich on "The Birth of A Nation," but the one whose genius was responsible for the unparalleled success of the epoch-making picture says he fared like most inventors and didn't get so rich. However, it probably didn't make Mr. Griffith so very unhappy, for so far he has seemingly got more satisfaction out of the art of picture making than out of the dollars the pictures bring.

Had the Epoch Company not sold State Rights on the picture when they did, Tom Dixon's interest would have been fabulous. But as the State Rights' privilege was not for life, only for a term of years, now soon expiring, or perhaps expired now, and as up to date the picture has brought in fifteen million dollars, it seems as though there's nothing much to be unhappy about for any of those concerned.

One of the State Rights buyers who took a sporting chance on the picture was Louis B. Mayer, who had begun his movie career with a nickelodeon in some place like East or South Boston, borrowing his chairs from an undertaker when they weren't being used for a funeral. Mr. Mayer managed to scrape together enough money to buy the State Rights for New England and he cleaned up a small fortune on the deal after the owners had figured they had skimmed all the cream off Boston and other New England cities.

Oh, well, what's money anyway? A little while and we all will rest in good old mother earth, and if we're lucky perhaps pink and white daisies may nod in the soft spring breezes overhead. Or we may be grand and have a mausoleum, or a shining shaft of stone, or a huge boulder to mark our spot, or perhaps we may just rest in a neat little urn—a handful of ashes.

And what then of the fêted days of Mary and Doug? Of the peals of laughter that rocked a Charlie Chaplin audience? Of the suspenseful rescue of a persecuted

Griffith heroine on the ice-blocked river? Of the storm-tossed career of Mabel Normand?

Of the magic city of Hollywood? And the Hollywooders? Of the exotic and hectic life of the beautiful stars? Of the saner careers of the domestically happy? Who was greatest? Who produced the best pictures? Who was the most popular? Who made the most money?

All this will be told of in books reposing on dusty library shelves. Possibly a name alone will be left to whisper to posterity of their endeavor, or tinned celluloid reels shown maybe on special occasions, only to be greeted by roars of laughter—even scenes of tender death-bed partings —so old-fashioned will the technique be.

But David Wark Griffith's record may yet perhaps shine with the steady bright light of his courage, of his patient laboring day by day, of his consecration to his work; and of his faithful love for his calling, once thought so lowly.

And so eventually "The Birth of A Nation" was finished. At the Liberty Theatre in West Forty-second Street, New York—1915 was the time—it had its première —one wholly novel for a moving picture—for it was the first time a movie was presented bedecked in the same fashion as the more luxurious drama, and shown at two dollars per seat. It was not the first picture to be given in a legitimate theatre, however, for Mr. Aitken had previously booked at the Cort Theatre "The Escape," the picture made from the Paul Armstrong play of the same name.

At this first public projection of "The Birth of A Nation," an audience sat spellbound for three hours. The picture was pronounced the sensation of the season. From critics, ministers, and historians came a flood of testimonials, treatises, and letters on the new art and artists of the cinema.

"The Birth of A Nation" remains unique in picture production. It probably never will be laid absolutely to rest, as it pictures so dramatically the greatest tragedy in the history of America, showing the stuff its citizens were made of and the reason why this nation has become such a great and wonderful country.

Through the success of "The Birth of A Nation" the two-dollar movie was born. But here let there be no misunderstanding: the two-dollar-a-seat innovation in the movies was H. E. Aitken's idea. He was opposed in it by both Mr. Griffith and Mr. Dixon, Mr. Dixon becoming so alarmed that he type-wrote a twelve-page argument against it. However, Mr. Aitken persisted and the result proved him right. The public will pay if they think your show is worth it.

Through the success of "The Birth of A Nation," the sole habitat of the movies was no longer Eighth Avenue, Sixth Avenue, Avenue A and Fourteenth Street; the movies had reached Broadway to stay. D. W. Griffith had achieved that, and had he stopped right there he would have done his bit in the magical development of the motion picture. For though "Bagdad Carpets" fly, and "Ten Commandments" preach, and "Covered Wagons" trek—miles and miles of movies unreel, and some of them awfully fine, they must all acknowledge that the narrow trail that led to their highway was blazed by Mr. Griffith.

Whoever might have had a dream that the degraded little movie would blossom into magnificence, now was beginning to see that dream come true. The two-dollar movie was launched; tickets were obtainable at the box office for what future dates one pleased; there were surroundings that made the wearing of an evening dress look quite inconspicuous; serious criticism and sober attention were to be had from the high-minded—these were the first stages of the dream's fulfillment.

But little we then dreamed that to-day's picture world was to be like an Arabian Night's tale! Kings and Queens and Presidents interested! A University proposed for the study of the motion picture alone! James M. Barrie consenting to "Peter Pan" in the movies and selecting the *Peter* himself!—Any one who had made such suggestions then would have been put where he could have harmed no one!

The wildest flights of fancy hardly visioned a salary of one thousand dollars a day for an actor. But it came, as every one now knows, and with the approach of dizzy salaries departed the simple happinesses and contentment, and the fun of the old days, when thirty or fifty dollars weekly looked like a small fortune.

We had to grow up. It was so written. I, for one, am glad I served my novitiate in a day when we could afford to be good fellows, and our hearts were young enough and happy enough to enjoy the gypsying way of things.

THE END

INDEX

Only names of persons (not fictional characters) and titles of films and plays are indexed. Illustration pages are referred to as 6A, 6B, 22A, 22B, etc.

Abbott, Emma, 2
Adam and Eva, 35
Adams, Maude, 13
Adolfi, John, 37
Adventures of Dollie (Dolly), The 48-51
After Many Years (Enoch Arden), 65, 66, 88
Aitken, Harry E., 245, 249, 251, 252, 254, 255
All on Account of a Cold, 138
All on Account of the Milk, 138
America, 19, 27
Anderson, 156, 158
Anderson, Mrs. A. A., 87
Apfel, Oscar, 74
Arcadian Maid, An, 182B
Armstrong, Paul, 254
Arvidson, Linda (Mrs. D. W. Griffith), xviii, 6 and throughout
As It Is in Life, 170
Assassination of the Duc de Guise, The, 66
At the Crossroads of Life, 40
Auer, Florence, 32, 33, 37, 38, 57
August, Edwin, 54A, 175, 181, 193, 227
Avenging Conscience, The, 249

Bacon, Frank, 8, 11
Bagdad Carpet, The, 255
Baggott, King, 191, 234
Balked at the Altar, 22B
Balshofer, Fred, 143

Bambrick, Elsie, 210
Bambrick, Gertrude, 210-216, 223, 227
Bambrick, Mrs., 212
Bara, Theda, 109
Barbarian, The, 38B
Barker, Florence, 137, 138, 144, 147, 193
Barrie, James M., 256
Barrymore, John, 219
Barrymore, Lionel, xix, 219, 227
Barthelmess, Caroline, 136, 137
Barthelmess, Richard, 86B, 136
Battle at Elderbush (of Elderberry) Gulch, The, 203
Battle of the Sexes, The, 249
Bauman, Charles O., 203, 240
Beaudine, William, 150B, 191
Beban, George, 145
Beck, Martin, 16
Behind the Scenes, 60
Belasco, David, 8, 13, 40, 43, 103, 104, 228, 229, 238
Belasco, Fred, 8, 15
Bell, Gaston, 230B, 234-236, 246, 247
Benedict XV, Pope, 68
Benedict, Commodore, 115, 175
Bennett, Enid, 145
Bernard, Barney, 11, 16
Bernard, Dorothy, xxii, xxiii, 181, 227
Bernhardt, Sarah, 105, 230B
Beside the Bonnie Brier Bush, 180
Betrayed by a Handprint, 60

257

Better Way, The, 136
Birth of a Nation, The, 112, 145, 198B, 249-255
Bitzer, Billy (G. W.), 46, 89, 94, 99, 117, 119, 120, 122, 128, 129, 147, 156, 202, 221, 230, 249
Bitzer, Mrs. Billy, 193
Blackwell, Carlyle, 143, 172
Blind Princess and the Poet, The, xx
Blythe, Betty, 17, 140, 141·
Boggs, Frank, 143
Boroff, 161, 162
Bracey, Clara T., xv, 17, 214A
Bracy, Sidney, 180
Brammall, Jack, 198B
Brennan, George H., 249
Brennon, Herbert, 86B
Brock, 248
Broken Blossoms, 180
Broken Doll, The, 139
Brown, 84
Browning, Robert, 97, 129, 130, 131, 133
Bruce, Kate, xvi, 109, 112, 139, 147, 193, 230, 230A
Bruenner, Herman, 57
Buchanan, Thompson, 9
Bunny, John, 35, 209
Burke, Billie, 145
Bush, W. Stephen, 208
Butler, Daddy, 57, 139, 147

Cabanne, Christy, 249
Cahill, Lily, 180, 181, 227
Caine, Hall, 8
Calder, Alexander Stirling, 6, 7
Call of the Wild, The, 60
Call to Arms, The, 176
Camille, 105
Camp, Walter, 184
Captain Barrington, 16
Carlton, 14
Carlton, Lloyd, 182
Carr, 41
Carr, Mrs. Mary, 41
Carroll, William, 164

Carter, Leslie, 13
Cartier, 35
Caruso, Enrico, 11
Caudebec, 118
Caught in the Rain, 234, 235
Chaney, Lon, Sr., 237
Chapin, Benjamin, 137
Chaplin, Charlie, 102, 238-244, 253
Child of the Ghetto, A, 174
Child Wife, The, 103
Choosing a Husband, 138
Christie, Howard Chandler, 181
Civilization, 145
Clansman, The, 20, 249-251
Clarges, Vernon, 139, 174
Clark, Marguerite, 105
Classmates, 227
Cohan, George M., 233
Collier, William, 234
Comata, the Sioux, 111
Compson, Betty, 237
Compson, John, 57, 61
Comrades, 166B
Concealing a Burglar, 60
Conover, Theresa Maxwell, 34
Converts, The, 118B, 160
Convict's Sacrifice, A, xvi
Coogan, Jackie, 86, 102, 244
Cooper, James Fenimore, 122
Corner in Wheat, A, xvii
Costello, Maurice, 209
Cotton, Lucy, 181
Course of True Love, The, 138
Covered Wagon, The, 180, 255
Craig, Charles, 144, 164, 193
Craig, John, 8
Craven, Frank, 113
Crews, Laura Hope, 238
Cricket on the Hearth, The, xv, 70A, 92
Crisp, Donald, 180, 193, 214B, 227
Crossing the American Prairies in the Early Fifties, 198
Cruze, James, 180
Curtain Pole, The, 79, 81

Dalton, Dorothy, 145

Daly, Augustin, 96, 136
Dancing Girl of Butte, The, 144
Dark Cloud, 180
Davenport, Dorothy, 181
Davenport, Fanny, 11
Davies, Marion, 22A, 34
Davidson, Max, 29
Day After, The, 139
Dean, Julia, 234
Deane, Jack, 25
De Cordoba, Pedro, 34
de Garde, Adele, 58, 118A, 139, 182A
Delaney, Leo, 209
de Longpré, Paul, 157, 158
DeMille, Cecil B., 71, 73, 74, 151, 228
DeMille, William, 74
Dickens, Charles, 66, 90
Dillon, Eddie, 37, 38, 57, 150B, 166B, 182, 193, 212, 249
Dillon, Jack, 193
Dispatch Bearer, The, 58
Dixon, Thomas, 20, 22, 249-253, 255
Donaldson, Arthur, 35
Dooley, John, 35
Dough and Dynamite, 241
Dougherty, Lee, 40, 51, 55, 62, 63, 65, 66, 67, 68, 69, 138, 142, 173, 176, 185, 207, 217, 218, 219, 248
Dougherty, Lee, Jr., 134B
Dream, The, 192
Dressler, Marie, 241
Drew, John, 13, 70, 192
Drunkard's Reformation, A (The), 118A
Duane, 25
Duke's Plan, The, 144
Dumas, Alexandre, *fils,* 105
Duveen, Sir Joseph, 35
Dwan, Allan, 216

Eagle's Nest, The: see Rescued from an Eagle's Nest
Edgar Allan Poe, 70A, 76
Edmund Burke, 103
Egan, Gladys, 58, 139, 170, 193

Ehrlich, Frederic, 5
Eliot, George, 130
Ellsner, Edward, 22
Eltinge, Julian, 231, 238
English Channel Flown, etc., The, 111
Englishman and the Girl, The, 144
Enoch Arden, 102B, 171, 195, 196; see also *After Many Years*
Erlanger, Abraham Lincoln, 25
Escape, The, 249, 254
Eternal Mother, The, xxi
Evans, "Big," 193
Evans, Millicent, 227

Fairbanks, Douglas, Sr., 136, 253
Fair Rebel, The, 214A
Farrar, Geraldine, 238, 239
Father Gets in the Game, 79
Fedora, 12
Fernandez, Mrs., 13
Fields, Lewis Maurice, 11
Fighting Blood, xix
Financier, The, 16
Finch, Flora, 35, 58, 75
Fisher Folk(s), xviii, 171
Fiske, Minnie Maddern, 13, 229
Flagg, James Montgomery, 181
Fleming, Charles H., 246
Fool and a Girl, A, 21, 25
Fools of Fate, 86A
Fool There Was, A, 109
Ford, Hugh, 85
For Love of Gold, 60
Forrest, Arthur, 34
Fox, William, 41, 109, 141, 182, 246
Frances, Mme., 231
Frederick, Pauline, 22
French, P. W., 35
Friend, Arthur, 74
Frohman, Charles, 13, 43, 76, 182
Frohman, Daniel, 247
From Out the Shadow: see Out from the Shadow
From the Manger to the Cross, 85, 223
Fugitive, The, 181

Fuller, Hector, 26

Gardner, Helen, 222
Gates, Eleanor, 9
Gauntier, Gene, 85, 209
Gebhardt, Frank, 57
Gebhardt, George, 22B
Gebhardt, Mrs., 49
Gelert, John S., 5
Genthe, Arnold, 10
George V, 245
Gerhardt, Jake, 64
Gest, Morris, 222, 238
Get-Rich-Quick Wallingford, 237
Gibson, Charles Dana, 181, 247
Gibson Goddess, The, xvi
Gidding, 35
Girl and Her Trust, The, xxiii
Girl and the Outlaw, The, 60
Gish, Dorothy, xxiii, 213-216 (incl. 214A and 214B), 227, 228, 232, 249
Gish, Lillian, xxiii, 213-216, 227, 228, 230-233, 249
Gish, Mrs., 215
Glendenning, Ernest, 17, 22A, 34
Glendenning, John, 17
Goddefroy, 121, 125, 178, 188
Goddess of Sagebrush Gulch, The, xxii
Goelet, Peter, 2
Golden Supper, The, 115
Goldfish (Goldwyn), Sam, 73, 74, 238
Gold Is Not All, 159
Gold-Seekers, The, 168
Good Little Devil, The, 104, 214, 229
Goodman, Jules E., 27
Goodwin, Nat, 172
Gordon, Eleanor, 8
Grandin, Frank, 77, 102B, 144, 147, 156, 193, 196
Graybill, Joseph, 150A, 174, 182B, 193
Greaser's Gauntlet, The, 82
Great Divide, The, 111
Greene, Clay, 182
Grey, 150

Griffith, David Wark ("Lawrence"), 1 and throughout
Griffith, Jacob Wark, 13
Griffith, "Mattie," 13
Griffith, Mrs. D. W.: *see* Arvidson, Linda
Groeber, George, 67
Gypsy Girl, The, 103

Hackett, James K., 22, 23, 25, 229
Hale, Alan, 227
Hall, Jessie Mae, 64
Ham, 83, 84
Hamilton, Mahlon, 247
Hamilton, Neil, 247
Hammer, R. H., 116, 142, 147, 149, 216
Harding, Lyn, 34
Harlam, Macy, 35
Harris, Caroline: *see* Barthelmess, Caroline
Harris, Elmer, 9
Harrison, Louis Reeves, 208
Harron, Robert, 35, 55, 57, 85, 93, 147, 156, 196, 217
Hart, Ruth, 58, 144
Harte, Bret, 90, 201
Hawkins, Col. Rush C., 2
Hearst, William Randolph, 34, 36, 149, 150
Heart of O Yama (Oyama), The, 60
Hearts of the World, 228
Hedlund, Guy, 193
Heir to the Hoorah, 82
Hello People, 73
Henderson, Dell, 137, 144, 147, 153, 164, 166B, 176, 177, 188, 193, 199, 201, 203, 204, 205, 206, 215, 221
Henderson, Grace, 136, 174, 193, 196
Henderson, Mrs. Dell, 147, 193, 215
Hendry, Anita, 58, 191
Henley, Homer, 9, 10
Henry, O. (William Sydney Porter), 90
Her Awakening, xxi
Hessian Renegades, The: see 1776
Heyman, Polly, 231

Hicks, Eleanor, 108, 125, 145, 147, 193
His Daughter, 209
His Duty, 109
His Wife's Visitor(s), 101
Hitchcock, Raymond, 238
Hoffman, Gertrude, 211, 212
Home, Sweet Home, 249
Honest Abe, 137
House That Jack Built, The, 198B
How She Triumphed, 150A, 184
Hughie, 84, 85
Hugo, Victor, 130

Ibsen, Henrik, 17
Ince, Eleanor Kershaw, 58, 137, 138, 144, 145
Ince, Ralph, 145
Ince, Thomas H., 33, 137, 145, 191, 234
Ince, William, 138
Indian Runner's Romance, The, 188
Ingomar the Barbarian, 38B
Ingrate, The, 60
In Old California, 156
In Old Kentucky, 112
Inslee, Charles, 49, 57, 86
In the Bishop's Carriage, 229
In the Good Old Summertime, 237
In the Hills of California, 8
In the Palace of the King, 16
In the Season of Buds, 173
Intolerance, 198B
In Washington's Time, 15
Irving, Henry, 11, 12
Italian Barber, The, 182B

Jackson, Helen Hunt, 16, 169
Jackson, Stonewall (Thomas Jonathan), 13
James Wobberts, Freshman, 9
Jefferson, Joseph, 2, 105
Jefferson, Thomas (actor), 227
Jefferson, William, 227
Jeffries, James J., 69

Johnson, Arthur, xvi, xviii, 38B, 49, 57, 90, 92, 118A, 118B, 124, 125, 127, 147, 148, 149, 170, 174, 192, 209
Johnson, Effie, 53
Joy, Leatrice, 171
Joyce, Alice, 143, 172, 181, 209, 226
Judith of Bethulia, 224, 225, 227, 248

Kahn, Felix, 252
Kahn, Otto, 252
Kant, Immanuel, 130
Karno, Fred, 239
Keene, Laura, 2
Kellogg, Clara Louise, 2
Kennedy, Jeremiah J., 69, 95-97, 116, 117, 119, 219
Kershaw, Eleanor: *see* Ince, Eleanor Kershaw
Kershaw, Willette, 137
Kessel, Adam, 203, 240
Kessel, Charles, 240, 241
Kid, The (Chaplin), 102, 244
Kid, The (Powell), 160
King, Rose, 137
King Lear, 33
Kingsley, Charles, 171
Kipling, Rudyard, 109
Kirkwood, James, xvi, xvii, 86A, 109-111, 112, 116, 124, 127, 174, 180, 192, 249
Klaw, Marc, 25
Kolb and Dill, 11, 16
Kreuske, Emil, 9

LaBadie, Florence, 180, 193, 196
Laemmle, Carl, 107, 241-243
Lambert, 176
Lampson, Teddy, 214B
La Shelle, Kirke, 82
Lasky, Blanche, 73
Lasky, Jesse, 73, 74, 238, 239
Last Drop of Water, The, xx, 134A, 197
Lawrence, Florence, 38B, 57, 58, 59, 60, 61, 77, 86A, 90, 92, 116, 141, 191, 209, 213

Lawrence, W. E., 214B
Leah Kleschna, 229
Leather Stocking, 120
Lee, Florence: *see* Henderson, Mrs., Dell
Lehrman, Henry, 91, 182, 223, 238, 244
Leo XIII, Pope, 68
Leonard, Marion, xvi, xvii, xviii, 57, 58, 86A, 92, 100, 118B, 122, 124, 127, 135, 147, 156, 157, 163, 176, 182A, 192
Le Saint, Jack, 246
Lester, 5
Lightnin', 8
Lincoln at the White House, 137
Linder, Max, 78, 79
Lines of White on a Sullen Sea, 111
Little Old New York, 35
Livingston, Crawford, 252
London, Jack, 60
Lonedale Operator, The, xix, 201
Lonely Villa, The, 100, 101, 182A
Longfellow, Henry Wadsworth, 136
Longfellow, Stephanie, 136, 180, 193, 201
Longman, Evelyn, 5
Lotta (Crabtree), 2
Love Among the Roses, 157
Love of Lady Irma, The, 144
Loveridge, Margaret: *see* Marsh, Margaret
Loveridge, Mrs., 216
Lubin, Sigmund, 41, 182
Lucas, Wilfred, xx, xxiii, 57, 82, 102B, 140, 141, 192, 196

Mabel's Predicament, 241
Macbeth, 223
MacDowell, Claire, 180, 193, 201, 251
MacDowell, Melbourne, 11, 14
Mace, Fred, 150B, 206, 223
Mack, Hayward, 191
Mackay, 198A
Mackley, Arthur, 188

Macpherson, Jeanie, 54A, 58, 71, 72, 73, 74, 102B, 125, 134A, 146, 180, 191, 196
Macphersons, the, 178
Magda, 17
Mahr, John, 85, 94, 147
Mailes, H. C (harles), xxii, 180
Major, Charles, 36
Mansfield, Richard, 11, 13
Man's Genesis, 217, 218
Marbury, Jane, 17
Marion, Frank J., 41
Markey, Enid, 145
Marlowe, Julia, 36
Marsh, Mae, 206, 207, 214B, 216, 217, 227, 228, 232, 249
Marsh, Margaret, 205, 206, 216
Marvin, Arthur, 46, 47, 48, 50, 128, 129, 147, 185, 186
Marvin, Henry Norton, 45, 46, 51, 52, 69, 95, 97, 111
Massacre, The, 218
Mauer, Oscar, 10
Maupassant, Guy de, 130, 137
Maxwell, Perriton, 24, 27
Mayer, Louis B., 253
Maytime, 35
McClure, Samuel Sidney, 24
McCutcheon, 30, 31, 32, 37, 42, 45, 48
McCutcheon, Wallace, 37, 38, 42, 48
McNamara, Walter, 223
Meighan, Thomas, 237-239, 244
Men and Women, 227
Mencher, Joseph, 222
Mended Lute, The, 86A, 116, 117
Miles, David, 57, 100, 182A, 191, 234-236, 246, 247
Miller, Christie, 139, 147, 156, 199
Miller, Henry, 26, 110
Million Dollar Mystery, The, 180
Mills of the Gods, The, 118B
Miracle, The, 222
Miracle Man, The, 237
Misérables, Les, 222
Mission Bells, 198A
Miss Petticoats, 11, 14

Monsieur Beaucaire, 13
Moore, Mrs. Victor : *see* Hart, Ruth
Moore, Owen, 57, 70A, 75, 86A, 90, 92, 101, 107, 109, 112, 116, 124, 127, 144, 148, 168, 176, 183, 191, 209, 213
Morosco, Oliver, 16
Morris, Clara, 249
Morris, William, 35
Moses, Vivian M., 27
Mother Love, 223
Mr. Jones at the Ball, 71
Mr. Jones Has a Card Party, 75
Mrs. Jones Entertains, xv, 74
Mulhal, Jack, 227
Mumming Birds, (The), 239
Murphy, 83
Music Master, The, 40

Nash, George, 35
Nazimova, Alla, 86B
Necklace, The, 137
Neilan, Marshall, 215, 216, 226, 227
Neilan, Marshall, Jr., 227
New Lid, The, 145
New York Life, 103
Nichols, George, 57, 137, 139, 147, 193, 196
Nichols, Mrs. George, 147, 193
Night in an English Music Hall (Music-Hall) (= Mumming Birds), 239, 240
Normand, Mabel, xxi, 134B, 136, 150B, 181, 193, 204, 207, 214, 223, 254
Norris, Frank, 90

Oberhardt, 5
Ogle, Charles, 171
Oil and Water, 224
Olcott, Chauncey, 103
Olcott, Sidney, 33, 85, 223
Old Isaacs, the Pawnbroker, 40
O'Moore, Barry : *see* Yost, Herbert
O'Neill, Eugene, 194
O'Neill, Nance, 17, 18
One Woman, The, 20, 21
O'Ramey, George, 11, 227

Ormsby, Helen, 137
Orth, Louise, 227
Osterman, Katherine, 11
Ostler Joe, 40
O'Sullivan, Tony, 57, 125, 147, 193, 221
Out from the Shadow, 54A
Over Silent Paths, 161
Over the Hill, 41

Paget, Alfred, 54A, 147, 180, 193, 225
Patti, Adelina, 2
Perley, Charles, 214A
Pete, 177, 178
Peter Pan, 136, 182, 256
Peyton, Col., 226
Phelan, James H., 10
Pickford, Charlotte, 102, 103, 107, 134, 135, 148, 179, 183, 191, 213, 228, 229
Pickford, Jack, 107, 135, 140, 148, 152, 153, 160, 164, 191
Pickford, Lottie, 106, 107, 140, 191
Pickford, Mary, xv, 1, 2, 8, 60, 70B, 75, 77, 78, 84, 99-107, 108, 110, 112, 113, 124, 128, 131, 134, 135, 138, 140, 144, 147, 148, 149, 152, 153, 155, 166A, 168, 170, 175, 176, 179, 182A, 182B, 183, 187, 189, 190, 191, 192, 209, 213, 214, 215, 217, 220, 221, 224, 227, 228, 229, 234, 253
Pippa Passes, 97, 98, 99, 110A, 137, 133
Pius X, Pope, 68
Planter's Wife, The, 60
Platt, George Foster, 86
Pocahontas, 24
Politician's Love Story, The, 38B, 80, 81
Porter, William Sydney : *see* Henry, O.
Potter, Mrs. James Brown, 40
Powell, David, 113
Powell, Frank, 86A, 108, 109, 112, 119, 125, 137, 138, 139, 143, 144, 145, 147, 160, 193, 204, 205

Powell, (Frank) Baden, 145, 193
Powell, Mrs. Frank: *see* Hicks, Eleanor
Predmore, 118, 119, 120, 124, 126
Predmore, Mrs., 123, 124, 126
Prescott, Vivian, 150A, 150B, 193
Primitive Man: see Man's Genesis
Prisoner of Zenda, The, 229
Pryor, Herbert, 57, 70A, 92, 137
Pueblo Legend, A, 220
Purviance, Edna, 238

Queen Elizabeth, 104, 229
Queen of Sheba, The, 141
Quimby, Harriet, 9, 10, 20, 111
Quirk, Billy, 101, 147, 170
Quo Vadis, 34, 222

Rae, Isabel, 191, 234
Rainous, 58, 59
Ramona (film), 169, 189, 196
Ramona (play), 16, 21
Ranger, The, 37
Rankin, McKee, 17
Ray, Charles, 145
Redman and the Child, The, 85, 86
Red Rose, The, 231
Reid, Hal, 103, 223
Reid, Mrs. Wallace, 238
Reid, Wallace, 103, 181, 223, 238
Reinhardt, Max, 222
Remington, Frederic, 180
Rennie, James, 232, 233
Rescued from an Eagle's Nest, 41
Resurrection, 90
Revere, Paul, 19
Richard the Third, 33
Rich Revenge, A, 170
Ring, Blanche, 237, 239
Ring, Frances, 237
Ring, Julie, 237
Rings on My Fingers, 237
Rip Van Winkle, 105
Ritchie, Franklin, 227
Roberts, Florence, 6A, 15
Robinson, Gertrude, 118A, 124, 128, 148, 174, 175, 213

Robinson, Spike, 136, 186, 193
Romance of a Jewess, The, 60
Romance of the Western Hills, A, 168
Roosevelt, Theodore, 165
Ruotolo, 5
Russell, Dorothy, 84
Russell, Lillian, 84, 230B, 247

Salome, 22
Salter, Harry, xv, 22A, 22B, 57, 59, 71, 72, 140, 141, 190
Salutary Lesson, A, 176
Sands of (o') Dee, (The), 217
Sardou, Victorien, 11, 17
Sargent, Epes Winthrop, 208
Scardon, Paul, 17, 140, 141
Scarlet Letter, The, 247
Schwartz, Milton, 9
Scott, Paul, 108
Scott, Sir Walter, 90
Sealed Room, The, 112
Sennett, Mack, xvi, 2, 22B, 38B, 57, 75, 77-81, 89, 100, 110, 124, 125, 135, 144, 145, 147, 150B, 164, 166B, 176, 177, 182B, 187, 193, 202, 203, 204, 223, 239, 240, 244
Seton, Ernest Thompson, 38B
1776, or The Hessian Renegades, 120
Seyffertitz, Gustav von, 35
Shakespeare, William, 90
Sharkey, Jack, 69
Shelter, Eddie, 147
Shepley, Ruth, 22A, 35
Sherlock Holmes, 239
Sherry, J. Barney, xvii, xx
Shuffle Along, 232
Silver King, The, 103
Skipworth, Alison, 25
Sleicher, John A., 24, 131, 132
Smiley, Joseph, 191
Smith, Charlotte: *see* Pickford, Charlotte
Smith, George Albert, 245
Smith, Gladys: *see* Pickford, Mary
Smith, Jack: *see* Pickford, Jack

Smith, John, 24
Smith, Lottie : see Pickford, Lottie
Smoked Husband, A, 61
Snow, Marguerite, 180
Snow, Mortimer, 35
Snow-man, The, 37, 38, 39, 42
Song of the Shirt, The, 60
Sorrows of the Unfaithful, The, 176
Sothern, Edward Hugh, 36
Squaw Man, The, 74
Stage Rustler, The, 40
Standing, Jack, 113
Stanley, Forrest, 22A
Starr, Frances, 8
Steck, 3, 4
Stevens, Ashton, 16
Stewart, Anita, 145
Stewart, Grant, 234
Stewart, Lucille Lee, 145
Stoughton, Mabel, 22B, 57
Strange Meeting, A, 136
Straton, John Roach, 232
Studio Party, A, 45
Sudermann, Hermann, 11, 17
Sue, Eugène, 222
Sunshine, Marion, 54A, 114, 183B
Surratt, Valeska, 231
Sweet, Blanche, xix, xx, 54A, 138, 139, 150A, 184, 188, 192, 201, 202, 204, 207, 212, 213, 224, 225, 227, 228, 230A, 249
Sweet and Twenty, 101

Taming of the Shrew, The, 60
Tansy, Johnny, 58, 86
Taylor, 162
Taylor, Charles, 103
Taylor, Laurette, 103
Taylor, Moses, 2
Taylor, Stanner E. V., 45, 46, 48, 111, 124, 192
Tell-Tale Heart, The (= The Avenging Conscience?), 249
Ten Commandments, The, 71, 255
Tenderfoot, The (The Tenderfoot's Triumph?), 188

Tennyson, Alfred, 65, 115, 195
Terry, Ellen, 11, 108, 113
Terwilliger, George, 64, 65
Tetrazzini, Luisa, 248
Thanhouser, 180, 182
Thaw, Harry, 38A
They Would Elope, 101, 106
Thomas, Augustus, 37
Thomas, E. R., 181
Thompson, Lydia, 17
Those Awful Hats, 75
Thread, The (Threads) of Destiny, 155
Through Fire to Fortune, 182
Tillie's Nightmare, 241
Tillie's Punctured Romance, 241
Tolstoy, Leo, 90, 130
Toncray, Kate, 193
Too Much Susette, 67
Torch Bearers, The, 25
Traffic in Souls, 223, 237
Trahern, A1, 64
Truex, Ernest, 104
Trunelle, Mabel, 137
Tucker, Ethel, 237
Tucker, George Loane, 191, 223, 234, 236, 237
Tully, Dick, 9
Tully, Richard Walton, 9
Turner, Florence, 209
Two Brothers, The, 165
Tynon, Brandon, 182

Unchanging Sea, The, 171
Unexpected Help, 170
Unseen Enemy, An (The), xxiii, 228
Urban, Charles, 243
Urban, Joseph, 35

Vail, Olive, 9
Vale, Louise, 227
Vale, Travers, 227
Valentino, Rudolph, 247
Vanderbilt, Cornelius, 117
Vaquero's Vow, The, 60
Varges, Capt., 68
Vignola, Robert G., 33, 35, 37

Village Cut-up, 33
Violin Maker of Cremona, The, 100, 182A
Volstead, Andrew J., 83

Wake, 63, 64
Waldrop, Oza, 8
Walker, Charlotte, 104
Waller, 5
Walthall, Henry B., xviii, 111, 112, 124, 127, 147, 168, 177, 180, 192, 224, 249
Wandering Jew, The, 222
War, 26, 27
War Brides, 86B
Ward, Fanny (Fannie), 25
Warrens of Virginia, The, 104
Way Down East, 38, 180
Way of Man, The, 101
Way of the World, The, 160
Webb, Austin, 114, 251
Weber, Joseph M., 11
Werner, Edgar S., 6
West, 182
West, Charles, 54A, 147, 148, 174, 193, 214A
West, Dorothy, 58, 115, 144, 147, 149, 152, 153, 174, 175, 193, 230

What the Daisy Said, 175
When Knighthood Was in Flower, 22A, 34, 35, 36
When Knights Were Bold, 22A, 34, 35
White, Pearl, 42
White, Stanford, 38A
White Rose of the Wilds, The, 202, 203
Wife, The, 228
Wildflower, 105
Wilful Peggy, 179, 188
William II of Germany, 36
Winninger, Charles, 237, 239
Wolff children, 139
Woman's Way, A, 60
Woods, Al, 231
Woods, Frank E., 9, 62-65, 246, 248, 249, 250, 251

Yost, Herbert (Barry O'Moore), 57, 70A, 76
Young, Clara Kimball, 222
Young, Mary, 8

Zukor, Adolph, 104, 105, 229
Zulu's Heart, The, 60

A CATALOGUE OF SELECTED DOVER BOOKS
IN ALL FIELDS OF INTEREST

A CATALOGUE OF SELECTED DOVER BOOKS
IN ALL FIELDS OF INTEREST

AMERICA'S OLD MASTERS, James T. Flexner. Four men emerged unexpectedly from provincial 18th century America to leadership in European art: Benjamin West, J. S. Copley, C. R. Peale, Gilbert Stuart. Brilliant coverage of lives and contributions. Revised, 1967 edition. 69 plates. 365pp. of text.

21806-6 Paperbound $3.00

FIRST FLOWERS OF OUR WILDERNESS: AMERICAN PAINTING, THE COLONIAL PERIOD, James T. Flexner. Painters, and regional painting traditions from earliest Colonial times up to the emergence of Copley, West and Peale Sr., Foster, Gustavus Hesselius, Feke, John Smibert and many anonymous painters in the primitive manner. Engaging presentation, with 162 illustrations. xxii + 368pp.

22180-6 Paperbound $3.50

THE LIGHT OF DISTANT SKIES: AMERICAN PAINTING, 1760-1835, James T. Flexner. The great generation of early American painters goes to Europe to learn and to teach: West, Copley, Gilbert Stuart and others. Allston, Trumbull, Morse; also contemporary American painters—primitives, derivatives, academics—who remained in America. 102 illustrations. xiii + 306pp.   22179-2 Paperbound $3.00

A HISTORY OF THE RISE AND PROGRESS OF THE ARTS OF DESIGN IN THE UNITED STATES, William Dunlap. Much the richest mine of information on early American painters, sculptors, architects, engravers, miniaturists, etc. The only source of information for scores of artists, the major primary source for many others. Unabridged reprint of rare original 1834 edition, with new introduction by James T. Flexner, and 394 new illustrations. Edited by Rita Weiss. 6⅝ x 9⅝.

21695-0, 21696-9, 21697-7 Three volumes, Paperbound $13.50

EPOCHS OF CHINESE AND JAPANESE ART, Ernest F. Fenollosa. From primitive Chinese art to the 20th century, thorough history, explanation of every important art period and form, including Japanese woodcuts; main stress on China and Japan, but Tibet, Korea also included. Still unexcelled for its detailed, rich coverage of cultural background, aesthetic elements, diffusion studies, particularly of the historical period. 2nd, 1913 edition. 242 illustrations. lii + 439pp. of text.

20364-6, 20365-4 Two volumes, Paperbound $6.00

THE GENTLE ART OF MAKING ENEMIES, James A. M. Whistler. Greatest wit of his day deflates Oscar Wilde, Ruskin, Swinburne; strikes back at inane critics, exhibitions, art journalism; aesthetics of impressionist revolution in most striking form. Highly readable classic by great painter. Reproduction of edition designed by Whistler. Introduction by Alfred Werner. xxxvi + 334pp.

21875-9 Paperbound $2.50

VISUAL ILLUSIONS: THEIR CAUSES, CHARACTERISTICS, AND APPLICATIONS, Matthew Luckiesh. Thorough description and discussion of optical illusion, geometric and perspective, particularly; size and shape distortions, illusions of color, of motion; natural illusions; use of illusion in art and magic, industry, etc. Most useful today with op art, also for classical art. Scores of effects illustrated. Introduction by William H. Ittleson. 100 illustrations. xxi + 252pp.
21530-X Paperbound $2.00

A HANDBOOK OF ANATOMY FOR ART STUDENTS, Arthur Thomson. Thorough, virtually exhaustive coverage of skeletal structure, musculature, etc. Full text, supplemented by anatomical diagrams and drawings and by photographs of undraped figures. Unique in its comparison of male and female forms, pointing out differences of contour, texture, form. 211 figures, 40 drawings, 86 photographs. xx + 459pp. 5⅜ x 8⅜.
21163-0 Paperbound $3.50

150 MASTERPIECES OF DRAWING, Selected by Anthony Toney. Full page reproductions of drawings from the early 16th to the end of the 18th century, all beautifully reproduced: Rembrandt, Michelangelo, Dürer, Fragonard, Urs, Graf, Wouwerman, many others. First-rate browsing book, model book for artists. xviii + 150pp. 8⅜ x 11¼.
21032-4 Paperbound $2.50

THE LATER WORK OF AUBREY BEARDSLEY, Aubrey Beardsley. Exotic, erotic, ironic masterpieces in full maturity: Comedy Ballet, Venus and Tannhauser, Pierrot, Lysistrata, Rape of the Lock, Savoy material, Ali Baba, Volpone, etc. This material revolutionized the art world, and is still powerful, fresh, brilliant. With *The Early Work,* all Beardsley's finest work. 174 plates, 2 in color. xiv + 176pp. 8⅛ x 11.
21817-1 Paperbound $3.00

DRAWINGS OF REMBRANDT, Rembrandt van Rijn. Complete reproduction of fabulously rare edition by Lippmann and Hofstede de Groot, completely reedited, updated, improved by Prof. Seymour Slive, Fogg Museum. Portraits, Biblical sketches, landscapes, Oriental types, nudes, episodes from classical mythology—All Rembrandt's fertile genius. Also selection of drawings by his pupils and followers. "Stunning volumes," *Saturday Review.* 550 illustrations. lxxviii + 552pp. 9⅛ x 12¼.
21485-0, 21486-9 Two volumes, Paperbound $7.00

THE DISASTERS OF WAR, Francisco Goya. One of the masterpieces of Western civilization—83 etchings that record Goya's shattering, bitter reaction to the Napoleonic war that swept through Spain after the insurrection of 1808 and to war in general. Reprint of the first edition, with three additional plates from Boston's Museum of Fine Arts. All plates facsimile size. Introduction by Philip Hofer, Fogg Museum. v + 97pp. 9⅜ x 8¼.
21872-4 Paperbound $2.00

GRAPHIC WORKS OF ODILON REDON. Largest collection of Redon's graphic works ever assembled: 172 lithographs, 28 etchings and engravings, 9 drawings. These include some of his most famous works. All the plates from *Odilon Redon: oeuvre graphique complet,* plus additional plates. New introduction and caption translations by Alfred Werner. 209 illustrations. xxvii + 209pp. 9⅛ x 12¼.
21966-8 Paperbound $4.00

DESIGN BY ACCIDENT; A BOOK OF "ACCIDENTAL EFFECTS" FOR ARTISTS AND DESIGNERS, James F. O'Brien. Create your own unique, striking, imaginative effects by "controlled accident" interaction of materials: paints and lacquers, oil and water based paints, splatter, crackling materials, shatter, similar items. Everything you do will be different; first book on this limitless art, so useful to both fine artist and commercial artist. Full instructions. 192 plates showing "accidents," 8 in color. viii + 215pp. 8⅜ x 11¼.   21942-9 Paperbound $3.50

THE BOOK OF SIGNS, Rudolf Koch. Famed German type designer draws 493 beautiful symbols: religious, mystical, alchemical, imperial, property marks, runes, etc. Remarkable fusion of traditional and modern. Good for suggestions of timelessness, smartness, modernity. Text. vi + 104pp. 6⅛ x 9¼.
20162-7 Paperbound $1.25

HISTORY OF INDIAN AND INDONESIAN ART, Ananda K. Coomaraswamy. An unabridged republication of one of the finest books by a great scholar in Eastern art. Rich in descriptive material, history, social backgrounds; Sunga reliefs, Rajput paintings, Gupta temples, Burmese frescoes, textiles, jewelry, sculpture, etc. 400 photos. viii + 423pp. 6⅜ x 9¾.   21436-2 Paperbound $4.00

PRIMITIVE ART, Franz Boas. America's foremost anthropologist surveys textiles, ceramics, woodcarving, basketry, metalwork, etc.; patterns, technology, creation of symbols, style origins. All areas of world, but very full on Northwest Coast Indians. More than 350 illustrations of baskets, boxes, totem poles, weapons, etc. 378 pp.
20025-6 Paperbound $3.00

THE GENTLEMAN AND CABINET MAKER'S DIRECTOR, Thomas Chippendale. Full reprint (third edition, 1762) of most influential furniture book of all time, by master cabinetmaker. 200 plates, illustrating chairs, sofas, mirrors, tables, cabinets, plus 24 photographs of surviving pieces. Biographical introduction by N. Bienenstock. vi + 249pp. 9⅞ x 12¾.   21601-2 Paperbound $4.00

AMERICAN ANTIQUE FURNITURE, Edgar G. Miller, Jr. The basic coverage of all American furniture before 1840. Individual chapters cover type of furniture—clocks, tables, sideboards, etc.—chronologically, with inexhaustible wealth of data. More than 2100 photographs, all identified, commented on. Essential to all early American collectors. Introduction by H. E. Keyes. vi + 1106pp. 7⅞ x 10¾.
21599-7, 21600-4 Two volumes, Paperbound $11.00

PENNSYLVANIA DUTCH AMERICAN FOLK ART, Henry J. Kauffman. 279 photos, 28 drawings of tulipware, Fraktur script, painted tinware, toys, flowered furniture, quilts, samplers, hex signs, house interiors, etc. Full descriptive text. Excellent for tourist, rewarding for designer, collector. Map. 146pp. 7⅞ x 10¾.
21205-X Paperbound $2.50

EARLY NEW ENGLAND GRAVESTONE RUBBINGS, Edmund V. Gillon, Jr. 43 photographs, 226 carefully reproduced rubbings show heavily symbolic, sometimes macabre early gravestones, up to early 19th century. Remarkable early American primitive art, occasionally strikingly beautiful; always powerful. Text. xxvi + 207pp. 8⅜ x 11¼.   21380-3 Paperbound $3.50

ALPHABETS AND ORNAMENTS, Ernst Lehner. Well-known pictorial source for decorative alphabets, script examples, cartouches, frames, decorative title pages, calligraphic initials, borders, similar material. 14th to 19th century, mostly European. Useful in almost any graphic arts designing, varied styles. 750 illustrations. 256pp. 7 x 10.   21905-4 Paperbound $4.00

PAINTING: A CREATIVE APPROACH, Norman Colquhoun. For the beginner simple guide provides an instructive approach to painting: major stumbling blocks for beginner; overcoming them, technical points; paints and pigments; oil painting; watercolor and other media and color. New section on "plastic" paints. Glossary. Formerly *Paint Your Own Pictures.* 221pp.   22000-1 Paperbound $1.75

THE ENJOYMENT AND USE OF COLOR, Walter Sargent. Explanation of the relations between colors themselves and between colors in nature and art, including hundreds of little-known facts about color values, intensities, effects of high and low illumination, complementary colors. Many practical hints for painters, references to great masters. 7 color plates, 29 illustrations. x + 274pp.
20944-X Paperbound $2.75

THE NOTEBOOKS OF LEONARDO DA VINCI, compiled and edited by Jean Paul Richter. 1566 extracts from original manuscripts reveal the full range of Leonardo's versatile genius: all his writings on painting, sculpture, architecture, anatomy, astronomy, geography, topography, physiology, mining, music, etc., in both Italian and English, with 186 plates of manuscript pages and more than 500 additional drawings. Includes studies for the Last Supper, the lost Sforza monument, and other works. Total of xlvii + 866pp. 7⅞ x 10¾.
22572-0, 22573-9 Two volumes, Paperbound $10.00

MONTGOMERY WARD CATALOGUE OF 1895. Tea gowns, yards of flannel and pillow-case lace, stereoscopes, books of gospel hymns, the New Improved Singer Sewing Machine, side saddles, milk skimmers, straight-edged razors, high-button shoes, spittoons, and on and on . . . listing some 25,000 items, practically all illustrated. Essential to the shoppers of the 1890's, it is our truest record of the spirit of the period. Unaltered reprint of Issue No. 57, Spring and Summer 1895. Introduction by Boris Emmet. Innumerable illustrations. xiii + 624pp. 8½ x 11⅝.
22377-9 Paperbound $6.95

THE CRYSTAL PALACE EXHIBITION ILLUSTRATED CATALOGUE (LONDON, 1851). One of the wonders of the modern world—the Crystal Palace Exhibition in which all the nations of the civilized world exhibited their achievements in the arts and sciences—presented in an equally important illustrated catalogue. More than 1700 items pictured with accompanying text—ceramics, textiles, cast-iron work, carpets, pianos, sleds, razors, wall-papers, billiard tables, beehives, silverware and hundreds of other artifacts—represent the focal point of Victorian culture in the Western World. Probably the largest collection of Victorian decorative art ever assembled—indispensable for antiquarians and designers. Unabridged republication of the Art-Journal Catalogue of the Great Exhibition of 1851, with all terminal essays. New introduction by John Gloag, F.S.A. xxxiv + 426pp. 9 x 12.
22503-8 Paperbound $4.50

A History of Costume, Carl Köhler. Definitive history, based on surviving pieces of clothing primarily, and paintings, statues, etc. secondarily. Highly readable text, supplemented by 594 illustrations of costumes of the ancient Mediterranean peoples, Greece and Rome, the Teutonic prehistoric period; costumes of the Middle Ages, Renaissance, Baroque, 18th and 19th centuries. Clear, measured patterns are provided for many clothing articles. Approach is practical throughout. Enlarged by Emma von Sichart. 464pp. 21030-8 Paperbound $3.50

Oriental Rugs, Antique and Modern, Walter A. Hawley. A complete and authoritative treatise on the Oriental rug—where they are made, by whom and how, designs and symbols, characteristics in detail of the six major groups, how to distinguish them and how to buy them. Detailed technical data is provided on periods, weaves, warps, wefts, textures, sides, ends and knots, although no technical background is required for an understanding. 11 color plates, 80 halftones, 4 maps. vi + 320pp. 6⅛ x 9⅛. 22366-3 Paperbound $5.00

Ten Books on Architecture, Vitruvius. By any standards the most important book on architecture ever written. Early Roman discussion of aesthetics of building, construction methods, orders, sites, and every other aspect of architecture has inspired, instructed architecture for about 2,000 years. Stands behind Palladio, Michelangelo, Bramante, Wren, countless others. Definitive Morris H. Morgan translation. 68 illustrations. xii + 331pp. 20645-9 Paperbound $2.50

The Four Books of Architecture, Andrea Palladio. Translated into every major Western European language in the two centuries following its publication in 1570, this has been one of the most influential books in the history of architecture. Complete reprint of the 1738 Isaac Ware edition. New introduction by Adolf Placzek, Columbia Univ. 216 plates. xxii + 110pp. of text. 9½ x 12¾. 21308-0 Clothbound $10.00

Sticks and Stones: A Study of American Architecture and Civilization, Lewis Mumford.One of the great classics of American cultural history. American architecture from the medieval-inspired earliest forms to the early 20th century; evolution of structure and style, and reciprocal influences on environment. 21 photographic illustrations. 238pp. 20202-X Paperbound $2.00

The American Builder's Companion, Asher Benjamin. The most widely used early 19th century architectural style and source book, for colonial up into Greek Revival periods. Extensive development of geometry of carpentering, construction of sashes, frames, doors, stairs; plans and elevations of domestic and other buildings. Hundreds of thousands of houses were built according to this book, now invaluable to historians, architects, restorers, etc. 1827 edition. 59 plates. 114pp. 7⅞ x 10¾. 22236-5 Paperbound $3.00

Dutch Houses in the Hudson Valley Before 1776, Helen Wilkinson Reynolds. The standard survey of the Dutch colonial house and outbuildings, with constructional features, decoration, and local history associated with individual homesteads. Introduction by Franklin D. Roosevelt. Map. 150 illustrations. 469pp. 6⅝ x 9¼. 21469-9 Paperbound $4.00

CATALOGUE OF DOVER BOOKS

THE ARCHITECTURE OF COUNTRY HOUSES, Andrew J. Downing. Together with Vaux's *Villas and Cottages* this is the basic book for Hudson River Gothic architecture of the middle Victorian period. Full, sound discussions of general aspects of housing, architecture, style, decoration, furnishing, together with scores of detailed house plans, illustrations of specific buildings, accompanied by full text. Perhaps the most influential single American architectural book. 1850 edition. Introduction by J. Stewart Johnson. 321 figures, 34 architectural designs. xvi + 560pp.
22003-6 Paperbound $4.00

LOST EXAMPLES OF COLONIAL ARCHITECTURE, John Mead Howells. Full-page photographs of buildings that have disappeared or been so altered as to be denatured, including many designed by major early American architects. 245 plates. xvii + 248pp. 7⅞ x 10¾.
21143-6 Paperbound $3.50

DOMESTIC ARCHITECTURE OF THE AMERICAN COLONIES AND OF THE EARLY REPUBLIC, Fiske Kimball. Foremost architect and restorer of Williamsburg and Monticello covers nearly 200 homes between 1620-1825. Architectural details, construction, style features, special fixtures, floor plans, etc. Generally considered finest work in its area. 219 illustrations of houses, doorways, windows, capital mantels. xx + 314pp. 7⅞ x 10¾.
21743-4 Paperbound $4.00

EARLY AMERICAN ROOMS: 1650-1858, edited by Russell Hawes Kettell. Tour of 12 rooms, each representative of a different era in American history and each furnished, decorated, designed and occupied in the style of the era. 72 plans and elevations, 8-page color section, etc., show fabrics, wall papers, arrangements, etc. Full descriptive text. xvii + 200pp. of text. 8⅜ x 11¼.
21633-0 Paperbound $5.00

THE FITZWILLIAM VIRGINAL BOOK, edited by J. Fuller Maitland and W. B. Squire. Full modern printing of famous early 17th-century ms. volume of 300 works by Morley, Byrd, Bull, Gibbons, etc. For piano or other modern keyboard instrument; easy to read format. xxxvi + 938pp. 8⅜ x 11.
21068-5, 21069-3 Two volumes, Paperbound $10.00

KEYBOARD MUSIC, Johann Sebastian Bach. Bach Gesellschaft edition. A rich selection of Bach's masterpieces for the harpsichord: the six English Suites, six French Suites, the six Partitas (Clavierübung part I), the Goldberg Variations (Clavierübung part IV), the fifteen Two-Part Inventions and the fifteen Three-Part Sinfonias. Clearly reproduced on large sheets with ample margins; eminently playable. vi + 312pp. 8⅛ x 11.
22360-4 Paperbound $5.00

THE MUSIC OF BACH: AN INTRODUCTION, Charles Sanford Terry. A fine, nontechnical introduction to Bach's music, both instrumental and vocal. Covers organ music, chamber music, passion music, other types. Analyzes themes, developments, innovations. x + 114pp.
21075-8 Paperbound $1.25

BEETHOVEN AND HIS NINE SYMPHONIES, Sir George Grove. Noted British musicologist provides best history, analysis, commentary on symphonies. Very thorough, rigorously accurate; necessary to both advanced student and amateur music lover. 436 musical passages. vii + 407 pp.
20334-4 Paperbound $2.75

JOHANN SEBASTIAN BACH, Philipp Spitta. One of the great classics of musicology, this definitive analysis of Bach's music (and life) has never been surpassed. Lucid, nontechnical analyses of hundreds of pieces (30 pages devoted to St. Matthew Passion, 26 to B Minor Mass). Also includes major analysis of 18th-century music. 450 musical examples. 40-page musical supplement. Total of xx + 1799pp.
(EUK) 22278-0, 22279-9 Two volumes, Clothbound $17.50

MOZART AND HIS PIANO CONCERTOS, Cuthbert Girdlestone. The only full-length study of an important area of Mozart's creativity. Provides detailed analyses of all 23 concertos, traces inspirational sources. 417 musical examples. Second edition. 509pp.   (USO) 21271-8 Paperbound $3.50

THE PERFECT WAGNERITE: A COMMENTARY ON THE NIBLUNG'S RING, George Bernard Shaw. Brilliant and still relevant criticism in remarkable essays on Wagner's Ring cycle, Shaw's ideas on political and social ideology behind the plots, role of Leitmotifs, vocal requisites, etc. Prefaces. xxi + 136pp.
21707-8 Paperbound $1.50

DON GIOVANNI, W. A. Mozart. Complete libretto, modern English translation; biographies of composer and librettist; accounts of early performances and critical reaction. Lavishly illustrated. All the material you need to understand and appreciate this great work. Dover Opera Guide and Libretto Series; translated and introduced by Ellen Bleiler. 92 illustrations. 209pp.
21134-7 Paperbound $1.50

HIGH FIDELITY SYSTEMS: A LAYMAN'S GUIDE, Roy F. Allison. All the basic information you need for setting up your own audio system: high fidelity and stereo record players, tape records, F.M. Connections, adjusting tone arm, cartridge, checking needle alignment, positioning speakers, phasing speakers, adjusting hums, trouble-shooting, maintenance, and similar topics. Enlarged 1965 edition. More than 50 charts, diagrams, photos. iv + 91pp.   21514-8 Paperbound $1.25

REPRODUCTION OF SOUND, Edgar Villchur. Thorough coverage for laymen of high fidelity systems, reproducing systems in general, needles, amplifiers, preamps, loudspeakers, feedback, explaining physical background. "A rare talent for making technicalities vividly comprehensible," R. Darrell, *High Fidelity*. 69 figures. iv + 92pp.   21515-6 Paperbound $1.25

HEAR ME TALKIN' TO YA: THE STORY OF JAZZ AS TOLD BY THE MEN WHO MADE IT, Nat Shapiro and Nat Hentoff. Louis Armstrong, Fats Waller, Jo Jones, Clarence Williams, Billy Holiday, Duke Ellington, Jelly Roll Morton and dozens of other jazz greats tell how it was in Chicago's South Side, New Orleans, depression Harlem and the modern West Coast as jazz was born and grew. xvi + 429pp.
21726-4 Paperbound $2.50

FABLES OF AESOP, translated by Sir Roger L'Estrange. A reproduction of the very rare 1931 Paris edition; a selection of the most interesting fables, together with 50 imaginative drawings by Alexander Calder. v + 128pp. 6½x9¼.
21780-9 Paperbound $1.50

AGAINST THE GRAIN (A REBOURS), Joris K. Huysmans. Filled with weird images, evidences of a bizarre imagination, exotic experiments with hallucinatory drugs, rich tastes and smells and the diversions of its sybarite hero Duc Jean des Esseintes, this classic novel pushed 19th-century literary decadence to its limits. Full unabridged edition. Do not confuse this with abridged editions generally sold. Introduction by Havelock Ellis. xlix + 206pp. 22190-3 Paperbound $2.00

VARIORUM SHAKESPEARE: HAMLET. Edited by Horace H. Furness; a landmark of American scholarship. Exhaustive footnotes and appendices treat all doubtful words and phrases, as well as suggested critical emendations throughout the play's history. First volume contains editor's own text, collated with all Quartos and Folios. Second volume contains full first Quarto, translations of Shakespeare's sources (Belleforest, and Saxo Grammaticus), Der Bestrafte Brudermord, and many essays on critical and historical points of interest by major authorities of past and present. Includes details of staging and costuming over the years. By far the best edition available for serious students of Shakespeare. Total of xx + 905pp. 21004-9, 21005-7, 2 volumes, Paperbound $7.00

A LIFE OF WILLIAM SHAKESPEARE, Sir Sidney Lee. This is the standard life of Shakespeare, summarizing everything known about Shakespeare and his plays. Incredibly rich in material, broad in coverage, clear and judicious, it has served thousands as the best introduction to Shakespeare. 1931 edition. 9 plates. xxix + 792pp. (USO) 21967-4 Paperbound $3.75

MASTERS OF THE DRAMA, John Gassner. Most comprehensive history of the drama in print, covering every tradition from Greeks to modern Europe and America, including India, Far East, etc. Covers more than 800 dramatists, 2000 plays, with biographical material, plot summaries, theatre history, criticism, etc. "Best of its kind in English," *New Republic.* 77 illustrations. xxii + 890pp. 20100-7 Clothbound $8.50

THE EVOLUTION OF THE ENGLISH LANGUAGE, George McKnight. The growth of English, from the 14th century to the present. Unusual, non-technical account presents basic information in very interesting form: sound shifts, change in grammar and syntax, vocabulary growth, similar topics. Abundantly illustrated with quotations. Formerly *Modern English in the Making.* xii + 590pp. 21932-1 Paperbound $3.50

AN ETYMOLOGICAL DICTIONARY OF MODERN ENGLISH, Ernest Weekley. Fullest, richest work of its sort, by foremost British lexicographer. Detailed word histories, including many colloquial and archaic words; extensive quotations. Do not confuse this with the Concise Etymological Dictionary, which is much abridged. Total of xxvii + 830pp. 6½ x 9¼. 21873-2, 21874-0 Two volumes, Paperbound $6.00

FLATLAND: A ROMANCE OF MANY DIMENSIONS, E. A. Abbott. Classic of science-fiction explores ramifications of life in a two-dimensional world, and what happens when a three-dimensional being intrudes. Amusing reading, but also useful as introduction to thought about hyperspace. Introduction by Banesh Hoffmann. 16 illustrations. xx + 103pp. 20001-9 Paperbound $1.00

POEMS OF ANNE BRADSTREET, edited with an introduction by Robert Hutchinson. A new selection of poems by America's first poet and perhaps the first significant woman poet in the English language. 48 poems display her development in works of considerable variety—love poems, domestic poems, religious meditations, formal elegies, "quaternions," etc. Notes, bibliography. viii + 222pp.

22160-1 Paperbound $2.00

THREE GOTHIC NOVELS: THE CASTLE OF OTRANTO BY HORACE WALPOLE; VATHEK BY WILLIAM BECKFORD; THE VAMPYRE BY JOHN POLIDORI, WITH FRAGMENT OF A NOVEL BY LORD BYRON, edited by E. F. Bleiler. The first Gothic novel, by Walpole; the finest Oriental tale in English, by Beckford; powerful Romantic supernatural story in versions by Polidori and Byron. All extremely important in history of literature; all still exciting, packed with supernatural thrills, ghosts, haunted castles, magic, etc. xl + 291pp.

21232-7 Paperbound $2.00

THE BEST TALES OF HOFFMANN, E. T. A. Hoffmann. 10 of Hoffmann's most important stories, in modern re-editings of standard translations: Nutcracker and the King of Mice, Signor Formica, Automata, The Sandman, Rath Krespel, The Golden Flowerpot, Master Martin the Cooper, The Mines of Falun, The King's Betrothed, A New Year's Eve Adventure. 7 illustrations by Hoffmann. Edited by E. F. Bleiler. xxxix + 419pp.

21793-0 Paperbound $2.50

GHOST AND HORROR STORIES OF AMBROSE BIERCE, Ambrose Bierce. 23 strikingly modern stories of the horrors latent in the human mind: The Eyes of the Panther, The Damned Thing, An Occurrence at Owl Creek Bridge, An Inhabitant of Carcosa, etc., plus the dream-essay, Visions of the Night. Edited by E. F. Bleiler. xxii + 199pp.

20767-6 Paperbound $1.50

BEST GHOST STORIES OF J. S. LEFANU, J. Sheridan LeFanu. Finest stories by Victorian master often considered greatest supernatural writer of all. Carmilla, Green Tea, The Haunted Baronet, The Familiar, and 12 others. Most never before available in the U. S. A. Edited by E. F. Bleiler. 8 illustrations from Victorian publications. xvii + 467pp.

20415-4 Paperbound $3.00

THE TIME STREAM, THE GREATEST ADVENTURE, AND THE PURPLE SAPPHIRE— THREE SCIENCE FICTION NOVELS, John Taine (Eric Temple Bell). Great American mathematician was also foremost science fiction novelist of the 1920's. *The Time Stream,* one of all-time classics, uses concepts of circular time; *The Greatest Adventure,* incredibly ancient biological experiments from Antarctica threaten to escape; The *Purple Sapphire,* superscience, lost races in Central Tibet, survivors of the Great Race. 4 illustrations by Frank R. Paul. v + 532pp.

21180-0 Paperbound $3.00

SEVEN SCIENCE FICTION NOVELS, H. G. Wells. The standard collection of the great novels. Complete, unabridged. *First Men in the Moon, Island of Dr. Moreau, War of the Worlds, Food of the Gods, Invisible Man, Time Machine, In the Days of the Comet.* Not only science fiction fans, but every educated person owes it to himself to read these novels. 1015pp.

20264-X Clothbound $5.00

LAST AND FIRST MEN AND STAR MAKER, TWO SCIENCE FICTION NOVELS, Olaf Stapledon. Greatest future histories in science fiction. In the first, human intelligence is the "hero," through strange paths of evolution, interplanetary invasions, incredible technologies, near extinctions and reemergences. Star Maker describes the quest of a band of star rovers for intelligence itself, through time and space: weird inhuman civilizations, crustacean minds, symbiotic worlds, etc. Complete, unabridged. v + 438pp. 21962-3 Paperbound $2.50

THREE PROPHETIC NOVELS, H. G. WELLS. Stages of a consistently planned future for mankind. *When the Sleeper Wakes,* and *A Story of the Days to Come,* anticipate *Brave New World* and *1984,* in the 21st Century; *The Time Machine,* only complete version in print, shows farther future and the end of mankind. All show Wells's greatest gifts as storyteller and novelist. Edited by E. F. Bleiler. x + 335pp. (USO) 20605-X Paperbound $2.25

THE DEVIL'S DICTIONARY, Ambrose Bierce. America's own Oscar Wilde—Ambrose Bierce—offers his barbed iconoclastic wisdom in over 1,000 definitions hailed by H. L. Mencken as "some of the most gorgeous witticisms in the English language." 145pp. 20487-1 Paperbound $1.25

MAX AND MORITZ, Wilhelm Busch. Great children's classic, father of comic strip, of two bad boys, Max and Moritz. Also Ker and Plunk (Plisch und Plumm), Cat and Mouse, Deceitful Henry, Ice-Peter, The Boy and the Pipe, and five other pieces. Original German, with English translation. Edited by H. Arthur Klein; translations by various hands and H. Arthur Klein. vi + 216pp.
20181-3 Paperbound $2.00

PIGS IS PIGS AND OTHER FAVORITES, Ellis Parker Butler. The title story is one of the best humor short stories, as Mike Flannery obfuscates biology and English. Also included, That Pup of Murchison's, The Great American Pie Company, and Perkins of Portland. 14 illustrations. v + 109pp. 21532-6 Paperbound $1.00

THE PETERKIN PAPERS, Lucretia P. Hale. It takes genius to be as stupidly mad as the Peterkins, as they decide to become wise, celebrate the "Fourth," keep a cow, and otherwise strain the resources of the Lady from Philadelphia. Basic book of American humor. 153 illustrations. 219pp. 20794-3 Paperbound $1.50

PERRAULT'S FAIRY TALES, translated by A. E. Johnson and S. R. Littlewood, with 34 full-page illustrations by Gustave Doré. All the original Perrault stories—Cinderella, Sleeping Beauty, Bluebeard, Little Red Riding Hood, Puss in Boots, Tom Thumb, etc.—with their witty verse morals and the magnificent illustrations of Doré. One of the five or six great books of European fairy tales. viii + 117pp. 8⅛ x 11. 22311-6 Paperbound $2.00

OLD HUNGARIAN FAIRY TALES, Baroness Orczy. Favorites translated and adapted by author of the *Scarlet Pimpernel.* Eight fairy tales include "The Suitors of Princess Fire-Fly," "The Twin Hunchbacks," "Mr. Cuttlefish's Love Story," and "The Enchanted Cat." This little volume of magic and adventure will captivate children as it has for generations. 90 drawings by Montagu Barstow. 96pp.
(USO) 22293-4 Paperbound $1.95

THE RED FAIRY BOOK, Andrew Lang. Lang's color fairy books have long been children's favorites. This volume includes Rapunzel, Jack and the Bean-stalk and 35 other stories, familiar and unfamiliar. 4 plates, 93 illustrations x + 367pp.
21673-X Paperbound $2.50

THE BLUE FAIRY BOOK, Andrew Lang. Lang's tales come from all countries and all times. Here are 37 tales from Grimm, the Arabian Nights, Greek Mythology, and other fascinating sources. 8 plates, 130 illustrations. xi + 390pp.
21437-0 Paperbound $2.50

HOUSEHOLD STORIES BY THE BROTHERS GRIMM. Classic English-language edition of the well-known tales — Rumpelstiltskin, Snow White, Hansel and Gretel, The Twelve Brothers, Faithful John, Rapunzel, Tom Thumb (52 stories in all). Translated into simple, straightforward English by Lucy Crane. Ornamented with headpieces, vignettes, elaborate decorative initials and a dozen full-page illustrations by Walter Crane. x + 269pp.
21080-4 Paperbound $2.50

THE MERRY ADVENTURES OF ROBIN HOOD, Howard Pyle. The finest modern versions of the traditional ballads and tales about the great English outlaw. Howard Pyle's complete prose version, with every word, every illustration of the first edition. Do not confuse this facsimile of the original (1883) with modern editions that change text or illustrations. 23 plates plus many page decorations. xxii + 296pp.
22043-5 Paperbound $2.50

THE STORY OF KING ARTHUR AND HIS KNIGHTS, Howard Pyle. The finest children's version of the life of King Arthur; brilliantly retold by Pyle, with 48 of his most imaginative illustrations. xviii + 313pp. 6⅛ x 9¼.
21445-1 Paperbound $2.50

THE WONDERFUL WIZARD OF OZ, L. Frank Baum. America's finest children's book in facsimile of first edition with all Denslow illustrations in full color. The edition a child should have. Introduction by Martin Gardner. 23 color plates, scores of drawings. iv + 267pp.
20691-2 Paperbound $2.25

THE MARVELOUS LAND OF OZ, L. Frank Baum. The second Oz book, every bit as imaginative as the Wizard. The hero is a boy named Tip, but the Scarecrow and the Tin Woodman are back, as is the Oz magic. 16 color plates, 120 drawings by John R. Neill. 287pp.
20692-0 Paperbound $2.50

THE MAGICAL MONARCH OF MO, L. Frank Baum. Remarkable adventures in a land even stranger than Oz. The best of Baum's books not in the Oz series. 15 color plates and dozens of drawings by Frank Verbeck. xviii + 237pp.
21892-9 Paperbound $2.00

THE BAD CHILD'S BOOK OF BEASTS, MORE BEASTS FOR WORSE CHILDREN, A MORAL ALPHABET, Hilaire Belloc. Three complete humor classics in one volume. Be kind to the frog, and do not call him names . . . and 28 other whimsical animals. Familiar favorites and some not so well known. Illustrated by Basil Blackwell. 156pp.
(USO) 20749-8 Paperbound $1.25

EAST O' THE SUN AND WEST O' THE MOON, George W. Dasent. Considered the best of all translations of these Norwegian folk tales, this collection has been enjoyed by generations of children (and folklorists too). Includes True and Untrue, Why the Sea is Salt, East O' the Sun and West O' the Moon, Why the Bear is Stumpy-Tailed, Boots and the Troll, The Cock and the Hen, Rich Peter the Pedlar, and 52 more. The only edition with all 59 tales. 77 illustrations by Erik Werenskiold and Theodor Kittelsen. xv + 418pp. 22521-6 Paperbound $3.00

GOOPS AND HOW TO BE THEM, Gelett Burgess. Classic of tongue-in-cheek humor, masquerading as etiquette book. 87 verses, twice as many cartoons, show mischievous Goops as they demonstrate to children virtues of table manners, neatness, courtesy, etc. Favorite for generations. viii + 88pp. 6½ x 9¼.
22233-0 Paperbound $1.25

ALICE'S ADVENTURES UNDER GROUND, Lewis Carroll. The first version, quite different from the final *Alice in Wonderland,* printed out by Carroll himself with his own illustrations. Complete facsimile of the "million dollar" manuscript Carroll gave to Alice Liddell in 1864. Introduction by Martin Gardner. viii + 96pp. Title and dedication pages in color. 21482-6 Paperbound $1.25

THE BROWNIES, THEIR BOOK, Palmer Cox. Small as mice, cunning as foxes, exuberant and full of mischief, the Brownies go to the zoo, toy shop, seashore, circus, etc., in 24 verse adventures and 266 illustrations. Long a favorite, since their first appearance in St. Nicholas Magazine. xi + 144pp. 6⅝ x 9¼.
21265-3 Paperbound $1.75

SONGS OF CHILDHOOD, Walter De La Mare. Published (under the pseudonym Walter Ramal) when De La Mare was only 29, this charming collection has long been a favorite children's book. A facsimile of the first edition in paper, the 47 poems capture the simplicity of the nursery rhyme and the ballad, including such lyrics as I Met Eve, Tartary, The Silver Penny. vii + 106pp. 21972-0 Paperbound $1.25

THE COMPLETE NONSENSE OF EDWARD LEAR, Edward Lear. The finest 19th-century humorist-cartoonist in full: all nonsense limericks, zany alphabets, Owl and Pussycat, songs, nonsense botany, and more than 500 illustrations by Lear himself. Edited by Holbrook Jackson. xxix + 287pp. (USO) 20167-8 Paperbound $2.00

BILLY WHISKERS: THE AUTOBIOGRAPHY OF A GOAT, Frances Trego Montgomery. A favorite of children since the early 20th century, here are the escapades of that rambunctious, irresistible and mischievous goat—Billy Whiskers. Much in the spirit of *Peck's Bad Boy,* this is a book that children never tire of reading or hearing. All the original familiar illustrations by W. H. Fry are included: 6 color plates, 18 black and white drawings. 159pp. 22345-0 Paperbound $2.00

MOTHER GOOSE MELODIES. Faithful republication of the fabulously rare Munroe and Francis "copyright 1833" Boston edition—the most important Mother Goose collection, usually referred to as the "original." Familiar rhymes plus many rare ones, with wonderful old woodcut illustrations. Edited by E. F. Bleiler. 128pp. 4½ x 6⅜. 22577-1 Paperbound $1.25

TWO LITTLE SAVAGES; BEING THE ADVENTURES OF TWO BOYS WHO LIVED AS INDIANS AND WHAT THEY LEARNED, Ernest Thompson Seton. Great classic of nature and boyhood provides a vast range of woodlore in most palatable form, a genuinely entertaining story. Two farm boys build a teepee in woods and live in it for a month, working out Indian solutions to living problems, star lore, birds and animals, plants, etc. 293 illustrations. vii + 286pp.

20985-7 Paperbound $2.50

PETER PIPER'S PRACTICAL PRINCIPLES OF PLAIN & PERFECT PRONUNCIATION. Alliterative jingles and tongue-twisters of surprising charm, that made their first appearance in America about 1830. Republished in full with the spirited woodcut illustrations from this earliest American edition. 32pp. 4½ x 6⅜.

22560-7 Paperbound $1.00

SCIENCE EXPERIMENTS AND AMUSEMENTS FOR CHILDREN, Charles Vivian. 73 easy experiments, requiring only materials found at home or easily available, such as candles, coins, steel wool, etc.; illustrate basic phenomena like vacuum, simple chemical reaction, etc. All safe. Modern, well-planned. Formerly *Science Games for Children*. 102 photos, numerous drawings. 96pp. 6⅛ x 9¼.

21856-2 Paperbound $1.25

AN INTRODUCTION TO CHESS MOVES AND TACTICS SIMPLY EXPLAINED, Leonard Barden. Informal intermediate introduction, quite strong in explaining reasons for moves. Covers basic material, tactics, important openings, traps, positional play in middle game, end game. Attempts to isolate patterns and recurrent configurations. Formerly *Chess*. 58 figures. 102pp.   (USO) 21210-6 Paperbound $1.25

LASKER'S MANUAL OF CHESS, Dr. Emanuel Lasker. Lasker was not only one of the five great World Champions, he was also one of the ablest expositors, theorists, and analysts. In many ways, his Manual, permeated with his philosophy of battle, filled with keen insights, is one of the greatest works ever written on chess. Filled with analyzed games by the great players. A single-volume library that will profit almost any chess player, beginner or master. 308 diagrams. xli x 349pp.

20640-8 Paperbound $2.75

THE MASTER BOOK OF MATHEMATICAL RECREATIONS, Fred Schuh. In opinion of many the finest work ever prepared on mathematical puzzles, stunts, recreations; exhaustively thorough explanations of mathematics involved, analysis of effects, citation of puzzles and games. Mathematics involved is elementary. Translated by F. Göbel. 194 figures. xxiv + 430pp.   22134-2 Paperbound $3.00

MATHEMATICS, MAGIC AND MYSTERY, Martin Gardner. Puzzle editor for Scientific American explains mathematics behind various mystifying tricks: card tricks, stage "mind reading," coin and match tricks, counting out games, geometric dissections, etc. Probability sets, theory of numbers clearly explained. Also provides more than 400 tricks, guaranteed to work, that you can do. 135 illustrations. xii + 176pp.

20338-2 Paperbound $1.50

MATHEMATICAL PUZZLES FOR BEGINNERS AND ENTHUSIASTS, Geoffrey Mott-Smith. 189 puzzles from easy to difficult—involving arithmetic, logic, algebra, properties of digits, probability, etc.—for enjoyment and mental stimulus. Explanation of mathematical principles behind the puzzles. 135 illustrations. viii + 248pp.
20198-8 Paperbound $1.75

PAPER FOLDING FOR BEGINNERS, William D. Murray and Francis J. Rigney. Easiest book on the market, clearest instructions on making interesting, beautiful origami. Sail boats, cups, roosters, frogs that move legs, bonbon boxes, standing birds, etc. 40 projects; more than 275 diagrams and photographs. 94pp.
20713-7 Paperbound $1.00

TRICKS AND GAMES ON THE POOL TABLE, Fred Herrmann. 79 tricks and games— some solitaires, some for two or more players, some competitive games—to entertain you between formal games. Mystifying shots and throws, unusual caroms, tricks involving such props as cork, coins, a hat, etc. Formerly *Fun on the Pool Table.* 77 figures. 95pp.
21814-7 Paperbound $1.00

HAND SHADOWS TO BE THROWN UPON THE WALL: A SERIES OF NOVEL AND AMUSING FIGURES FORMED BY THE HAND, Henry Bursill. Delightful picturebook from great-grandfather's day shows how to make 18 different hand shadows: a bird that flies, duck that quacks, dog that wags his tail, camel, goose, deer, boy, turtle, etc. Only book of its sort. vi + 33pp. 6½ x 9¼.
21779-5 Paperbound $1.00

WHITTLING AND WOODCARVING, E. J. Tangerman. 18th printing of best book on market. "If you can cut a potato you can carve" toys and puzzles, chains, chessmen, caricatures, masks, frames, woodcut blocks, surface patterns, much more. Information on tools, woods, techniques. Also goes into serious wood sculpture from Middle Ages to present, East and West. 464 photos, figures. x + 293pp.
20965-2 Paperbound $2.00

HISTORY OF PHILOSOPHY, Julián Marias. Possibly the clearest, most easily followed, best planned, most useful one-volume history of philosophy on the market; neither skimpy nor overfull. Full details on system of every major philosopher and dozens of less important thinkers from pre-Socratics up to Existentialism and later. Strong on many European figures usually omitted. Has gone through dozens of editions in Europe. 1966 edition, translated by Stanley Appelbaum and Clarence Strowbridge. xviii + 505pp.
21739-6 Paperbound $3.00

YOGA: A SCIENTIFIC EVALUATION, Kovoor T. Behanan. Scientific but non-technical study of physiological results of yoga exercises; done under auspices of Yale U. Relations to Indian thought, to psychoanalysis, etc. 16 photos. xxiii + 270pp.
20505-3 Paperbound $2.50

Prices subject to change without notice.
Available at your book dealer or write for free catalogue to Dept. GI, Dover Publications, Inc., 180 Varick St., N. Y., N. Y. 10014. Dover publishes more than 150 books each year on science, elementary and advanced mathematics, biology, music, art, literary history, social sciences and other areas.